LAWS AND LEGISLATION

LABOR RELATIONS

MAJOR LAWS AND A GUIDE TO THE NATIONAL LABOR RELATIONS ACT

Laws and Legislation

Additional books in this series can be found on Nova's website under the Series tab.

Additional e-books in this series can be found on Nova's website under the e-books tab.

Congressional Policies, Practices and Procedures

Additional books in this series can be found on Nova's website under the Series tab.

Additional e-books in this series can be found on Nova's website under the e-books tab.

LAWS AND LEGISLATION

LABOR RELATIONS

MAJOR LAWS AND A GUIDE TO THE NATIONAL LABOR RELATIONS ACT

ALLEN DANIELS
AND
RUTH J. HOFFMAN
EDITORS

nova publishers
New York

For permission to use material from this book please contact us:
Telephone 631-231-7269; Fax 631-231-8175
Web Site: http://www.novapublishers.com

NOTICE TO THE READER

Additional color graphics may be available in the e-book version of this book.

LIBRARY OF CONGRESS CATALOGING-IN-PUBLICATION DATA

ISBN: 978-1-62257-420-9

Published by Nova Science Publishers, Inc. † New York

CONTENTS

PREFACE

Since 1926, Congress has enacted three major laws that govern labor-management relations for private sector and federal employees. An issue for Congress is the effect of these laws on employers, workers, and the nation's economy. The Bureau of Labor Statistics estimates that, nationwide, 9.2 million employees are represented by unions. In the 112th Congress alone, more than 30 bills have been introduced to amend federal labor relations statutes. The proposals range from making union recognition without a secret ballot election illegal to further modifying runoff election procedures. This legislative activity, and the significant number of employees affected by federal labor relations laws, illustrate the current relevance of labor relations issues to legislators and their constituents. The three major labor relations statutes in the U.S. are the Railway Labor Act, the National Labor Relations Act, and the Federal Service Labor-Management Relations Statute. Each law governs a distinct population of the U.S. workforce. This book provides a brief history and overview of the aims of each of these statutes and discusses key statutory provisions for each statute.

Chapter 1 - Since 1926, Congress has enacted three major laws that govern labor-management relations for private sector and federal employees. An issue for Congress is the effect of these laws on employers, workers, and the nation's economy. The Bureau of Labor Statistics estimates that, nationwide, 9.2 million employees are represented by unions. In the 112th Congress alone, more than 30 bills have been introduced to amend federal labor relations statutes. The proposals range from making union recognition without a secret ballot election illegal to further modifying runoff election procedures. This legislative activity, and the significant number of employees affected by federal labor relations laws, illustrate the current relevance of labor relations issues to legislators and their constituents.

The three major labor relations statutes in the United States are the Railway Labor Act, the National Labor Relations Act, and the Federal Service Labor-Management Relations Statute. Each law governs a distinct population of the U.S. workforce.

The Railway Labor Act (RLA) was enacted in 1926, and its coverage extends to railway and airline carriers, unions, and employees of the carriers. The RLA guarantees employees the right to organize and collectively bargain with their employers over conditions of work and protects them against unfair employer and union practices. It lays out specific procedures for selecting employee representatives and provides a dispute resolution system that aims to efficiently resolve labor disputes between parties, with an emphasis on mediation and arbitration. The RLA provides multiple processes for dispute resolution, depending on whether the dispute is based on a collective bargaining issue or the application of an existing collective bargaining agreement.

The National Labor Relations Act (NLRA) was enacted in 1933. The NLRA's coverage extends to most other private sector businesses that are not covered by the RLA. Like the RLA, the NLRA guarantees employees the right to organize and collectively bargain over conditions of employment and protects them against unfair employer and union activities. However, its dispute resolution system differs from the RLA's in that it is arguably more adversarial in nature; many disputes are resolved through adjudication, rather than through mediation and arbitration.

The Federal Service Labor-Management Relations Statute (FSLMRS) was enacted in 1978, and its coverage extends to most federal employees. The basic framework of the FSLMRS is similar to that of the NLRA; however, employee rights are more restricted under the FSLMRS, given the unique nature of their employer, the federal government. Federal employees have the right to organize and collectively bargain, but they cannot bargain over wages or strike. Additionally, the President has the power to unilaterally exclude an agency or subdivision from coverage under the FSLMRS if he determines that its primary work concerns national security.

This report provides a brief history and overview of the aims of each of these statutes. It also discusses key statutory provisions for each statute.

Congress has enacted three major laws that govern labor-management relations. The first law, the Railway Labor Act (RLA), was enacted in 1926. The RLA applies to railway and airline carriers. In 1935, Congress passed the National Labor Relations Act (NLRA), which applies to private sector employers other than railroad and airline carriers, and in 1978, Congress enacted the Federal Service Labor-Management Relations Statute (FSLMRS), which applies to most federal employees. This report provides an overview of these three labor relations laws by giving a brief history of each law and discussing how each statute operates and is administered.

This report uses specific "terms of art" relevant to these acts. Appendix A defines these "terms of art." Appendix B provides a list of acronyms used in this report. Appendix C contains a table that compares provisions of all three laws.

Chapter 2 - The National Labor Relations Act of 1935 (NLRA) gives private sector workers the right to join or form a labor union and to bargain collectively over wages, hours, and other working conditions. An issue before Congress is whether to change the procedures under which a union is certified as the bargaining representative of a union chosen by a majority of workers.

Under current law, the National Labor Relations Board (NLRB) conducts a secret ballot election when a petition is filed requesting one. A petition can be filed by a union, worker, or employer. Workers or a union may request an election if at least 30% of workers have signed authorization cards (i.e., cards authorizing a union to represent them). The NLRA does not require secret ballot elections. An employer may voluntarily recognize a union if a majority of workers have signed authorization cards.

In recent Congresses, legislation has been introduced that, if enacted, would change current union certification procedures. The Employee Free Choice Act would require the NLRB to certify a union if a majority of employees sign authorization cards. The Secret Ballot Protection Act would make it an unfair labor practice for an employer to recognize or bargain with a union without a secret ballot election.

Proponents of both measures sometimes use similar language to support their positions. Employers argue that, under card check certification, workers may be pressured or coerced into signing authorization cards and may only hear the union's point of view. Unions argue that, during an election campaign, employers may pressure or coerce workers into voting against a union. Supporters of secret ballot elections argue that casting a secret ballot is private and confidential. Unions argue that, during an election campaign, employers have greater access to workers. Unions argue that card check certification is less costly than a secret ballot election. Employers maintain that unionization may be more costly to workers, because union members must pay dues and higher union wages may result in fewer union jobs.

Requiring card check certification may increase the level of unionization, while requiring secret ballot elections may decrease it. Research suggests that, where card check recognition is required, unions undertake more union drives and the union success rate is higher. The union success rate is also greater where card check recognition is combined with a neutrality agreement (i.e., an agreement where the employer agrees to remain neutral during a union organizing campaign).

To the extent that requiring secret ballot elections or requiring certification when a majority of employees sign authorization cards would affect the level of unionization, the economic effects may depend on how well labor markets fit the model of perfect competition. Requiring card check certification may improve worker benefits and reduce earnings inequality—if more workers are unionized. Requiring secret ballot elections may increase inequality in compensation—if fewer workers are unionized.

The National Labor Relations Act of 1935 (NLRA), as amended, gives private sector workers the right to join or form a labor union and to bargain collectively over wages, hours, and other conditions of employment.[1] The act also requires employers to bargain in good faith with a union chosen by a majority of employees. An issue before Congress is whether to change the procedures under which a union is certified as the bargaining representative of a union chosen by a majority of workers.

In recent Congresses, legislation has been introduced that, if enacted, would change current union certification procedures. This report begins by summarizing legislation introduced in the 112th and 111th Congresses. The report then reviews the rights and responsibilities of workers and employers under the NLRA and the different ways that workers may form or join a union. Next, the report analyzes the potential effects of changes in union certification procedures. Finally, the report considers whether there is an economic rationale for protecting the rights of workers to organize and bargain collectively.

Chapter 3 - This report discusses legislative attempts to amend the National Labor Relations Act ("NLRA") to allow for union certification without an election, based on signed employee authorizations. The Employee Free Choice Act ("EFCA"), introduced in the 111th Congress as H.R. 1409 and S. 560, would have allowed union certification based on signed authorizations, provided a process for the bargaining of an initial agreement, and prescribed new penalties for certain unfair labor practices. This report reviews the current process for selecting a bargaining representative under the NLRA, and discusses the role of the Federal Mediation and Conciliation Service in resolving bargaining disputes under that act. The EFCA has been introduced in the past four Congresses. During the 110th Congress, the measure was passed by a vote of 241-185 in the House. In the Senate, proponents of the EFCA fell nine votes short of the 60 votes needed to limit debate and proceed to final consideration of the measure. The EFCA is widely expected to be reintroduced in the 112th Congress.

Legislation that would allow a union to become the exclusive bargaining representative of a unit of employees without an election has been introduced in the past four Congresses. The Employee Free Choice Act ("EFCA" or "the act"), introduced in the 111th Congress as H.R. 1409 and S. 560, would have amended the National Labor Relations Act ("NLRA") to allow union certification based on signed employee authorizations, provided a process for the bargaining of an initial agreement, and prescribed new penalties for certain unfair labor practices. Labor officials indicated that the EFCA was "the most important work we'll be doing, because it's a key to succeeding on everything else."

This report reviews the current process for selecting a bargaining representative under the NLRA, and examines how the EFCA would have altered that process. In addition, this report discusses the other changes proposed by the act. Some of these changes had been previously suggested in other past measures. For example, legislation that would have established a process for the bargaining of an initial agreement was first introduced in the 105th Congress.

Chapter 4 - Faced with distressed state budgets and lower revenue, many governors and state legislatures have focused on the collective bargaining rights of public employees as a way to control expenses. Legislation that would limit such rights has reportedly been introduced in at least 22 states. In general, the sponsors of such legislation contend that unionized state and local employees enjoy unsustainable salaries and benefits as a result of collective bargaining.

According to the Bureau of Labor Statistics, 26.8% of all federal employees are members of a union. A slightly higher percentage of state employees—31.1%—are union members. At the local government level, 42.3% of employees are union members. Although all of these employees engage in some form of collective bargaining through their unions, the scope of such bargaining is generally different for federal and state and local workers. In addition, because the collective bargaining rights of state and local employees are defined by state law, other variations in bargaining may exist among these workers. Subjects that are negotiable in one state, for example, may not be negotiable in another state.

This report examines the collective bargaining rights of federal, state, and local workers. The report also discusses the constitutional concerns that may be raised by state legislation that attempts to invalidate existing collective bargaining agreements. In Michigan, the Local Government and School District Fiscal Accountability Act ("Fiscal Accountability Act") was adopted on March 16, 2011. Under the Fiscal Accountability Act, the governor may appoint an emergency manager if he determines that a local government financial emergency exists. The emergency manager would have broad powers to rectify the financial emergency, including the ability to reject, modify, or terminate one or more terms and conditions of an existing collective bargaining agreement. If the emergency manager were to reject, modify, or terminate one or more terms and conditions of an existing agreement, constitutional concerns would likely be raised under the Contract Clause of the U.S. Constitution, which prohibits a state from passing any law "impairing the Obligation of Contracts."

Faced with distressed state budgets and lower revenue, many governors and state legislatures have focused on the collective bargaining rights of public employees as a way to control expenses. Legislation that would limit such rights has reportedly been introduced in at least 22 states. In general, the sponsors of such legislation contend that unionized state and local employees enjoy unsustainable salaries and benefits as a result of collective bargaining.

This report examines the collective bargaining rights of federal, state, and local workers, and discusses the constitutional concerns that may be raised by state legislation that attempts to invalidate existing collective bargaining agreements.

Chapter 5 - The Regional Offices of the National Labor Relations Board have found that, more than six decades after its enactment, there is still a lack of basic information about the National Labor Relations Act. Staff members have expressed a need for a simply stated explanation of the Act to which anyone could be referred for guidance. To meet this demand, the basic law under the Act has been set forth in this pamphlet in a nontechnical way so that those who may be affected by it can better understand what their rights and obligations are.

Any effort to state basic principles of law in a simple way is a challenging and unenviable task. This is especially true about labor law, a relatively complex field of law. Anyone reading this booklet must bear in mind several cautions.

First, it must be emphasized that the Office of the General Counsel does not issue advisory opinions and this material cannot be considered as an official statement of law. It represents the view of the Office of the General Counsel as of the date of publication only. It is important to note that the law changes and advances. In fact, it is the duty of the Agency to keep its decisions abreast of changing conditions, yet within the basic statute. Accordingly, with the passage of time no one can rely on these statements as absolute until and unless a check has been made to see whether the law may have been changed substantially or specifically.

Furthermore, these are broad general principles only and countless subprinciples and detailed rules are not included. Only by evaluation of specific fact situations in the light of current principles and with the aid of expert advice would a person be in a position to know definitely where the proposed conduct may fit under the statute. No basic primer or text can constitute legal advice in particular fact situations. This effort to improve basic education about the statute should not be considered as such. Many areas of the statute remain untested. Legal advisers and other experts can find the total body of "Board law" reported in other Agency publications.

One other caution: This material does not deal with questions arising under other labor laws, but only with the National Labor Relations Act. Laws administered by other Government agencies, such as the Labor-Management Reporting and Disclosure Act of 1959, the Employee Retirement Income Security Act, the Occupational Safety and Health Act, the Railway Labor Act, the Fair Labor Standards, Walsh-Healey and Davis-Bacon Acts, Title VII of the Civil Rights Act of 1964, Americans with Disabilities Act, the Federal Mine Safety and Health Act, and the Veterans' Preference Act, are not treated herein.

Lastly, this material does not reflect the view of the National Labor Relations Board as the adjudicating agency that in the end will decide each case as it comes before it.

It is hoped that with this cautionary note this booklet may be helpful to those in need of a better basic understanding of the National Labor Relations Act.

In: Labor Relations
Editors: A. Daniels and R. Hoffman

ISBN: 978-1-62257-420-9

Chapter 1

FEDERAL LABOR RELATIONS STATUTES: AN OVERVIEW*

Alexandra Hegji

SUMMARY

Since 1926, Congress has enacted three major laws that govern labor-management relations for private sector and federal employees. An issue for Congress is the effect of these laws on employers, workers, and the nation's economy. The Bureau of Labor Statistics estimates that, nationwide, 9.2 million employees are represented by unions. In the 112th Congress alone, more than 30 bills have been introduced to amend federal labor relations statutes. The proposals range from making union recognition without a secret ballot election illegal to further modifying runoff election procedures. This legislative activity, and the significant number of employees affected by federal labor relations laws, illustrate the current relevance of labor relations issues to legislators and their constituents.

The three major labor relations statutes in the United States are the Railway Labor Act, the National Labor Relations Act, and the Federal Service Labor -Management Relations Statute. Each law governs a distinct population of the U.S. workforce.

The Railway Labor Act (RLA) was enacted in 1926, and its coverage extends to railway and airline carriers, unions, and employees of the carriers. The RLA guarantees employees the right to organize and collectively bargain with their employers over conditions of work and protects them against unfair employer and union practices. It lays out specific procedures for selecting employee representatives and provides a dispute resolution system that aims to efficiently resolve labor disputes between parties, with an emphasis on mediation and arbitration. The RLA provides multiple processes for dispute resolution, depending on whether the dispute is based on a collective bargaining issue or the application of an existing collective bargaining agreement.

---

* This is an edited, reformatted and augmented version of the Congressional Research Service Publication, CRS Report for Congress R42526, dated May 11, 2012.

The National Labor Relations Act (NLRA) was enacted in 1933. The NLRA's coverage extends to most other private sector businesses that are not covered by the RLA. Like the RLA, the NLRA guarantees employees the right to organize and collectively bargain over conditions of employment and protects them against unfair employer and union activities. However, its dispute resolution system differs from the RLA's in that it is arguably more adversarial in nature; many disputes are resolved through adjudication, rather than through mediation and arbitration.

The Federal Service Labor-Management Relations Statute (FSLMRS) was enacted in 1978, and its coverage extends to most federal employees. The basic framework of the FSLMRS is similar to that of the NLRA; however, employee rights are more restricted under the FSLMRS, given the unique nature of their employer, the federal government. Federal employees have the right to organize and collectively bargain, but they cannot bargain over wages or strike. Additionally, the President has the power to unilaterally exclude an agency or subdivision from coverage under the FSLMRS if he determines that its primary work concerns national security.

This report provides a brief history and overview of the aims of each of these statutes. It also discusses key statutory provisions for each statute.

Congress has enacted three major laws that govern labor-management relations. The first law, the Railway Labor Act (RLA), was enacted in 1926. The RLA applies to railway and airline carriers. In 1935, Congress passed the National Labor Relations Act (NLRA), which applies to private sector employers other than railroad and airline carriers, and in 1978, Congress enacted the Federal Service Labor-Management Relations Statute (FSLMRS), which applies to most federal employees. This report provides an overview of these three labor relations laws by giving a brief history of each law and discussing how each statute operates and is administered.

This report uses specific "terms of art" relevant to these acts. **Appendix A** defines these "terms of art." **Appendix B** provides a list of acronyms used in this report. **Appendix C** contains a table that compares provisions of all three laws.

THE RAILWAY LABOR ACT

Background

By the late 19th Century, the railroad industry had a significant impact on the U.S. economy. It helped connect the coasts, making settlement of the western United States much easier. Farmers were able to ship their goods to cities hundreds of miles away, and consumers were able to purchase products made in factories across the nation.[1] The railroad industry was also a major consumer of U.S. goods. It used over 75% of the steel produced in the United States, a large portion of the United States' extracted coal, and was the nation's primary employer.[2]

As the public began to depend on railroads and their regular availability, railroad workers also began to unionize.[3] Because the nation grew dependent on railroads, labor-management disputes that grew into work stoppages adversely affected the nation's welfare.

Enacted in 1926, the Railway Labor Act (RLA) continued a pattern of federal attempts at regulating labor relations in the industry.[4] It was the product of an agreement between industry and labor that Congress adopted. The act was intended to help maintain labor-management peace within the railway industry and thereby avoid work stoppages that could carry with them adverse economic and social effects.[5] The act's five major purposes are to

- prevent any interruption to commerce or to the operation of any carrier;
- ensure employees the right to organize or join a labor union;
- ensure railway carriers and employees the right to select bargaining representatives without interference from the other party;
- provide timely settlement of disputes over rates of pay, rules, or working conditions; and
- provide timely settlement of disputes growing out of grievances or over interpretation or application of existing union contracts.[6]

To accomplish these goals, Congress established a system based on collective bargaining between labor and management, relying on mediation facilitated by the newly created National Mediation Board (NMB) and voluntary arbitration if neither collective bargaining nor mediation worked.

Major Amendments

1934 Amendments

The original RLA called for parties to establish by agreement special adjustment boards (SBAs) to resolve disputes over contract interpretation or application concerning changes in rates of pay, rules, or working conditions. These boards could be national, regional, or local in scope and would typically be composed of an equal number of carrier and employee representatives. If an adjustment board was unable to resolve a dispute because of a deadlock, the dispute could be referred to the Board of Mediation.[7] In the 1934 amendments, Congress created the National Railroad Adjustment Board (NRAB), which has jurisdiction over contract interpretation and administration disputes that cannot be resolved through direct negotiations. If the NRAB is deadlocked, it selects a referee to make an award in the dispute.[8] A referee is a neutral person who sits with the NRAB as a member and makes an award in the dispute at issue. Additionally, Congress replaced the Board of Mediation with the NMB, which can resolve disputes between parties concerning changes in rates of pay, rules, working conditions, and any other dispute not referable to NRAB.

Congress also strengthened the RLA's provisions that allow carriers and employees to select representatives freely and without interference from each other. It added language specifically stating that employees have the right to organize and collectively bargain and added a provision requiring that a majority of employees in a craft or class must support a union before it is recognized as their representative. Additionally, the amendments prohibited carriers from denying or questioning an employee's right to organize or join a union and tasked the NMB with investigating representation disputes. The amendments also provided for both civil and criminal means to enforce the RLA's provisions.[9]

Congress explicitly prohibited carriers from unilaterally changing pay rates, rules, and working conditions and added a "status quo" provision, which prohibits changes to pay rates, rules, and working conditions for 30 days after

parties are released from the NMB's services.[10] Finally, the definition of "carrier" was broadened to include companies that perform operations integral to railway transportation but not already covered by the act.[11]

1936 Amendments

In 1936, Congress extended most of the RLA's provisions to commercial airline carriers that operate in interstate or foreign commerce and airlines that transport mail for, or under contract with, the U.S. government.[12] Although the airline industry was relatively new in 1936, Congress acknowledged that it was part of the national transportation system that was vital to the economic well-being of the nation and that it too would need mechanisms to assist in dispute resolution and avoiding work stoppages. While the National Labor Relations Act (NLRA) was enacted in 1935 and covered most private sector employees, labor wanted airline carriers to be included under the RLA, because it believed the RLA's mediation/arbitration dispute resolution mechanisms provided more flexibility for the constantly changing, fledging industry.[13]

Additional Amendments

Between 1951 and 1981, the RLA was the subject of much congressional action. The major changes enacted are discussed below. This is followed by a depiction of the NLRA provisions currently in effect.

1951 Amendments

In 1951, Congress amended the RLA to allow carriers and unions to enter into union security agreements. These agreements require employees to pay union dues equal to the cost of representation as a condition of employment. However, under a union security agreement, employees are not required to become formal members of the union. State right-to-work laws that prohibit or restrict union security agreements are preempted by the RLA.[14]

1966 and 1981 Amendments

In 1966, Congress amended the RLA to provide for Public Law Boards (PLBs) that can be established upon the request of either party. Unlike an SBA, the parties do not need to agree on the creation of a PLB. PLBs are composed of one person selected by the carrier and one person selected by the union. Each selected board member is compensated by the carrier or union who selected them. If these selected board members deadlock on an issue, they designate a neutral third party to decide the dispute. If the selected board members are unable to agree on a neutral party, the NMB designates the neutral party. The neutral party is compensated by the NMB.[15] Finally, in 1981, Congress established emergency procedures for certain publicly funded and operated carriers that provide commuter rail services.[16]

FAA Modernization and Reform Act of 2012

The RLA was most recently amended in 2012 during the 112th Congress as part of the Federal Aviation Administration (FAA) Modernization and Reform Act of 2012. Under these amendments, for the NMB to conduct an election or otherwise certify a union for a craft of unrepresented employees, the NMB must receive, along with an application for certification, authori-zation cards signed by at least 50% of the employees in the craft or class seeking representation. Before this amendment, those parties filing an application for certification were required to include authorization cards signed by 35% of employees in the craft or class seeking representation.[17]

The 2012 amendments also changed the rules for runoff elections. Previously, only the names of the two unions that received the most votes in the first election were on the runoff ballot. If more employees voted not to have a union than voted for one or both of the unions that received the most votes, the runoff ballot did not include the choice of not being represented by a union.[18] Under the 2012 amendments, the runoff ballot has the two choices, including the choice not to be represented, that received the most votes in the initial election.[19]

The 2012 amendments also mandate periodic NMB evaluations and audits.[20]

Overview

The RLA seeks to prevent labor-management disputes that could interrupt railroad and airline service and harm the economy. It grants certain rights to both workers and carriers, seeks to prevent practices that could frustrate a peaceful worker-carrier relationship, and provides mechanisms for workers and carriers to resolve disputes.

To achieve these goals, the RLA regulates the labor-management relation-ship between workers and carriers in the railway and airline industries. It provides parties with a standard process for choosing a union to act as an employee representative in the collective bargaining process and details which individuals can participate in the process. Once a union is selected, the RLA governs which subjects workers and unions can negotiate. The RLA also regulates how workers, carriers, and unions should behave towards each other during the union selection and collective bargaining processes and prohibits certain unfair actions.

The RLA provides for several entities to administer and enforce its provisions. The National Mediation Board (NMB) is the primary agency charged with administration and enforcement of the act and also provides mediation service to parties who cannot reach a resolution in a dispute. The National Railway Adjustment Board (NRAB) is an NMB tribunal that hears and decides (arbitrates) grievances in the railway industry. Additionally, the RLA allows parties to a dispute in the railway industry to establish their own arbitration tribunals, known as Special Boards of Adjustment (SBAs), or a single party to request that the NMB create a Public Law Board (PLB) to arbitrate its dispute. Various System Boards of Adjustment (System Boards), created jointly by labor and management, arbitrate disputes in the airline carrier industry. Additionally, if an unresolved dispute threatens to substantially interrupt commerce, the President can create a Presidential Emergency Board (PEB) to investigate and aid in the resolution of the dispute.

Scope of Coverage

The RLA regulates the collective bargaining rights and duties of carriers and employees in the railway and airline carrier industries. "Collective bargaining" refers to the process of negotiation between these parties regarding working conditions. Employers are referred to as "carriers" in the RLA. The term "carrier" is used throughout this discussion for consistency with the act. The preliminary sections of the act define "carrier" and "employee," and those definitions are used to determine who is covered by the act and its accompanying regulations.

Carrier Defined

Under the RLA, a carrier is defined as:

> any company which is directly or indirectly owned or controlled by or under common control with any carrier by railroad and which operates any equipment or facilities or performs any service (other than trucking service) in connection with the transportation, receipt, delivery, elevation, transfer in transit, refrigeration or icing, storage, and handling of property transported by railroad, and any receiver, trustee, or other individual or body, judicial or otherwise, when in the possession of the business of any such "carrier" [21]

In addition to railroads, later adopted provisions cover airline carriers. The RLA also applies to any company that is directly or indirectly controlled by, or under common control with, a railroad or airline carrier that falls under the coverage of the act.

The RLA specifically excludes "trucking service" and most "street, interurban, or suburban electric railways" from its scope. However, if a trucking company almost exclusively performs services for a rail carrier, the trucking exemption may not apply.[22]

Employee Defined

The RLA defines an employee as any "person in the service of a carrier ... who performs any work defined as that of an employee or subordinate official."[23] Temporary, probationary and furloughed employees generally are within the RLA's definition of "employee."[24]

Rights and Duties under the Law

The act both mandates and prohibits certain actions of all parties involved in a labor-management dispute. The act grants employees the right to organize and collectively bargain. It also sets forth the procedures and standards to be applied in the selection of a union as an employee representative and the subsequent relations between the union, the carrier, and the employees.

Employees can select a union that will represent their craft or class's interests in bargaining with carriers over working conditions. A craft or class is a group of employees who are or wish to be represented by a union. A union can be recognized as a representative through either a secret ballot election or voluntary carrier recognition.

Certain conduct is prohibited in the carrier-union-employee relationship. Carriers and unions cannot interfere with employees' right to organize and select a union representative.

Carriers can only bargain with the employee-selected union, and the parties cannot use self-help until they have reached an impasse in negotiations and have exhausted all of the RLA's dispute resolution mechanisms. Self-help is a way in which one party can exert pressure on the other party and occurs outside of the formal dispute resolution process. For example, strikes and worker lockout are forms of self-help.

Union Selection

The RLA specifically states that employees have a right to select a union free from carrier interference or influence. A majority of a craft or class determines the union to represent that craft or class.[25] The NMB has exclusive jurisdiction to certify unions. A union can be certified as an employee representative if at least one party to a representation dispute petitions the NMB to conduct a secret ballot election and the union receives a majority of votes cast. However, the NMB will recognize the validity of a carrier-union agreement under which a carrier voluntarily recognizes a union as an employee representative. The NMB also has exclusive jurisdiction to determine a craft or class of employees, and this decision is practically unreviewable by courts.[26]

Determination of a Craft or Class

In defining a class or craft, the NMB will consider many factors including historical or traditional crafts and similarity of job functions between employees.[27] The NMB generally adheres to the traditional railroad craft or class distinctions.[28] When Congress extended coverage of the RLA to airlines, the industry was relatively new and did not have historical crafts. However, over the years, the NMB has come to distinguish several crafts within the industry.[29]

A union may only be certified on a system-wide basis. Union certification extends to members of that craft throughout the carrier's organization. The craft or class must include all employees who are eligible to be in the craft or class, including those at different locations.[30]

Eligibility to Vote in a Secret Ballot Election

Employees who regularly work in a craft or class are eligible to vote in a secret ballot election.[31] Employees who are furloughed, on a leave of absence, or probationary are eligible to vote. Contractors, retirees, and managers are ineligible to vote. Part-time, temporary, and dismissed employees may be eligible to vote, and the determination is made on a case-by-case basis.[32]

Certification

To determine a union, the NMB can conduct elections or use "any [other] appropriate method."[33]

Before the NMB selects a method to determine a union, it must complete an investigation to determine whether a representation dispute exists. To begin the investigation process, either party can petition for an investigation. The petition must be supported by a showing of interest in which a majority of workers in the craft or class involved sign authorization cards.[34] An NMB investigator compares the authorization cards with the list of system-wide, potential eligible voters provided by the carrier to determine if a sufficient percentage of authorization cards was submitted. An investigator reports his findings to the NMB's General Counsel (see discussion of "RLA Enforcement and Adjudication Processes" below). If an investigator finds that a dispute exists, the General Counsel will establish the way in which the dispute will be resolved (e.g., secret ballot election).[35]

The NMB may conduct elections by mail, telephone, Internet, or in-person ballot. A union must receive a *majority of votes cast* to be certified by the NMB as the employees' bargaining representative. In 2010, this rule replaced a 75-year-long NMB practice that required that a *majority of workers vote* for representation before a union was certified. The former practice effectively counted all those workers who did not vote in the election as "no union" votes. Now, an employee who does not vote, is no longer counted in the vote tally.[36] If no choice receives a majority of the votes, the NMB may conduct a runoff election between the two choices that receive the most votes.[37]

The RLA does not preclude a carrier from voluntarily recognizing a union as an employee representative. If employees are unrepresented, the union seeking certification is the only organization involved, and the parties agree in writing, the NMB can certify the union based solely on the union's presenting authorization cards signed by a majority of employees in the craft.[38] However, if the union is for a group of employees not generally recognized as a craft or class or if the craft or class is not represented system-wide, the voluntary recognition does not control the NMB's determination in a later representation dispute.[39]

Decertification

A union can have its certification revoked through decertification. The NMB does not have a formal procedure for decertifying a union, but has several practices that effectively removes an incumbent union's certification.[40] A union will be decertified when an individual or union petitions for a secret ballot election and less then 50% of voting employees cast ballots for the incumbent union or when the existing union freely renounces its certification.[41]

Bargaining Subjects

The RLA expressly mandates that all carriers and employees use "every reasonable effort" to create and maintain agreements on pay rates, rules, and working conditions and to settle all disputes arising out of such agreements (known as "direct negotiations").[42]

Prohibited Conduct

The RLA does not specifically list the unfair labor practices that it prohibits. Instead, the NMB looks to general considerations of fair dealing in defining the few bounds that the RLA does set. "Fair dealing" includes both unions' and carriers' responsibility to bargain in good faith, to recognize and respect each parties' representatives and concerns, and to refrain from interfering with each parties' rights.[43]

During Union Organization Efforts

The act protects employees' right to organize by prohibiting "interference, influence, or coercion by either party over the designation of representatives by the other."[44] Carriers may not deny or question an employee's right to organize, and carriers cannot use funds to maintain or assist a union in carrying out its duties or to influence an employee to leave or remain in a union.[45] Carriers cannot require prospective employees to sign an agreement to join or not to join a union.[46] Any carrier who willfully violates any of these provisions may be subject to civil and criminal penalties.[47] Additionally, the NMB can order rerun elections to eliminate the potential effects of any interference.[48]

During an Ongoing Carrier-Union Relationship

After certification of a union, carriers have the duty to bargain with that union.[49] A carrier has the duty to bargain only with the union and not directly with employees. Carriers cannot engage in direct communications with employees that give the impression that a carrier is unwilling to negotiate or communications that may disrupt negotiations or destroy a union's bargaining powers.[50]

During Self-Help

Self-help is the way in which one party can exert pressure on the other party and occurs outside of the formal dispute resolution process. Self-help includes peaceful striking, picketing, and locking out employees. Parties may not engage in self-help until they have exhausted the RLA's dispute resolution mechanisms; any self-help used afterwards must be lawful. Among the permissible actions employees can take are peaceful picketing, intermittent striking, and selective striking.

Additionally, employees may be able to engage in "secondary activity," through which they exert pressure on an entity with which they do not have a dispute.[51]

A carrier may hire permanent replacements for striking employees and keep those replacements at the end of the strike. However, a carrier may not discharge or eliminate the jobs of striking employees as retaliation for a strike.[52] A court has the ability to order parties to stop self-help (i.e., issue an injunction), if it finds that a carrier or a union has violated the status quo (i.e., neither party can change the current practices under an agreement).[53]

RLA Enforcement and Adjudication Processes

The RLA established several entities to administer and enforce the act. The National Mediation Board (NMB) is the primary agency charged with administration and enforcement and also provides mediation services to parties to a dispute. The National Railroad Adjustment Board (NRAB) is a tribunal under the NMB that hears and decides (arbitrates) grievances in the railway industry. Alternatively, parties in the railway industry can create their own arbitration tribunals, known as Special Boards of Adjustment (SBAs), or a single party can request that the NMB create a Public Law Board (PLB) to arbitrate the dispute. In the airline industry, various System Boards of Adjustment (System Boards), created jointly by labor and management, arbitrate disputes. The decisions of these entities can be reviewed by federal courts in limited circumstances.

National Mediation Board

The NMB is an independent agency that was created to administer and enforce the RLA. It is headed by a three member board. Each member serves full time and is appointed by the President and confirmed by the Senate for a term of three years. No more than two members can be of the same political party.[54] The three members self-designate a chairman on a yearly basis. The NMB has delegated its powers to investigate and adjudicate representation disputes to its General Counsel and oversees mediation and arbitration under the RLA.[55]

Adjustment Boards

The NRAB, SBAs, and System Boards are adjustment boards. An adjustment board is an entity that arbitrates disputes. Under the RLA, three types of adjustment boards exist for the railway industry (NRAB, SBAs, PLBs) and one exists for the airline carrier industry (System Boards).

The NRAB is a federal tribunal under the NMB that arbitrates grievances in the railroad industry. The NRAB consists of 34 members; seventeen are selected by carriers, and seventeen are selected by labor organizations of national scope.[56] The NRAB is divided into four divisions that generally operate independently of each other and process disputes involving specific types of employees.[57] Parties may seek compliance with NRAB decisions in federal district courts. District courts can also affirm or set aside, in whole or in part, NRAB orders.[58]

Alternatively, parties to a railway industry dispute can voluntarily agree to create an SBA, an arbitration tribunal. The NMB provides a list of potential arbitrators, known as the Roster of Arbitrators, to the parties, and the parties select the arbitrator from that list.

Finally, in the railway industry, a single party can request the establishment of a PLB to settle disputes for an individual railroad. Again, the parties choose arbitrators from the NMB's Roster of Arbitrators. The party upon whom the request is made must then enter into an agreement with the requesting party, establishing the board within 30 days of the request. If that party fails to agree to the creation of a PLB or fails to designate a member to the PLB, the requesting party may ask that the NMB designate an arbitrator.[59]

In all railway arbitration proceedings, the NMB pays the salaries and travel expenses of the arbitrators.[60]

When the RLA was amended to include airline carriers, it maintained the requirement of compulsory arbitration in certain disputes and established the National Air Transit Adjustment Board,[61] however, it was never created. Rather, airline carriers and unions created their own temporary special boards of adjustment, System Boards. Like railway carrier disputes, parties to an airline carrier dispute are required to engage in direct bargaining, but System Boards have no formal procedures and are limited in the jurisdiction agreed upon by the parties. System Boards must, therefore, look to collective bargaining agreements to determine how to proceed with a grievance.[62]

Unlike railway arbitration proceedings, the NMB does not pay the salaries and travel expenses to arbitrators in airline carrier industry disputes.[63]

Judicial Review

Grounds for judicial review and overturning either an NMB order or an adjustment board award are very narrow. A court can overturn an NMB order releasing parties from mediation if the order is outside of the NMB's jurisdiction or contrary to specific prohibitions in the RLA.[64]

Adjustment board awards may be reviewed and overturned if the award is affected by fraud, an adjustment board oversteps its jurisdiction, or the award does not conform to the RLA.[65] Additionally, an award can be called into question, referred to in the RLA as "impeached." To do so, a party must file a petition to impeach within 10 days of the final judgment. A decision can be impeached for several reasons: (1) if the award or proceedings do not conform to the substantive or procedural requirements of the RLA; (2) if the parties made a voluntary agreement to arbitrate and the award does not conform to the agreement; or (3) if a member of the board that rendered the award or a party to the arbitration was found guilty of fraud or corruption, and that fraud or corruption affected the outcome of the arbitration.[66]Any decision reached by an adjustment board is final and binding on the parties and can be enforced in the U.S. district courts.[67]

Dispute Resolution

Upon certification, a carrier has the duty to negotiate with, and only with, the certified union.[68] If parties fail to reach an agreement through direct negotiations, further RLA procedures may be invoked. The RLA divides disputes into two categories: major and minor disputes, and each type has its own dispute resolution mechanism. If a dispute cannot be resolved and the President believes that the dispute may substantially disrupt interstate commerce, he may invoke emergency procedures to resolve the dispute.

"Major" Disputes

"Major" disputes are those related to the process of collective bargaining (i.e., the parties cannot reach an agreement as to pay rates, rules, and working conditions). In the railway industry, agreements generally do not have expiration dates.[69] Rather, they become subject to change on a specified date within the original agreement. Major disputes, therefore, include both bargaining on the terms of an initial labor-management agreement and on any subsequent changes to the agreement the parties may wish to make.

Carriers and employees must give 30 days' written notice of any intended changes to the agreement to the other party. This is known as a "Section 6 notice." The parties must then agree on the time and place of a conference about the proposed changes within 10 days of receipt of the notice, and the conference between the parties must take place within the 30 days. Once the Section 6 notice has been served, each party must maintain the status quo.[70]

At any time during this direct bargaining process, either party may invoke the NMB's mediation services.[71] Parties continue to negotiate in the presence of an NMB mediator, and the mediator works with both parties, helping them to resolve their dispute. The NMB has sole discretion to decide when the parties can discontinue mediation because they have either reached an agreement or they are at an impasse and cannot reach an agreement.[72]

If the parties cannot reach an agreement, the NMB will "proffer arbi-tration" and invite the parties to submit their dispute to an arbitrator. This arbitration is voluntary-but-binding and is held before the appropriate adjustment board. If either or both parties refuse arbitration, the NMB sends written notice to the parties terminating its services. The parties then enter into a 30-day "coolingoff" period during which they cannot change the terms of the agreement.[73] After the cooling-off period, if the parties have not reached a mutual agreement, then they may exercise self-help, including strikes, lock outs, and imposition of new rules on the workforce.[74]

If parties do agree to arbitration, the arbitration board will comprise three members. Each party will select one arbitrator. These two arbitrators will then select a third. If the two arbitrators fail to select another within five days after their first meeting, the NMB will select the third arbitrator.[75] The arbitrators' decision is final as to all issues placed before them.[76]

"Minor" Disputes

A "minor" dispute is one involving the interpretation or application of an already existing agreement. As with major disputes, the parties have a duty to first engage in direct negotiations,[77] but, generally, a carrier may act on its own interpretation of the existing agreement while waiting for resolution of the dispute by an Adjustment Board.[78]

The RLA mandates that minor disputes be submitted to compulsory arbitration in front of the appropriate adjustment board, the NRAB for the railway industry and System Boards of Adjustment for airline carriers. In arbitration, members of the NRAB conduct hearings and make findings on the disputes. The parties must comply with the orders of the NRAB.[79]

Alternatively, the parties can mutually agree to form their own, temporary, adjustment board, a Special Board of Adjustment (SBA) that decides specific issues agreed upon by the parties. If one of the parties is dissatisfied with the SBA, it may give 90 days' notice to the other party to be brought under the jurisdiction of the NRAB or the System Boards of Adjustment.[80]

Finally, a single party can request of the other party that a PLB be created to resolve a dispute. The requesting party can select an arbitrator and if the other party does not agree to the establishment of a PLB or fails to select an arbitrator, the NMB will designate an arbitrator to sit on the PLB. If members of the PLB are unable to agree on an issue, they must select a neutral member of the board to decide the matter. If PLB members cannot agree on a neutral member within 10 days of their failure to agree on an issue, either member can request the NMB to appoint a neutral board member. [81]

Emergency Actions

Although a carrier and a union may exercise self-help at the end of the dispute resolution process, the NMB may determine that an unresolved dispute threatens "substantially to interrupt interstate commerce." It may then recommend that the President create a Presidential Emergency Board (PEB). The President may, in his discretion, create a PEB to investigate and issue a report on the dispute within 30 days of its creation. Parties must maintain the status quo upon the creation of a PEB and for the 30 days following the release of its report, unless the parties reach an agreement to the dispute.[82]

Publicly funded and operated commuter rails have a different set of PEB procedures. If the President decides not to create a PEB under the above mentioned procedures, parties to the dispute or the governor of a state through which the commuter rail runs may request that the President establish a PEB. If the parties have not settled within 60 days of the establishment of the PEB, the NMB is required to conduct a public hearing at which the parties explain why they have not accepted the PEB's dispute resolution recommendations. If the parties have still not reached a resolution 120 days after the PEB's creation, then any party or governor of a state through which the commuter rails run can request a second PEB. Upon such a request, the President must establish a second PEB. The parties must then submit to the NMB an offer for settlement within 30 days. The PEB than has 30 days to report to the President which offer it finds most reasonable. Throughout this process, parties may not engage in self-help.[83]

For both commuter and non-commuter rails, Congress may intervene (e.g., adopt PEB recommendations) in a dispute to prevent a work stoppage. On several occasions, Congress has either created another study commission or adopted PEB recommendations, effectively imposing a new agreement on the parties.[84]

NATIONAL LABOR RELATIONS ACT

Background

In 1933, the United States was in the midst of the Great Depression. President Franklin D. Roosevelt and Congress pursued policies to stabilize a weak economy and reduce unemployment. To these ends, the National Industrial Recovery Act of 1933 (NIRA) was enacted, which guaranteed workers the right to organize and to collectively bargain. By enabling unions to exert pressure on employers to increase wages, Congress believed workers would spend their higher wages, thus increasing the nation's purchasing power.[85]

NIRA did not prohibit so-called company-dominated unions, unions that are organized or assisted by an employer to such an extent that they appear to be an employer's creation and not an employee bargaining representative. Also, some employers refused to recognize employee-selected unions, which prompted some employees to strike.[86] Ultimately, the U.S. Supreme Court declared that NIRA was unconstitutional. Congress then enacted the National Labor Relations Act (NLRA), which is often called the Wagner Act, after its Senate sponsor, Senator Robert Wagner. Unlike its predecessor, the Wagner Act prohibited company-dominated unions and established the majority rule principle for worker representation. The act proved more effective than NIRA in protecting and guaranteeing employee rights.[87]

Major Amendments

The Taft-Hartley Act

Although the Wagner Act, by many accounts, accomplished Congress's goals, some critiqued it as one-sided and believed it too heavily favored unions, enabling excessive union power and disrupting the labor-management equilibrium.[88] In 1947, Congress passed the Taft-Hartley Act, named after its sponsors Senator Robert Taft and Representative Fred Hartley. This act placed some restrictions on unions and guaranteed certain freedoms of conduct and speech to employers.

Specifically, the Taft-Hartley Act enumerated prohibited unfair labor practices for unions,[89] required unions to give notification before striking, prohibited closed shops,[90] and outlawed secondary boycotts.[91] The act allowed states to enact right-to-work laws and gave employers the right to request an election to determine which of multiple unions claiming to represent employees was in fact the employee representative.[92] Supervisors were prohibited from joining unions,[93] and employees were given the right to petition to decertify a union.[94] Additionally, Congress restructured the National Labor Relations Board (NLRB), the federal agency charged with enforcing the NLRA.[95]

The Landrum-Griffin Act

Ten years following the enactment of the Taft-Hartley Act, in response to allegations of union corruption, Congress passed the Labor Management Reporting and Disclosure Act of 1959, commonly called the Landrum-Griffin Act after its sponsors Representative Phillip Landrum and Senator Robert Griffin.[96] The act applies to parties covered under both the NLRA and the Railway Labor Act (RLA). It added a union member "Bill of Rights" that enumerated five basic rights of union members: equality of rights, safeguards against improper disciplinary actions, freedom of speech, freedom from interference with the right to sue, and freedom from increased dues except by majority vote. The act also increased internal union transparency by mandating that each union enact by-laws and issue yearly financial disclosures.[97] Additionally, the act set forth specific election procedures to help ensure that internal union elections were free of corruption.[98]

Overview

The NLRA seeks to prevent labor-management disputes that could burden or obstruct commerce and harm the economy. It grants certain rights to both workers and employers, seeks to prevent practices that could frustrate a peaceful worker-employer relationship, and provides mechanisms for workers and employers to resolve disputes.

To achieve these goals, the NLRA regulates the labor-management relationship between workers and employers in the private sector, excluding the railway and airline carrier industries. It provides parties with a standard process for choosing a union to act as an employee representative in the collective bargaining process and details which individuals can participate in the process. Once a union is selected, the NLRA governs which subjects workers and unions can negotiate. The NLRA also regulates how workers, employers, and unions should behave towards each other during the union selection and collective bargaining processes and prohibits certain unfair actions.

To administer and enforce the act, the NLRA established the National Labor Relations Board (NLRB). The NLRB investigates and adjudicates representation disputes, complaints of unfair labor practices (ULPs), and contract disputes. The NLRB's General Counsel investigates and prosecutes ULP claims, and the General Counsel has delegated its authority to issue ULP complaints to regional directors.

Additionally, the President has the ability to create a Presidential Emergency Board (PEB) to investigate and aid in dispute resolution when he believes that a threatened or actual strike or lockout will endanger national health.

Scope of Coverage

The NLRA regulates collective bargaining rights and duties for employers, employees, and unions in the private sector, excluding the railway and airline carrier industries. While commercial airline carriers fall under the RLA's jurisdiction, the aviation manufacturing (defense, space, and commercial) and general aviation (e.g., flight training, intercontinental jet transportation of executives and public officers) industries fall under the NLRA's jurisdiction.[99] As with the RLA, the NLRA's preliminary sections define "employer" and "employee," and those definitions determine who is covered by the act's regulations.

Employer Defined

The NLRB has jurisdiction over employers whose operations affect interstate commerce.[100] The NLRB can assert jurisdiction over any employer whose operations affect commerce. However, the NLRB has established administrative standards, limiting its jurisdiction to those cases involving employers with a substantial effect on commerce. If an employer meets these administrative standards, the NLRB *must* review the case. These standards are based on an employer's annual sales or gross revenue. For example, retailers must have annual sales of at least $500,000 and privately operated hospitals must have an annual revenue of at least $250,000.[101]

The NLRA's definition of employer includes any person "acting as an agent of an employer, directly or indirectly." This definition does not include the United States, a wholly owned government corporation, a state or its subdivisions, or any Federal Reserve Bank.[102] International organizations, while not specifically enumerated, are excluded from NLRA coverage.[103]

Employee Defined

An employee includes anyone who works for another for hire. Individuals who have stopped working because of a current labor dispute or unfair labor practice and who have not obtained equivalent employment are also included in the definition. Agricultural workers, domestic workers employed by a family or person within their home, individuals employed by their parent or spouse, independent contractors, and supervisors are not employees for the purposes of the NLRA.[104]

If a person does not fall under one of the excluded categories, he is assumed to be an employee under the act. Therefore, nonresident aliens and hospital resident physicians are considered employees. However, graduate students working in teaching positions and unpaid volunteers are not employees.[105]

A supervisor is not an employee. An individual is a supervisor if he has the authority to "hire, transfer, suspend, lay off, recall, promote, discharge, assign, reward, or discipline other employees, or responsibly direct them, or to adjust their grievances" and if that authority requires the use of independent judgment.[106] Individuals who are temporarily holding a supervisory position are usually considered employees and, therefore, afforded NLRA protections.[107] Managerial employees, although they may not exercise supervisory functions, are exempt from NLRA coverage because they "formulate and effectuate management policies" and have discretion in performing their jobs.[108]

Rights and Duties under the Law

The act both mandates and prohibits certain actions of all parties involved in a labor-management dispute. The act grants employees the right to organize and collectively bargain and sets forth the procedures and standards to be applied in the selection of a union as an employee representative and the subsequent relations between the union and the employer.

During organization, employees can select a union that will represent their bargaining unit's interests in bargaining with employers over working conditions. A bargaining unit is a group of employees who are or wish to be represented by a union. A union can be recognized as a representative through a union security agreement, a secret ballot election, or voluntary employer recognition.

Bargaining topics are divided into those that unions and employers must bargain over (mandatory subjects), those that parties may bargain over (permissive subjects), and those that parties are prohibited from bargaining over (illegal subjects).

Certain conduct is prohibited in the employer-union relationship during union organization and collective bargaining. Employers and unions cannot interfere with employees' right to organize and select a union. Employers and unions are required to bargain with each other in good faith over conditions of employment, and employers can only bargain with the employee-selected union. In limited circumstances, the parties can use some forms of self-help if they have reached an impasse in the bargaining process.

Union Selection

Employees have the right to choose their union representative.[109] A majority vote by the members of an appropriate bargaining unit determines the union.[110] A union must either be certified by the NLRB or voluntarily recognized by the employer before collective bargaining can begin.[111]

Union Security Agreements

Unions and employers are generally allowed to enter into union security agreements under which employees may be required, as a condition of employment, to become union members by paying dues and initiation fees. A job applicant cannot be required to be a union member for hiring consideration, but a newly hired employee can be required to become a dues-paying member on or 30 days after the start of employment. This type of union-security agreement is known as a union shop agreement. Agency shops may also be created. In an agency shop, employees who do not join the union pay a fee to the union for its services as a bargaining agent, in lieu of dues.[112]

The union's authority to enter into security agreements can be revoked if a majority of affected employees vote to do so. Only one deauthorization election per twelve-month period can be held. Petitions for deauthorization elections must be supported by at least 30% of employees in the affected bargaining unit. Any employees, including those not required to join the union by the terms of the collective bargaining agreement, but excluding supervisors, may petition for a deauthorization election.[113]

Most provisions of the NLRA preempt state law, however, the NLRA specifically allows states to enact "right-to-work" laws.[114] Right-to-work laws prohibit or restrict union security agreements and give employees the option of employment without requiring them to join a union or to pay union dues.[115]

Determination of a Bargaining Unit

A bargaining unit is a group of employees represented or seeking representation by a union. If a union and employer do not agree on an appropriate bargaining unit, the issue is settled by the NLRB.

A bargaining unit is generally determined on the basis of a "community of interest" of the employees involved and whether those employees can be reasonably grouped together. To determine a "community of interest," the NLRB will look to several factors including historical or traditional units; employee wishes; and whether employees have the same or similar interests with respect to pay rates, hours, and other working conditions. A bargaining unit may include the employees of one employer location or multiple employer locations; it may also include employees of multiple employers. A bargaining unit may include both professional and nonprofessional employees, however, a majority of professional employees must vote to be members of the unit.[116]

Eligibility to Vote in a Secret Ballot Election

Employees who work in the bargaining unit during the eligibility period set by the NLRB and who are employed at the time of an election may vote in an election. Employees who are on a leave of absence or furloughed are eligible to vote. Economic strikers[117] who have been replaced by permanent employees may be allowed to vote in elections held within 12 months after the beginning of the strike; their permanent replacements can vote in the same election.[118] Unfair labor practice strikers are entitled to vote in elections but their temporary replacements are not.[119]

Certification

A union can be recognized as an employee representative in a number of ways, including through a secret ballot election. To initiate a secret ballot election, an individual or union must file a representation petition with the NLRB alleging that a "substantial number of employees" want union representation or that a recognized union no longer represents a majority of employees in the bargaining unit. An employer can also file a petition alleging that one or more organizations claim recognition. Petitions filed by employees or unions must be accompanied by authorization cards signed by at least 30% of employees.[120]

Consent Agreements

Before an election, the NLRB's regional staff will try to secure one of three types of consent-election agreement from the parties. Consent agreements are agreed upon by the parties and lay out the terms of an election, including which choices are to be included on the ballot and the method to determine voting eligibility.[121] A regional director of the NLRB must approve any consent-election agreement.[122] The three types of consent-election agreements are:

- **Pure consent agreement.** The parties agree to have the regional director resolve any disputes arising from the election, and the regional director's rulings are final.
- **Stipulated election agreement.** The regional director's rulings are subject to review by the adjudicatory arm of the NLRB.
- **Full consent agreement.** The parties agree that the regional director will resolve both pre- and post-election disputes.[123]

Each type of agreement usually gives the NLRB regional director the authority to conduct the election, but parties can agree to an election conducted by a third party, such as an arbitrator or a mediation board.[124]

NLRB-Administered Elections

If parties do not enter into a consent-election agreement, a formal representation hearing is held. The hearing provides a forum for the parties to present their arguments regarding the representation election and may include the examination of witnesses and introduction of evidence. After the hearing, the hearing officer gives a summary of the issues and evidence to the regional director and the regional director makes a decision on the issues.[125]

After the hearing, the NLRB can direct a secret ballot election. The NLRB can certify a union receiving the majority of votes cast in an election. If an election has more than one union on the ballot and no choice receives a majority of the vote, the two choices with the most votes face each other in a runoff election.[126]

Parties can file an objection to the election if they believe the NLRB's election standards have not been met. An election may be set aside if it was accompanied by interference with the employees' freedom of choice. Examples of interference with employee freedom of choice include threats of job or benefits loss, threats of violence, and incentives to influence an employee's vote.[127]

If a union is NLRB-certified, the employer must bargain with it in good faith for one year.[128]

Voluntary Recognition

The NLRA does not preclude employers from voluntarily recognizing a union as an employee representative. An employer may do this if a majority of employees in a bargaining unit have signed authorization cards. A union and employer can also enter into a card check agreement, under which an employer agrees to recognize a union before the union begins to collect authorization cards. A card check agreement may require the union to collect more than a majority of authorization cards from bargaining unit employees.[129]

If an employer voluntarily recognizes a union, employees can file a decertification petition or an election petition requesting representation by another union after a reasonable amount of time. A reasonable amount of time is defined by the NLRA as at least six months, but no more than one year after the parties' first bargaining session.[130]

The NLRB may also require an employer to recognize and bargain with a union if a majority of employees signed authorization cards and the employer engaged in unfair labor practices that make a fair election unlikely.[131] The employer must bargain with the union, in good faith, for one year.[132]

Decertification

The NLRB requires a secret ballot election to decertify either certified or voluntarily recognized unions. A decertification petition may be filed by employees or a union acting on their behalf. The petition must be signed by at least 30% of the employees in the bargaining unit represented by the union. Parties cannot file a decertification or election petition for unions certified in an NLRB-conducted election until one year after certification.[133]

Withdrawal of Recognition

Union recognition can be withdrawn under two circumstances. It can be withdrawn if

1. one year after certification the employer and union have not reached a contract agreement. Both parties must have bargained in good faith, and the employer must doubt that a majority of employees currently support the certified union. The employer's doubt must be based on objective information (e.g., a petition signed by a majority of employees), or
2. no contract agreement has been reached after a reasonable amount of time and the employer has a reasonable doubt, supported by objective information, that the union is no longer supported by a majority of unit employees.[134]

Bargaining Subjects

The NLRA mandates that employers must bargain with unions regarding "rates of pay, wages, hours of employment, and other conditions of employment."[135] Because the statute does not provide further explanation, the NLRB and courts have divided bargaining subjects into three distinct categories: mandatory, permissive, and illegal.

Mandatory Subjects

Mandatory bargaining subjects are those that "vitally affect" employees. Employers must bargain with unions over such subjects, are prohibited from taking unilateral action related to them, and cannot make agreements with individual union members about them.[136]

The NLRA defines the following terms: "wage," "hours of employment," and "other conditions of employment." The term "wage" includes

- overtime pay,
- shift differentials,
- paid holidays and vacations,
- commissions,
- severance pay,
- pensions,
- health insurance, and
- profit-sharing plans.

The term "hours of employment" includes work schedules. The term "other conditions of employment" include provisions for grievance procedures, work loads, and sick leave.[137]

Permissive Subjects

Permissive bargaining subjects are those that either party may propose for inclusion in collective bargaining but neither party is required to bargain over them. When a permissive subject is included in a collective bargaining agreement, that subject does not then become a mandatory subject. Permissive subjects include the definition of a bargaining unit, selection of bargaining representatives, and union-recognition clauses.[138]

Illegal Subjects

The NLRA specifically prohibits either party from requiring the other party to contract for provisions that are illegal or that go against Congress's intent in enacting the NLRA. Closed-shop and hot-cargo clauses are examples of such provisions.[139] Additional illegal subjects of bargaining include separation of employees by race, rules requiring preference for union members, and an employer's right to terminate and employee for union activity.[140]

Prohibited Conduct

The NLRA defines and prohibits certain conduct as unfair labor practices (ULPs) to protect the rights of both employees and employers.[141] Through its provisions, the NLRA attempts to prevent and remedy, but not punish, ULPs. The NLRB can issue cease-and-desist orders to stop ULPs, and it can require employers to reinstate and give back pay to employees who were improperly discharged for union activities.[142] A union may be required to give an employee back pay if it is responsible for a ULP that caused an employer to discharge a worker. Punitive damages, however, are generally unavailable.[143]

During Union Organization Efforts

The NLRA imposes restrictions on employers and unions during the process of union organization. The act prohibits employers and unions from interfering with or coercing employees exercising their right to organize.[144] The NLRB does not require a showing of intent to violate the act, rather, an employer's or union's conduct must tend to interfere with employees' right to organize.[145]

During union organization, neither an employer nor a union can threaten discharge, loss of benefits, or plant closure if employees exercise their right to organize. An employer cannot raise wages to discourage workers from unionizing or discriminate against employees regarding conditions of employment (e.g., give unfavorable work assignments), and a union cannot cause an employer to discriminate against employees regarding employment conditions.[146]

Employers are prohibited from dominating a union. An employer dominates a union when it has participated in the union's organization and assisted and supported its activities to such an extent that the union appears to be the employer's creation and not the employees' bargaining representative. Additionally, employers cannot interfere with or contribute money or other support to a union, such as supporting one union over another in an election or pressuring employees to financially support a union, absent a valid union security agreement.[147]

Unions are prohibited from interfering with employers' choice of selecting who will or will not represent them in the collective bargaining process.[148] A union cannot influence an employee's choice of representative in procedures to address individual employee complaints.[149]

During an Ongoing Employer-Union Relationship

Both employers and unions are required to bargain collectively and in good faith with one another over "wages, hours of employment, and other terms and conditions of employment."[150] "Good faith" has not been specifically defined, but factors surrounding the bargaining process are used to determine whether parties bargained in good faith, including the justification for proposals and a willingness to make concessions. Some actions, such as unilateral changes and bargaining directly with employees, are considered by the NLRB to be in and of themselves refusals to bargain and in violation of the requirement to bargain in good faith.[151]

Neither employers nor unions can "restrain or coerce employees" in exercising their right to bargain collectively.[152] Employers cannot discriminate against employees to encourage or discourage union membership or because they have filed charges or given testimony under the NLRA.[153] A union cannot cause an employer to discriminate against employees to encourage or discourage union membership.[154]

Unions can fine and discipline members, so long as those sanctions are consistent with NLRB policy. For instance, a union cannot fine, expel, or use violence against a member for filing a ULP charge, for testifying against other members in arbitration, or for refusing to participate in unlawful or unprotected activity. A union can, however, fine or suspend a member for violating internal union rules.[155]

During Self-Help

In certain situations, the NLRA protects employees when they exercise self-help. When self-help is protected, employers violate the act by taking adverse or discriminatory action against employees who are using self-help. Protected activities are those used by employees, in a peaceful manner, to exercise their rights under the act, such as certain economic strikes, sympathy strikes, filing grievances, and activity opposing union leadership.[156] Unprotected activities include those that are violent or unlawful. Unprotected employee activities include sit-down strikes, intermittent strikes, partial strikes, strikes in violation of a contract's no-strike clause, acts of disloyalty,[157] and disruptive or vulgar behavior.[158]

During a strike, employee rights differ depending on the reason for the strike. If the strike is economic, employees retain their employment status and cannot be discharged, but employers can replace them. After the strike, if the employer has hired replacements, the striking employees are not entitled to job reinstatement. However, if the striking employees cannot find regular and substantially equivalent work, they are entitled to be recalled by the employer to jobs for which they are qualified, when jobs become available.[159]

During a strike protesting an employer's unfair labor practices, employees can neither lose their job nor be permanently replaced. After the strike, absent serious misconduct[160] on their part, striking employees are entitled to return to their jobs.[161]

Employers can also engage in certain self-help activities. An employer can prevent employees from working (i.e., a lockout) but not over a dispute about non-mandatory bargaining subjects. During a strike, an employer can unilaterally establish employment terms and conditions for workers hired as striker replacements, but without a bargaining impasse, an employer may not alter employment terms and conditions of non-striking employees.[162]

NLRA Enforcement and Adjudication Processes

The NLRA established the National Labor Relations Board (NLRB) to administer and enforce the act. The NLRB has the power to investigate and adjudicate representation disputes, ULP complaints, and contract disputes. NLRB decisions can be reviewed by federal courts in limited circumstances (see discussion below).

National Labor Relations Board

The NLRB is an independent federal agency charged with administering and enforcing the NLRA. It comprises a five-member Board and a General Counsel. Hereafter, the "NLRB" is used to refer to both the five-member Board and the General Counsel as a collective body. "The Board" refers to the five-member Board alone.

The Board and General Counsel are appointed by the President and confirmed by the Senate. Traditionally, the Board is comprised of two Democrats, two Republicans, and a fifth member who belongs to the same party as the President. If a position is vacant and the Senate is in recess, the President can make a "recess appointment." The appointment expires at the end of the next Senate session.[163]

The Board adjudicates objections and challenges to secret ballot elections, decides questions about the composition of bargaining units, and determines all ULP cases prosecuted by the General Counsel.[164] The General Counsel has authority over ULP investigations and the issuance of ULP complaints; it has delegated its authority to issue ULP complaints to 51 field offices, which are composed of approximately 1,680 full-time employees.[165]

Judicial Review

Only final orders issued by the Board in ULP cases are subject to judicial review by the courts.[166] Board orders do not have the force of law, and parties can only be compelled to comply with NLRB orders through the U.S. courts of appeals.[167]

Generally, U.S. district courts cannot review Board decisions on ULP or representation cases. District courts can review representation decisions in connection with the review of an order in a ULP case. District courts can review representation cases if the Board made an order in excess of its jurisdiction or contrary to a specific provision in the NLRA.[168] The Board and federal courts are not allowed to review General Counsel decisions not to issue a ULP complaint, unless they are in connection with a review of a Board final order.[169] If, after an investigation, the regional director has "reasonable cause to believe" that the ULP charge is true and that a complaint should be issued, the regional director must petition the district court for appropriate relief.[170]

Dispute Resolution

Unfair Labor Practice Disputes

An employee, employer, union, or any other person can initiate a ULP investigation against an employer or a union by filing a charge with the NLRB no more than six months after the alleged incident.[171] The charge is then investigated by the regional director, and the regional director determines whether a formal complaint should be issued. A refusal to issue a complaint can be appealed to the General Counsel. However, parties do not have a right to Board or court review.[172]

If the General Counsel determines that a charge has merit, he may try to settle the matter either formally or informally. In an informal settlement, parties generally agree to withdraw the charge upon remedial action and notice of the proposed settlement terms to affected employees. If the charged party does not comply with the agreement terms, the settlement will be withdrawn, and the case will be prosecuted. The settlement is not subject to judicial review.[173]

Formal settlements are used in cases where the General Counsel finds a persistent or deliberate violation of the NLRA. In a formal settlement, the charged party agrees to the Board's issuing a formal remedial order. If the charged party violates the settlement, the NLRB may institute judicial proceedings, or the party may be held in contempt.[174]

When a settlement is not reached in a meritorious case, the regional office will issue a complaint. Hearings are then held before an administrative law judge (ALJ), who issues a decision and recommendations to the Board. If a party does not object to the ALJ's decision, the Board can adopt the ALJ's decision as its own. Otherwise, the Board can review the ALJ's decision and issue its own orders. The General Counsel is responsible for ensuring compliance with the Board's orders.[175]

Contract Disputes

Arbitration is the primary mechanism for resolving contract disputes. In arbitration, the union and employer present their positions to an arbitrator who resolves the dispute. When arbitration is not possible, a party can bring a suit for contract violations in either state or federal court. However, if state law regarding contract interpretation or substance contradicts federal law, federal law prevails.[176] The Board also has the authority to interpret collective bargaining contracts, but courts generally do not defer to the Board in contract interpretation.[177] Both courts and the Board can issue injunctions to prevent certain actions, such as strikes that are in breach of a no-strike contract clause that requires arbitration.[178]

Emergency Actions

When the President believes that a threatened or actual strike or lockout that affects an entire industry or a substantial part of it will endanger national health or safety, he or she may appoint a "board of inquiry" to investigate the issue. A board of inquiry can include a chairman and any other members the President chooses. The board then issues a report on the facts of the dispute to the President. However, the report cannot include recommendations.[179]

After a report is issued, the President may direct the Attorney General to petition a U.S. district court to order a party to end the strike or lockout. If the court finds that the activity does indeed affect at least a substantial portion of an industry and threatens national health or safety, it will order a party to end the strike or lockout. A district court's orders may be appealed to a federal court of appeals.[180]

While the injunction is in effect, the parties to the dispute are encouraged to settle the matter on their own, and the board of inquiry reconvenes. After 60 days, the board reports to the President the current state of relations between the parties. Within 15 days of the issuance of the report, the NLRB must then conduct a secret ballot election of the employees involved in the dispute on whether they wish to accept a final offer of settlement made by their employer.[181]

After either the certification of the secret ballot election or a settlement, the injunction is discharged. The President submits a report detailing the process and any other recommendations of appropriate action to Congress.[182]

THE FEDERAL SERVICE LABOR-MANAGEMENT RELATIONS STATUTE

Background

While many private sector employees gained statutory rights to collective bargaining and remedies to unfair labor practices throughout the 1920s and 1930s, many of their public counterparts remained unprotected until the 1960s.[183] Traditional concepts of government sovereignty and public employees' general satisfaction with their job security contributed to this disparity.[184] However, by the 1960s, many federal public employees found their jobs to be less secure due to organizational and technological changes. Moreover, many commentators thought the federal government's willingness to extend collective bargaining rights to private employees but not to its own employees was inconsistent.[185]

Executive Order 10988

Union recognition bills were introduced in each Congress throughout the 1950s, but both President Harry Truman and President Dwight Eisenhower strongly opposed them. In 1961, President John F. Kennedy formed the Task Force on Employee-Management Relations in the Federal Service, which evaluated and made recommendations about federal employee unionization. In 1962, President Kennedy implemented the Task Force recommendations through Executive Order 10988.[186] The order granted federal employees the right to join, or not to join, labor unions and to collectively bargain. These new rights, however, were not as extensive as those of private employees. For instance, federal employees could not negotiate over wages and were prohibited from striking. Additionally, an agency could require that employees negotiate over a collective bargaining agreement only during non-official time (i.e., at times when employees were not on duty and entitled to compensation).[187]

Executive Order 11491

In 1969, President Richard Nixon issued Executive Order 11491, which further developed the framework of federal labor-management relations. It provided that majority exclusive recognition would be the only form of union recognition,[188] established the Federal Labor Relations Council (the predecessor to the current Federal Labor Relations Authority, FLRA) and the Federal Service Impasses Panel (FSIP), and listed prohibited unfair labor practices for both unions and management. It also allowed employees to use limited "official time" to negotiate a collective bargaining agreement.[189]

The Federal Service Labor-Management Relations Statute

Although federal employees were given collective bargaining rights under the executive orders (EOs) issued by Presidents Kennedy and Nixon, those rights were not necessarily secure, as EOs are subject to unilateral change or termination by the President. In 1978, however, Congress codified and adopted many of the EOs' provisions as Title VII of the Civil Service Reform Act of 1978, commonly referred to as the Federal Service Labor-Management Relations Statute (FSLMRS). While the statute followed the general principles of the EOs, it also made several changes, such as establishing the Federal Labor Relations Authority (FLRA), limiting the statute's coverage, and allowing employees official time to negotiate collective bargaining agreements.[190]

Recent Developments

In 2009, President Barack Obama issued Executive Order 13522, which created the National Council on Federal Labor-Management Relations (the Council). In this EO, the Council was charged with creating pilot labor-management forums within the federal government to allow agency managers and unions to discuss labor-management issues in a nonadversarial setting. The pilot project is in its second year and continues to implement new initiatives and advise the President on how to improve labor-management relations in the federal government.[191]

Other Federal Workforce Labor-Relations Statutes and Policies

Although several agencies were explicitly excluded from FSLMRS coverage see "Employer Defined" below), some of them are covered by separate labor-relations statutes or policies.

The Government Accountability Office (GAO) is excluded from FSLMRS coverage, but the General Accounting Office Personnel Act of 1980 gave GAO employees the right to organize and bargain collectively.[192]

Neither the FSLMRS nor the Tennessee Valley Authority (TVA) Act of 1933 granted TVA employees collective bargaining rights. However, in 1935, TVA adopted a policy that allows employees to organize and bargain over wages.[193]

Without actually changing the language of the National Labor Relations Act (NLRA), Congress incorporated most NLRA provisions into the Postal Reorganization Act of 1970. This action gave enforceable collective bargaining rights to U.S. postal workers.[194]

Overview

The FSLMRS seeks to prevent labor-management disputes that could burden or obstruct federal government operations. It grants certain rights to both workers and employers, seeks to prevent practices that could frustrate a peaceful worker-employer relationship, and provides mechanisms for workers and employers to resolve disputes.

To achieve these goals, the FSLMR regulates the labor-management relationship between workers and employers in most federal agencies. It provides parties with a standard process for choosing a union to act as an employee representative in the collective bargaining process and details which individuals can participate in the process. Once a union is selected, the FSLMR governs which subjects workers and unions can negotiate. The FSMLRS also regulates how workers, employers, and unions should behave towards each other during the union selection and collective bargaining processes and prohibits certain unfair actions.

To administer and enforce the statute, the FSLMRS established the Federal Labor Relations Authority (FLRA) as the primary agency to administer and enforce the statute. The FLRA has the authority to investigate and adjudicate representation disputes, ULP complaints, and contract disputes. The Federal Mediation and Conciliation Service (FMCS) is an independent agency that provides voluntary mediation services to parties who cannot resolve a bargaining dispute. The Federal Service Impasses Panel (FSIP) is an entity within the FLRA that provides additional assistance in resolving disputes if FMCS services cannot resolve the dispute or if the parties specifically request FSIP's services.

Scope of Coverage

The FSLMRS regulates collective bargaining rights and duties for most federal agencies, employees, and unions. The preliminary sections of the FSLMRS define "employer," "employee," and "labor organization," and those definitions determine who is covered by the statute's regulations.

State and local laws govern state and local public employees.

Employer Defined

The FSLMRS applies to most federal executive agencies, along with the Library of Congress, the Government Printing Office, and the Smithsonian Institution. Several agencies are specifically excluded from the statute's coverage. Those excluded agencies are the Government Accountability Office, the Federal Bureau of Investigation, the Central Intelligence Agency, the National Security Agency, the Tennessee Valley Authority, the Federal Labor Relations Authority, the Federal Impasses Panel, and the U.S. Secret Service.[195]

The President has the power to unilaterally exclude an agency or subdivision from coverage under the FSLMRS if he determines the entity's "primary function" is "intelligence, counterintelligence, investigative, or national security work" and that the provisions of the statute cannot be applied "in a manner consistent with national security requirements and considerations."[196] With this power, the President has excluded additional agencies and agency subdivisions, including the National Nuclear Security Administration, the Federal Air Marshall Service, and several subdivisions of each branch of the military.[197]

Employee Defined

An employee includes any individual employed in an agency or an individual who is no longer employed at an agency because of unfair labor practices and who has not obtained regular and substantially similar employment elsewhere. The definition specifically excludes some individuals from the definition of employee, including noncitizens, members of the uniformed services, supervisors, management officials, officers or employees in the Foreign Service, and individuals who participate in a strike in violation of the statute.[198]

Labor Organization Defined

A labor organization is defined as an organization composed, at least in part, of employees who participate in and pay dues to that organization. The organization must have the purpose of dealing with an agency regarding conditions of employment and grievances. Organizations that deny membership on the basis of sex, color, race, creed, national origin, and other similar characteristics; advocate the overthrow of the U.S. government; are sponsored by an agency; or participate or assist in a strike are not labor organizations recognized under the statute.[199]

Rights and Duties under the Law

The statute both mandates and prohibits certain actions of all parties involved in a labor-management dispute. The statute grants employees the right to organize and collectively bargain and sets forth the procedures and standards to be applied in the selection of a union as an employee representative and the subsequent relations between the union and the employer.

Unions and agencies can bargain over working conditions but cannot bargain over those topics already governed by another law (i.e., rates of pay as determined by the General Schedule). Working conditions might include work hours and allocation of employee offices. Employees must share a "community of interest" to be recognized as an appropriate unit for union representation. The union selection process is more limited in the federal sector than in the private sector, as a union can only be certified as an employee representative through a secret ballot election and union-security agreements are illegal.

Certain conduct is prohibited in the employer-union relationship during union organization and collective bargaining. Employers and unions cannot interfere with employees' right to organize and select a union. Employers and unions are required to bargain with each other in good faith, and employers can only bargain with an employee-selected union. If a bargaining impasse is reached, federal employees are prohibited from participating in strikes, work stoppages, slowdowns, or picketing that interferes with agency operations.

Bargaining Subjects

The FSLMRS gives federal employees the right to collectively bargain over conditions of employment.[200] Conditions of employment include "personnel policies, practices, and matters ... affecting work conditions." An employee's right to participate in political activities, the classification of positions, and any matters covered by other federal statutes (e.g., wages)[201] are specifically excluded from this definition.[202]

Employees and their unions are also not allowed to bargain over the statutory rights of management that are set forth in the statute. These nonnegotiable managerial rights include the authority to determine the organization's mission or budget and the authority to hire, discharge, or assign work to an employee.[203] The parties may, however, bargain over grievance procedures for adversely affected employees, the way in which management will exercise its authority, and, at the agency's election, the number of employees or positions assigned to a work project,[204]

Union Selection

Federal employees have the right to select their union, and agencies must give exclusive recognition to the union selected by employees.[205]

Union Security Agreements

Union security agreements are prohibited under the FSLMRS. Unions representing federal employees must represent all unit employees, regardless of whether they pay dues.[206]

Determination of a Bargaining Unit

Unions can represent those employees who are grouped together in an appropriate unit. To find a unit "appropriate" for representation, the FSLMRS requires that three criteria be met.

1. The unit must encompass employees who share a clear "community of interest," identifiable employment concerns distinct from those of other groups of employees.[207]
2. The unit must promote an effective relationship with the agency.
3. The unit must promote efficient operations of the agency.[208]

Management officials and supervisors cannot be included in a bargaining unit unless they have historically been included in the unit.[209] Additional employees prohibited from a unit include employees who administer FSLMRS provisions and employees whose work affects national security.[210]

Eligibility to Vote

The Federal Labor Relations Authority (FLRA) determines which employees are eligible to vote in secret ballot elections.[211] Regularly scheduled intermittent employees who work in positions that exist year round or who have a reasonable expectation of continued employment can vote in elections.[212] Temporary employees can also vote, if they have a reasonable expectation of continued employment beyond their initial six months of work and share a community of interest with the permanent employees included in the bargaining unit.[213]

Certification

Under the FSLMRS, a union can only be certified as an employee representative through a secret ballot election. To initiate a secret ballot election, an individual, a union, or an agency must first file a representation petition and a "showing of interest" that either 30% of unit employees wish to be represented by a union or that 30% of unit employees allege that the union no longer represents a majority of the unit employees.[214]

The regional director of the FLRA's General Counsel (see discussion of "FLRA Enforcement and Adjudication Processes" below) will determine whether the showing of interest is sufficient and meet with parties to resolve any preliminary disputes. It then conducts an investigation into any allegations made, including identifying related cases, identifying other parties who may be affected, and making any other necessary determinations.[215]

After an investigation and any hearings, the regional director can order a secret ballot election. If an election is ordered, parties are encouraged to enter into consent-election agreements that include the choices to be on the ballot and the method of election. However, if parties cannot agree to these terms, the regional director will issue a "direction of election." A direction of election sets out the election procedures. Parties have the opportunity to bring any nonprocedural issues before the regional director in a hearing.[216]

Once an election is held, a union will be certified as an employee representative if it receives the majority of votes cast. If an election has more than one union on the ballot and no choice receives a majority of the votes, the two choices with the most votes face each other in a runoff election.[217]

A party can file an objection to procedural aspects of an election or conduct that may have adversely impacted the election within five days of the vote tally.[218] While the results of an election are pending, parties must maintain the terms of any existing collective bargaining agreement.[219]

National Consultation Rights

The FSLMRS gives employees who are unrepresented by a certified union an additional collective bargaining protection. National Consultation Rights (NCRs)[220] entitle a union to be informed of agency-proposed substantive changes in employment conditions and to present its views and recom-mendations on the matter, even if the union does not have exclusive agency recognition. An agency must consider any views and recommendations submitted to it by a union with NCRs before making a final decision. A union gains NCRs if a unit does not have a recognized exclusive representative within its agency and the union is the exclusive representative of at least 3,500 or 10% of employees in the agency.[221]

Decertification

An election can also be held to determine if a bargaining unit no longer wishes to be represented by its union. As with a petition for a representation election, an individual, union, or agency can file a petition for an election, and the petition must be signed by or accompanied by authorization cards of 30% of the unit employees who allege that the union no longer represents a majority of the unit employees.[222]

Additionally, a regional director can revoke certification if a union disclaims its interest in representing the unit or if the regional director determines that the unit is no longer appropriate because of a "substantial change in character and scope of the unit" and that an election is unnecessary.[223]

Prohibited Conduct

The FSLMRS defines and prohibits certain conduct as unfair labor practices (ULPs) to protect the rights of both workers and employers.[224] The FLRA can issue cease-and-desist orders to stop a ULP, require employers to reinstate and give backpay to employees who were improperly discharged for union activities, and require parties to renegotiate contracts in accordance with its orders. A union may be required to give an employee backpay if it caused an employer to discharge that employee.[225]

During Union Organization Efforts

The FSLMRS protects employees' right to organize and imposes restrictions on employers and unions during this process. The statute prohibits employers and unions from interfering with or coercing employees exercising their right to organize. For instance, neither an employer nor a union can threaten discharge or make threatening statements to employees to influence their decision to join a union. A union cannot cause an employer to discriminate against employees regarding employment conditions.[226]

Agencies are prohibited from sponsoring, controlling, or assisting a union. Prohibited conduct includes actively assisting a union in organizing its employees or campaigning for a particular union or individual running for union office.[227]

During an Ongoing Employer-Union Relationship

Both employers and unions are required to negotiate in good faith with one another over conditions of employment. This obligation to negotiate includes, if requested by either party, the duty to enter into a written collective bargaining agreement. This obligation does not require either party to make a concession or agree to a proposal by the other party.[228]

The duty to bargain in good faith includes coming to the bargaining table with a willingness to reach a collective bargaining agreement and meeting at reasonable times and places. For instance, both employers and unions are required to bargain on negotiable matters proposed by the other that are not already in the collective bargaining agreement. Additionally, employers cannot unilaterally change working conditions. Working conditions might include work hours or allocation of employee offices. Neither employers nor unions can refuse to cooperate in impasse procedures and decisions. Failure to cooperate includes failing to comply with a final order from the Federal Service Impasses Panel, the FLRA's dispute resolution entity.[229]

Employers cannot discipline or discriminate against employees who file complaints under the statute. A union cannot coerce, discipline, fine, or attempt to coerce a union member as punishment or to hinder their work. Employees are protected from union harassment when they are performing their official work duties.[230] Additionally, unions cannot discriminate against employees regarding union membership because of race, color, creed, national origin, sex, age, civil service status, political affiliation, marital status, or handicap.[231] Neither employers nor unions can refuse to comply with any other provision of the statute.[232]

During Self-Help

Federal employees can use self-help to exert pressure on an employer, but the types of self-help available are more limited than under other labor relations laws. Federal employees can engage in peaceful, informational picketing so long as the activity does not interfere with agency operations. However, unlike private-sector employees, federal employees cannot participate in, and unions cannot encourage, strikes, work stoppages, slowdowns, or pickets that interfere with agency operations. Additionally, a union commits a ULP if it fails to prevent such activity. If a union willfully or intentionally supports such actions, the FLRA can revoke its exclusive recognition status.[233]

FSLMRS Enforcement and Adjudication Processes

The FSLMRS established the Federal Labor Relations Authority (FLRA) as the primary agency to administer and enforce the statute. The FLRA has the authority to investigate and adjudicate representation disputes, ULP complaints, and contract disputes. The Federal Mediation and Conciliation Service (FMCS) provides voluntary mediation services to parties who have reached a negotiation impasse. The Federal Service Impasses Panel (FSIP) is an entity within the FLRA that provides additional assistance in resolving disputes if FMCS services cannot resolve the dispute or if the parties specifically request FSIP's services. The FLRA's General Counsel investigates and prosecute ULP complaints. FLRA decisions can be reviewed by federal courts in limited circumstances; judicial review of FSIP decisions is unavailable.

The Federal Labor Relations Authority

The FLRA is an independent federal agency charged with administering and enforcing the FSLMRS. It is composed of three members (the Authority) who are appointed by the President for five-year terms. No more than two can be of the same political party. Hereafter, "FLRA" refers to the three-member board, the General Counsel, and the FSIP as a collective body. The "Authority" refers to the three-member board alone. The Authority's response-bilities include hearing ULP cases, determining the appropriateness of units, and conducting secret ballot elections.[234]

The FLRA's General Counsel investigates and prosecutes complaints before the Authority and is appointed by the President for a five-year term. The FLRA can delegate its power to determine election issues and to investigate and prosecute ULP complaints to its seven regional offices.[235]

The Federal Mediation and Conciliation Service

FMCS provides mediation services for parties who have reached an impasse in negotiations. FMCS services are available to both private and public workers and employers.

In the federal sector, use of FMCS services is voluntary. If federal parties are unable to resolve their dispute using FMCS services, they can request that FSIP consider the matter or they can agree to binding arbitration procedures. The arbitration procedures must be approved by FSIP.[236] To aid in arbitration, the FMCS maintains a list of approximately 1,400 independent arbitrators who can hear and decide disputes over collective bargaining interpretation or application.[237]

The Federal Service Impasses Panel

FSIP is an entity within the FLRA and provides assistance in resolving disputes between agencies and unions over working conditions.[238] FSIP comprises seven members who are appointed by the President and serve staggered five-year terms.[239]

If parties cannot resolve an impasse by using a third-party mediator or if either party requests FSIP's services, FSIP can make recommendations to the parties and assist them in resolving the dispute. If the parties still cannot come to an agreement, FSIP can impose an agreement on the parties.[240]

Judicial Review

Issues delegated to a regional director or administrative law judge can be reviewed and then affirmed, reversed, or modified by the Authority. In some cases, a party can also seek court review of a final order made by the Authority.[241] For a court to review a decision, generally, the Authority's determinations must be arbitrary or contrary to the law.[242] Direct judicial review of FSIP orders is unavailable.[243]

Dispute Resolution

Unfair Labor Practice Disputes

An employee, union, or agency can initiate a ULP investigation by filing a charge with an FLRA regional director. Generally, a charge must be filed no more than six months after the alleged ULP occurred. The charge is investigated by regional office staff, and the regional director, in his discretion, may issue a complaint, which sets forth the alleged ULP and the hearing date before an ALJ. If the regional director decides not to issue a complaint, the decision can be appealed to the General Counsel.[244]

Throughout the processing of a charge, the Authority offers parties voluntary alternative dispute resolution services, including training, education, and intervention at its Collaboration and Alternative Dispute Resolution Office (CADRO).[245] If the regional director decides to issue a complaint and the parties are still unable to settle the dispute, the General Counsel prosecutes the complaint before an ALJ. The ALJ's decision can be reviewed by the Authority. If the Authority does not review the decision, the decision becomes the Authority's decision.[246]

If the Authority finds that a ULP has occurred, it can order an agency to reinstate an employee with backpay, the parties to enter into a collective bargaining agreement, a party to stop committing the ULP (cease-and-desist order), or any other action that would carry out the purpose of the statute.[247] Additionally, district courts can issue temporary relief (e.g., cease-and-desist orders) during the processing of a complaint if the General Counsel believes that not maintaining the status quo would frustrate the intent of the statute.[248]

Contract Disputes

Negotiability

Disputes over whether parties have an obligation to negotiate over a specific contract term generally fall into one of two categories: negotiability disputes and bargaining obligation disputes. In a negotiability dispute, the agency and union disagree about whether a proposed contract term is contrary to the law such that the agency is not required to negotiate over it. If the agency contends it is not required to negotiate over a matter, the union may initiate a negotiability appeal in which it asks the Authority to review the matter.[249] In a bargaining obligation dispute, an agency usually argues that it has no obligation to bargain over a matter because the proposal is already covered by an existing collective bargaining agreement, the union has waived the right to bargain, a change initiated by the agency is too minor to warrant bargaining, or the matter does not cover a condition of employment. These disputes can be resolved through ULP resolution procedures, negotiated grievance procedures, or negotiability appeal procedures.[250] To initiate procedures in a negotiability appeal, the union must file a petition with the Authority's Office of Case Control, not the regional office. The parties then explain their dispute to the Authority in a conference and a series of written allegations, and the Authority makes a decision. If at any time during the appeal, the parties express an interest in mediation, they will be referred to CADRO.[251]

Negotiated Grievance Procedures

All collective bargaining agreements are required to contain negotiated grievance procedures, which lay out procedures for settling grievances. These procedures must provide for binding arbitration if a grievance cannot be settled by the parties. Usually, the procedures set forth in negotiated grievance procedures are the only procedures available for resolving grievances.[252]

A negotiated grievance procedure automatically covers all issues, except those excluded by law or those that parties explicitly exclude. Those subjects that are excluded from negotiated grievance procedures by the FSLMRS include retirement, life insurance, or health insurance benefits and suspension or removal for reasons of national security. Procedures other than the negotiated grievance procedures exist for disputes involving a removal or demotion for unacceptable performance; serious adverse actions, such as a reduction in grade or pay; employment discrimination allegations; personnel actions prohibited by statute; and unfair labor practices.[253] Either party can file an exception to most arbitration awards with the Authority within 30 days of the award being served on the parties.[254] The Authority can make recom-mendations and take appropriate action regarding the award if it finds the award is contrary to law or on "other grounds similar to those applied by Federal courts in private sector labor-management relations."[255]

Impasses

Parties have several dispute resolution options when they have reached an impasse in the collective bargaining process. The agency and union may agree on a method to help resolve the dispute, such as binding private arbitration.[256] Parties can also voluntarily go to the FMCS for assistance to resolve an impasse.[257] If parties have exhausted voluntary attempts to settle an impasse, either party can request that FSIP consider the issue. If FSIP asserts juris-diction, it can either recommend dispute resolution procedures to the parties (e.g., refer the parties to CADRO) or assist them in resolving the impasse. FSIP's procedures are generally informal, but it can hold hearings, administer oaths, issue subpoenas, and take any other necessary actions to resolve the impasse. Afterwards, FSIP makes a final decision and order, which is binding on the parties for the term of their agreement.[258]

Emergency Actions

Unlike the RLA and FLRA, the FSLMRS does not have any emergency dispute resolution provisions.

Appendix A. Glossary of Terms

Adjustment Board	An entity that provides dispute resolution services.
Agency Shop	A type of union-security through which employees who do not become union members pay a fee to the union for its services as a bargaining agent.
Arbitration	Dispute resolution procedure in which parties present their arguments to a neutral party (arbitrator) who determines what the resolution to an issue should be. In binding arbitration, the arbitrator's decision is imposed on both parties. In nonbinding arbitration, the parties may choose to accept or reject the arbitrator's decision.
Authorization Card	A form evidencing that an individual employee wishes to be represented by a union.
Bargaining Unit/Craft/Class	A group of employees who are or wish to be represented by a union.
Certification	The determination of the administrator of a secret ballot election that the results are the voting employees' wishes. The union that receives the majority valid votes cast will be certified as the employee representative.
Closed Shop	A type of union security that makes membership in a particular union a precondition to employment. Closed shops are generally prohibited.
Collective Bargaining	The process of negotiation about working conditions between a union and an employer.
Consent-Election Agreement	An employer-union agreement that contains terms of a secret ballot election agreed on by the parties and can include the election's time and place, choices to be included on the ballot, and the method to determine voting eligibility.
Decertification	The process through which a union loses NLRB recognition as a bargaining unit's exclusive representative.

APPENDIX A.

Economic Strike	An employee work stoppage for the purpose of obtaining economic concessions.
Injunction	A court order requiring or restraining specifics acts.
Intermittent Strike	A series of employee work stoppages for a short period of time, followed by resumptions of work.
Mediation	A dispute resolution procedure in which parties work with a neutral party (mediator) who helps the parties reach an agreement on their issues. Mediators do not have the authority to impose a settlement on the parties.
Partial Strike	An action in which employees remain on work premises and refuse to work overtime, engage in work slowdowns, or choose to do some tasks but not others.
Presidential Emergency Board	A special entity created by the President if he believes that a labor dispute will substantially affect the nation's commerce. It can investigate and issue reports to the President on the labor dispute at hand.
Right-to-Work Law	A law that prohibits or restricts union security agreements.
Secondary Activity	An employee action to exert pressure on an entity outside of a specific dispute.
Secondary Boycott	An union attempt to influence an employer by either appealing to consumers to discontinue the use or purchase of a business's products or services or attempting to dissuade employees from working for a particular employer.
Secret ballot election	An election in which a person's vote is secret. This is the primary way in which a union gains certification as an exclusive employee representative.
Selective Striking	An employee work stoppage against one or a small number of employers as a means to reach an agreement with all the employers concerned.
Self-Help	A way in which one party can exert pressure on the other party that occurs outside of the formal dispute resolution process.
Sit-Down Strike	An employee work stoppage in which employees take possession of the employer's property and exclude others from entering.
Status Quo	The rates of pay, rules, and work conditions in effect before a dispute arises.
Sympathy Strike	An employee work stoppage for the purpose of supporting a cause or another group of strikers.

Unfair Labor Practice	An action taken by an employer or a union that interferes with a party's rights under federal labor-management relations statutes.
Unfair Labor Practice Strike	An employee work stoppage for the purpose of protecting an unfair labor practice.
Union Security Agreement	An employer-union agreement that requires employees to pay union dues equal to the cost of representation as a condition of employment.
Union Shop	A type of union security that requires employees to become and remain a union member as a condition of employment after 30 days of employment. Union shops are generally legal.
Voluntary Recognition	An employer's choice to recognize a union as the exclusive employee representative without the use of a secret ballot election.

APPENDIX B. LIST OF ACRONYMS

ALJ	Administrative Law Judge
CADRO	Collaboration and Alternative Dispute Resolution Office
EO	Executive Order
FAA	Federal Aviation Administration
FLRA	Federal Labor Relations Authority
FMCS	Federal Mediation and Conciliation Service
FSIP	Federal Service Impasses Panel
FSLMRS	Federal Service Labor-Management Relations Statute
GAO	Government Accountability Office
NCR	National Consultation Right
NLRA	National Labor Relations Act
NLRB	National Labor Relations Board
NMB	National Mediation Board
NRAB	National Railroad Adjustment Board
PEB	Presidential Emergency Board
RLA	Railway Labor Act
SBA	Special Board of Adjustment
TVA	Tennessee Valley Authority
ULP	Unfair Labor Practice

Appendix C. Comparison of RLA, NLRA, and FSLMRA Key Provisions

Statutory Provision	RLA	NLRA	FSLMRS
Statute Citation	45 U.S.C. §151 et seq.	29 U.S.C. §141 et seq.	5 U.S.C. §7101 et seq.
Administrative Agency	• National Mediation Board • National Railroad Adjustment Board • System Boards of Adjustment	• National Labor Relations Board	• Federal Labor Relations Authority • Federal Mediation and Conciliation Service • Federal Service Impasses Panel
Statute Citation	45 U.S.C. §151 et seq.	29 U.S.C. §141 et seq.	5 U.S.C. §7101 et seq.
Coverage	Railway and airline carriers	Private employers, excluding railway and airline carriers	Federal agencies, excluding those specifically excepted
Union Selection	• Secret Ballot Election • Voluntary Recognition	• Secret Ballot Election • Voluntary Recognition • NLRB-Mandated Recognition	• Secret Ballot Election
Union Security Clauses	Allowed	Allowed, unless prohibited by state law	Prohibited
Bargaining Subjects	"Rates of pay, rules, and working conditions"	"Rates of pay, wages, hours of employment, and other conditions of employment"	"Personnel policies, practices, and matters" not otherwise provided for by statute or relating to position classification
Unfair Labor Practices	General rules of fair dealing found in 45 U.S.C. §152.	Specific provisions found in 29 U.S.C. §158.	Specific provisions found in 5 U.S.C. §7116.
Dispute Resolution	Mediation and Arbitration	Voluntary settlement or formal adjudicatory proceedings	Voluntary dispute resolution services or formal adjudicatory proceedings
Self-Help	Most self-help is allowed, so long as it is not unlawful or "inherently destructive" of union or employer activity. Some allowed activities are intermittent and selective striking and secondary activity.	Self-help is allowed, so long as it is not violent, unlawful, or unjustifiably injurious to employer interests. Some prohibited activities include intermittent and partial strikes, acts of disloyalty, and some secondary activities.	Limited forms of self-help are allowed, including informational picketing. Prohibited self-help includes strikes, work stoppages, slowdowns, and pickets that interfere with agency operations.
Emergency Procedures	Presidential emergency board potential congressional action	Presidential "board of inquiry" with potential congressional action	None

Source: CRS analysis.

End Notes

[1] Rudolph Daniels, *Trains Across the Continent: North America Railroad History*, 2nd ed. (Bloomington: Indiana University Press, 2000), p. 49.

[2] Frank N. Wilner, *The Railway Labor Act and the Dilemma of Labor Relations* (Omaha: Simmons-Boardman Books, Inc., 1991), p. 25.

[3] The Brotherhood of Locomotive Engineers was the first railway union, organizing in 1863; the Order of the Railway Conductors, the Brotherhood of Locomotive Firemen, and the Brotherhood of Railroad Trainmen formed shortly thereafter. Ibid., p. 26.

[4] Previous legislative efforts to regulate labor relations include Arbitration Act of 1888, 25 Stat. 501 (1888); Erdman Act, 30 Stat. 424 (1898); Newlands Act 38 Stat. 103 (1913); Adamson Act 39 Stat. 721 (1916); and Transportation Act of 1920, 41 Stat. 456 (1920). For an overview of this legislative history, see Wilner, *The Railway Labor Act & the Dilemma of Labor Relations*, pp. 29-49.

[5] Ibid., pp. 47-49.

[6] 45 U.S.C. §151a.

[7] American Bar Association, "Introduction," in *The Railway Labor Act*, ed. Douglas L. Leslie (Washington, D.C.: BNA Books, 1995), p. 47 (Hereafter cited as ABA, *The Railway Labor Act*).

[8] 45 U.S.C. §153, First (l).

[9] 45 U.S.C. §152, Third, Tenth.

[10] 45 U.S.C. §156.

[11] 45 U.S.C. §151, First.

[12] Most provisions of the RLA, 45 U.S.C. §§151-163, apply to air carriers. 45 U.S.C. §153, which establishes the National Railroad Adjustment Board, does not apply to air carriers. Title III of the RLA codifies the inclusion of air carriers under the RLA. The aviation manufacturing (defense, space, and commercial) and general aviation (e.g., flight training, intercontinental jet transportation of executives and public officers) industries fall under the NLRA's jurisdiction.

[13] U.S. Congress, Senate Committee on Interstate Commerce, *To Amend the Railway Labor Act to Cover Every Common Carrier by Air Engaged in Interstate or Foreign Commerce*, hearing on S. 2496, 74th Cong., 2nd sess., May 20, 1935, pp. 4-10. Carriers neither supported nor actively opposed the legislation. ABA, "Introduction," in *The Railway Labor Act*, p. 56.

[14] 45 U.S.C. §152, Eleventh.

[15] 45 U.S.C. §153, Second. Jacob Seidenberg, "Grievance Adjustment in the Railroad Industry," in *The Railway Labor Act at Fifty: Collective Bargaining in the Railroad and Airline Industries*, ed. Charles M. Rehmus (Washington, D.C.: National Mediation Board, 1977), pp. 223-224.

[16] 45 U.S.C. 159a (c).

[17] 29 C.F.R. §1206.2. Larry Swisher, "NMB Ends Longstanding Policy, Adopts Rule for Majority Vote in Representation Elections," *Daily Labor Report*, May 11, 2010, p. AA-1.

[18] 29 C.F.R §1206.1(b).

[19] *FAA Modernization and Reform Act of 2012*, P.L. 112-95 (2012).

[20] Ibid.

[21] 45 U.S.C. §151, First.

[22] 45 U.S.C. §151.

[23] 45 U.S.C. §151, Fifth.

[24] National Mediation Board, *Representation Manual*, March 21, 2011, §9.2, http://www.nmb.gov/representation/representation-manual.pdf (hereafter cited as NMB, *Representation Manual*).

[25] 45 U.S.C. §152, Third, Fourth.

[26] 45 U.S.C. §152, Ninth.

[27] NMB, *Representation Manual*, §9.1.

[28] The following is a list of some of the well-recognized traditional crafts or classes: Locomotive Engineers; Locomotive Firemen and Hostlers; Conductors; Trainmen; Yardmen; Yardmasters; Office, Station, and Store Employees; Telegraph Workers; Dispatchers; Signalmen; Maintenance of Way Employees; Machinists; Boilermakers and Blacksmiths; Sheet Metal Workers; Electrical Workers; Dining Car Attendants; Carmen and Coach Cleaners; and Powerhouse Employees and Shop Laborers. ABA, "Selecting A Bargaining Representative," in *The Railway Labor Act*, pp. 98-99.

[29] Some of the traditional crafts or classes within the airline industry include ground personnel (mechanics, ground service personnel, and plant maintenance personnel), clerical and office employees, fleet and passenger service employees, deck crew, and cabin crew. ABA, "Selecting A Bargaining Representative," in The Railway Labor Act, pp. 100-105.

[30] National Mediation Board, *Annual Performance and Accountability Report FY2011*, November 14, 2011, p. 27, http://www.nmb.gov/documents/2011annual-report/pdf/NMB2011_00_ full.pdf (hereafter cited as NMB, *FY2011*).

[31] An individual must be employed in the craft on and after the cut-off date. The cut-off date is the last day of the payroll period ending before an application was submitted to the NMB.

[32] NMB, *Representation Manual*, §9.2.

[33] 45 U.S.C. §152, Ninth.

[34] 45 U.S.C. §152, Twelfth. The NMB can dismiss applications for investigation under one of several election bar doctrines. Under these doctrines, the NMB, generally, will dismiss an application for a specific amount of time after an election has been held or a previous application has been filed between the same craft and carrier as in the current election or application before it. 29 C.F.R. §1206.4.

[35] NMB, *Representation Manual*, §§2.0-5.0.

[36] 29 C.F.R. §1202.4. Bureau of National Affairs, "NMB Ends Longstanding Policy, Adopts Rule For Majority Vote in Representation Elections," *Daily Labor Report*, no. 89, May 11, 2010, p. AA-1.

[37] *FAA Modernization and Reform Act of 2012*, Public Law No: 112-95 (2012).

[38] NMB, *Representation Manual*, §7.0.

[39] ABA, "Selecting a Bargaining Representative," in *The Railway Labor Act*, p. 107.

[40] ABA, "Selecting a Bargaining Representative," in *Railway Labor Act*, pp. 135-137.

[41] See 45 U.S.C. §152, Fourth.

[42] 45 U.S.C. §152, First.

[43] William E. Thoms and Frank J. Dooley, "Collective Bargaining Under the Railway Labor Act," *Transportation Law Journal*, vol. 20 (1991), p. 280.

[44] 45 U.S.C. §152, Third. Instances of carrier interference include firing or demoting employees for supporting a union, giving employees inaccurate information about an election, favoring one union candidate over another, granting or withholding benefits, and making threats. ABA, "Protection of Employees' Right of Self-Organization," in *The Railway Labor Act*, pp. 163-173.

[45] 45 U.S.C. §152, Fourth.

[46] 45 U.S.C. §152, Fifth.

[47] 45 U.S.C. §152, Tenth.

[48] 45 U.S.C. §152, Ninth.

[49] Ibid.

[50] ABA, "Protection of Employees' Right to Self-Organization," in *The Railway Labor Act*, pp. 186-187, 200-202.

[51] For instance, a union may appeal to consumers to discontinue use or purchase of a business's products or services or attempt to dissuade employees from working for a particular employer.

[52] ABA, "Exercise of Economic Weapons," in *The Railway Labor Act*, pp. 320-321.

[53] ABA, "Negotiation of Collective Bargaining Agreements," in *The Railway Labor Act*, pp. 241-242.

[54] 45 U.S.C. §154, First.

[55] See NMB, *FY2011*, pp. 4, 8.

[56] 45 U.S.C. §153, First, (a).

[57] The NRAB's First Division processes disputes involving "operating" employees (e.g., engineers). The Second Division processes disputes involving "shop" employees (e.g., repairmen). The Third Division processes dispute involving employees in miscellany crafts, and the Fourth Division processes disputes involving employees who transport passengers or property by water. 45 U.S.C. §153, First, (h).

[58] 45 U.S.C. §153, First, (p) and (q).

[59] 45 U.S.C. §153, Second.

[60] NMB, FY2011, p. 21. The daily pay rate for arbitrators on the NMB's Roster of Arbitrators is $300 per day. National Mediation Board, *Frequently Asked Questions: Arbitration*, http:// www.nmb.gov/ arbitration/ afaq.html.

[61] 45 U.S.C. §185.

[62] 45 U.S.C. §184.

[63] NMB, *FY2011*, p. 21.

[64] 45 U.S.C. §159.

[65] 45 U.S.C. §153, First (p) & (q).

[66] 45 U.S.C. §159, Second.

[67] ABA, "Enforcement of Collective Bargaining Agreements," in *The Railway Labor Act*, p. 269.

[68] See 45 U.S.C. §152, Ninth.

[69] ABA, "Negotiation of Collective Bargaining Agreements," in *The Railway Labor Act*, p. 251.

[70] 45 U.S.C. §156. "Status quo" refers to the rates of pay, rules, and work conditions in effect before a dispute arises. The purpose of maintaining the status quo during a dispute is to prevent either party from engaging in self-help until all negotiation and mediation procedures have been exhausted. ABA, "Negotiation of Collective Bargaining Agreements," in *The Railway Labor Act*, p. 232.

[71] 45 U.S.C. §155.

[72] ABA, "Selecting a Bargaining Representative," in *The Railway Labor Act*, pp. 128-129.

[73] 45 U.S.C. §155, First.

[74] 45 U.S.C. §156.

[75] 45 U.S.C. §157, First. The parties can also choose a six-member arbitration board where each party selects two members of the board; those four members, by a majority vote, then select two other arbitrators. If they fail to select the remaining two arbitrators, the NMB will select them.

[76] 45 U.S.C. §159, Second.

[77] 45 U.S.C. §152.

[78] ABA, "Negotiation of Collective Bargaining Agreements," in *The Railway Labor Act*, p. 234. Although carriers are not required to maintain the status quo in minor disputes, injunctions may be issued to preserve the status quo until the dispute is resolved. The Norris-LaGuardia Act, which generally prohibits courts from issuing injunctions in labor disputes, does not apply to disputes under the RLA. Injunctions are allowed against parties

who violate the status quo provisions of the RLA. See ABA, "Enforcement of Collective Bargaining Agreements," in *The Railway Labor Act*, pp. 290-295.

[79] 45 U.S.C. §153, First, (j) and (o).

[80] 45 U.S.C. §153, Second.

[81] Ibid.

[82] 45 U.S.C. §160.

[83] 45 U.S.C. §159a.

[84] ABA, "Negotiation of Collective Bargaining Agreements," in *The Railway Labor Act*, p. 221. For example, in P.L. 88-108, Congress established an arbitration board to resolve a dispute over the use of railroad firemen and manning levels for railroad crews. Congress has also created its own compromise packages and imposed settlements from other disputes on uncompromising unions. William E. Thoms and Frank J. Dooley, "Collective Bargaining Under the Railway Labor Act," *Transportation Law Journal*, vol. 20 (1991), pp. 224, 279.

[85] Benjamin J. Taylor and Fred Whitney, *U.S. Labor Relations Law: Historical Development* (Englewood Cliffs, NJ: Prentice Hall, 1992), pp. 153-154 (hereafter cited as Taylor & Whitney, *U.S. Labor Relations Law*).

[86] NIRA also did not provide enforcement procedures, specify prohibited antiunion conduct, require employers to bargain with employee-chosen representatives, or prohibit employer discrimination against employees for union activities. Ibid., pp. 154-155.

[87] Richard D. Polenberg, *The Era of Franklin D. Roosevelt 1933-1945* (Boston: Bedford/St. Martin's, 2000), pp. 68-69. For a statistical assessment of union growth after the NLRA was enacted, see Taylor & Whitney, *U.S. Labor Relations Law*, pp. 198-200.

[88] For instance, under the NLRA as originally enacted, no remedy existed against unions who imposed their will on employees, therefore, some unions used intimidation to garner support, rather than campaign for votes. Gerard D. Reilly, "The Legislative History of the Taft-Hartley Act," *George Washington Law Review*, vol. 29 (1960), pp. 286-287.

[89] 29 U.S.C. §158.

[90] 29 U.S.C. §158(a)(1) & (b)(1)(A). A closed shop is one in which an employer is required to employ only members of a particular union. Employers may hire anyone, but that person will be required to join the union within a specified amount of time. While these are prohibited under the NLRA, they are permitted under the Railway Labor Act. See "Railway Labor Act: Union Security Agreements," *supra*.

[91] 29 U.S.C. §158 (b)(3)(A).

[92] 29 U.S.C. §159(c)(1)(B).

[93] 29 U.S.C. §152.

[94] 29 U.S.C. §159(c)(1)(A).

[95] 29 U.S.C. §153.

[96] In the statute's declaration of findings, purposes, and policies, Congress stated:

> [T]here have been a number of instances of breach of trust, corruption, disregard of the rights of individual employees, and other failures to observe high standards of responsibility and ethical conduct which require further and supplementary legislation that will afford necessary protection of the rights and interests of employees and the public generally as they relate to the activities of labor organizations, employers, labor relations consultants, and their officers and representatives. (29 U.S.C. §401(b))

[97] 29 U.S.C. §§411, 431.

[98] 29 U.S.C. §481.

[99] Robert W. Kaps, *Air Transport Labor Relations* (Southern Illinois University Press, 1997), pp. 5-9.

[100] 29 U.S.C. §152.

[101] NLRB, *Basic Guide to the NLRA*, pp. 33-34, https://www.nlrb.gov/sites/default/files/ documents/224/ basicguide.pdf. CRS Report RL32930, *Labor Union Certification Procedures: Use of Secret Ballots and Card Checks*, by Gerald Mayer.

[102] 29 U.S.C. §152(2).

[103] ABA, "Jurisdiction: Coverage of the Act," in *The Developing Labor Law*, vol. 2, p. 2253.

[104] 29 U.S.C. §152(3). The Re-empowerment of Skilled and Professional Employees and Construction Tradeworkers (RESPECT) Act, S. 2168, was introduced in March, 2012. This amendment to the NLRB would narrow the definition of "supervisor," allowing employees who spend small amounts of time performing supervisory functions to participate in union activities.

[105] The NLRB reasons that the relationship between a university and a graduate student is primarily an educational one, such that graduate students who are also teaching assistants are not covered by the NLRA. *Brown University and International Union*, 432 NLRB, pp. 488-489 (2004).

[106] 29 U.S.C. §152(11).

[107] ABA, "Jurisdiction: Coverage of the Act," in *The Developing Labor Law*, vol. 2, pp. 2271-2272.

[108] *General Dynamics Corp., Convair Aerospace Division and National Engineers and Professionals Association*, 213 NLRB 857 (1974).

[109] 29 U.S.C. §157.

[110] 29 U.S.C. §159(a).
[111] CRS Report RL32930, *Labor Union Certification Procedures: Use of Secret Ballots and Card Checks*, by Gerald Mayer.
[112] 29 U.S.C. §158(a)(3).
[113] 29 U.S.C. §158(e).
[114] 29 U.S.C. §164(b).
[115] ABA, "Union Security," in *The Developing Labor Law*, pp. 2149-2150. The construction industry standards for union security agreements are covered by a separate section of the act, 29 U.S.C. §158(f), because of the irregular nature of construction employment.
[116] CRS Report RL32930, *Labor Union Certification Procedures: Use of Secret Ballots and Card Checks*, by Gerald Mayer. NLRB, *Basic Guide to the NLRA*, pp. 12-13. The NLRB recently issued a new rule to expedite pre-election proceedings. 29 C.F.R. §102.64. The new rule goes into effect April 30, 2012. Members of both houses have filed joint resolutions "disapproving" of the rule, stating that expedited pre-election procedures would deprive workers of sufficient time to make important decisions about union representation. Lawrence E. Dubé, "Legislators File Senate, House Resolutions," *Daily Labor Report*, February 16, 2012, p. A-17.
[117] An economic strike is one for the purpose of obtaining economic concessions, like higher wages.
[118] NLRB, *Basic Guide to the NLRA*, p. 16.
[119] ABA, "The Primary Strike," in *The Developing Labor Law*, p. 1597.
[120] 29 U.S.C. §159.
[121] NLRB, *Basic Guide to the NLRA*, p. 16.
[122] See 29 C.F.R. §101.19. NLRB, *Basic Guide to the NLRA*, p. 16.
[123] 29 C.F.R. §101.19.
[124] CRS Report RL32930, *Labor Union Certification Procedures: Use of Secret Ballots and Card Checks*, by Gerald Mayer. NLRB, *Basic Guide to the NLRA*, p. 16.
[125] 29 C.F.R. §§102.66-102.67.
[126] 29 U.S.C. §159.
[127] NLRB, *Basic Guide to the NLRA*, pp. 16-17.
[128] CRS Report RL32930, *Labor Union Certification Procedures: Use of Secret Ballots and Card Checks*, by Gerald Mayer. NLRB, Basic Guide to the NLRA, p. 16.
[129] CRS Report RL32930, *Labor Union Certification Procedures: Use of Secret Ballots and Card Checks*, by Gerald Mayer.
[130] The "reasonable amount of time" rule was the long-held NLRB rule until 2007 when the NLRB decided that employees could file a petition within 45 days of recognition. In August, 2011, the NLRB revised its position, stating that it was wholly unsupported by any empirical evidence. The NLRB will look to several factors in determining a reasonable amount of time, including progress made in the negotiation process, whether the parties are negotiating an initial contract, and whether the parties are at an impasse. *Lamons Gasket Company and United Steel, Paper and Forestry, Rubber, Manufacturing, and Energy, Allied Industrial and Service Workers International Union*, 357 NLRB No. 72, p. 10 (2011), http://nlrb.gov/case/16-RD-001597.
[131] CRS Report RL32930, *Labor Union Certification Procedures: Use of Secret Ballots and Card Checks*, by Gerald Mayer.
[132] Ibid. NLRB, *Basic Guide to the NLRA*, p. 37.
[133] CRS Report RL32930, *Labor Union Certification Procedures: Use of Secret Ballots and Card Checks*, by Gerald Mayer. NLRB, *Basic Guide to the NLRA*, p. 14.
[134] CRS Report RL32930, *Labor Union Certification Procedures: Use of Secret Ballots and Card Checks*, by Gerald Mayer.
[135] 29 U.S.C. §159(a).
[136] ABA, "Subjects of Bargaining," in *The Developing Labor Law*, vol. 1, pp. 1247, 1263.
[137] Ibid., pp. 1264-1299.
[138] Ibid., pp. 1362-1386.
[139] The Taft-Hartley Act prohibited closed shops. Hot-cargo clauses are those in which the employer agrees to stop handling, using, or selling products of another employer. 29 U.S.C. §158(e).
[140] ABA, "Subjects of Bargaining," in *The Developing Labor Law*, vol. 1, pp. 1393-1397.
[141] 29 U.S.C. §158. 29 U.S.C. §160(c).
[142] 29 U.S.C. §160(c). NLRB, *Basic Guide to the NLRA*, p. 35, 38.
[143] 29 U.S.C. §160(c). NLRB, *Basic Guide to the NLRA*, p. 38. The amount of back pay awarded is the amount of compensation (i.e., wages plus benefits) that a worker would have received if he or she had not been unlawfully fired, less the amount of compensation received (less the expenses from looking for work) from other work during the back pay period, plus interest accrued. National Labor Relations Board, *NLRB Casehandling Manual, Part 3, Compliance Proceedings*, §10536, http://www.nlrb.gov/sites/default/files/documents/44/ compliancemanual.pdf.
[144] 29 U.S.C. §§158(a)(1), (b)(1)(A).
[145] ABA, "Interference with Protected Rights," in *The Developing Labor Law*, vol. 1, p. 93.

[146] CRS Report RL32930, *Labor Union Certification Procedures: Use of Secret Ballots and Card Checks*, by Gerald Mayer.
[147] 29 U.S.C. §158(a)(2). NLRB, *Basic Guide to the NLRA*, p. 18.
[148] 29 U.S.C. §158(b)(1)(B).
[149] 29 U.S.C. §158(b)(1)(A).
[150] 29 U.S.C. §§158(a)(5), (b)(3), (d).
[151] ABA, "The Duty to Bargain," in *The Developing Labor Law*, vol. 1, pp. 827-846.
[152] 29 U.S.C. §§158(a)(1), (b)(1)(A).
[153] 29 U.S.C. §§158(a)(3), (a)(4).
[154] 29 U.S.C. §158(b)(2).
[155] ABA, "Interference with Protected Rights," in *The Developing Labor Law*, vol. 1, pp. 256-276.
[156] To be a "protected" activity, conduct must be for collective bargaining or for "mutual aid or protection" and concerted in nature. 29 U.S.C. §157.
[157] Acts of disloyalty include breach of confidentiality and false allegations about the employer.
[158] ABA, "Interference with Protected Rights," in *The Developing Labor Law*, vol. 1, pp. 196-254.
[159] NLRB, *Basic Guide to the NLRA*, p. 10.
[160] Serious misconduct includes violence and threats of violence and physically blocking individual from entering or leaving the workspace. Ibid., p. 11.
[161] Ibid., p. 10.
[162] ABA, "Interference with Protected Rights," in *The Developing Labor Law*, vol. 1, pp. 984-988.
[163] In January, 2012, President Barack Obama made three recess appointments to the NLRB during a three-day intra-session recess. Past Department of Justice (DOJ) briefs implied that the President may make a recess appointment during a recess lasting longer than three days. These appointments were considered by some to be controversial, because Congress had apparently scheduled its recesses to prevent recess appointments, but DOJ indicated that "the Administration does not regard congressional scheduling practices ... as an impediment to the exercise of the recess appointment power." CRS Report R42329, *Recess Appoin-tments Made by President Barack Obama*, by Henry B. Hogue and Maureen Bearden. CRS Report RS21308, *Recess Appointments: Frequently Asked Questions*, by Henry B. Hogue.
[164] The Board has complete authority over all representation matters but has delegated much of this power to its regional directors. It still retains the power to review any regional director's decision. NLRB, *Basic Guide to the NLRA*, p. 7, 33. Feldacker, *Labor Guide to Labor Law*, pp. 39-44.
[165] NLRB, *Basic Guide the NLRA*, p. 33. Lawrence E. Dubé, "Obama Seeks 5 Percent NLRB Budget Rise," *Daily Labor Report*, February 13, 2012, p. C-2.
[166] 29 U.S.C. §160(f).
[167] The Board, not the parties, files a petition to enforce its order. 29 U.S.C. §160(e).
[168] For instance, a court set aside NLRB certification when it found that the NLRB had exceeded its statutory authority by certifying a union that included both professional and nonprofessional employees without giving the professional employees a separate election to determine whether they wished to be included in the unit. *Leedom v. Kyne*, 258 U.S. 184 (1958).
[169] ABA, "Judicial Review and Enforcement," in *The Developing Labor Law*, pp. 2803-2805.
[170] 29 U.S.C. §160(l).
[171] 29 U.S.C. §160(b).
[172] NLRB, *A Basic Guide the NLRA*, p. 36.
[173] ABA, "The NLRB Procedures," in *The Developing Labor Law*, vol. 2, pp. 2683-2688.
[174] Ibid., p. 2691.
[175] ABA, "NLRB Procedures," in *The Developing Labor Law*, vol. 2, pp. 2692-2701.
[176] 29 U.S.C. §185(a). ABA, "Board Action and Contract Enforcement," in *The Developing Labor Law*, vol. 1, pp. 1424-1427.
[177] The Taft-Hartley Act gave courts jurisdiction over contract disputes as a way to make collective bargaining agreements more readily enforceable. ABA, "Board Action and Contract Enforcement," in *The Developing Labor Law*, vol. 1, pp. 1408, 1476-1480.
[178] ABA, "Board Action and Contract Enforcement," in *The Developing Labor Law*, vol. 1, pp. 1435-1448.
[179] 29 U.S.C. §§176-177.
[180] 29 U.S.C. §178.
[181] 29 U.S.C. §179.
[182] 29 U.S.C. §180.
[183] By 1960, approximately 30% of nonagricultural private sector employees were represented by unions. Charles M. Rehmus, "Labor Relations in the Public Sector in the United States," *International Labour Review*, vol. 109, no. 3 (1974), p. 200. Although an estimated 30% of federal employees were represented by unions in 1961, most of those were U.S. Postal Service employees. The Government Printing Office and the Tennessee Valley Authority also held some collective bargaining rights, but most employees from other agencies did not. Approximately 16% of non-postal service federal employees were union members. See Kenneth Bullock,

"Official Time as a Form of Union Security in Federal Sector Labor-Management Issues," *The Air Force Law Review*, vol. 59 (2007), pp. 164-167.

[184] Charles M. Rehmus, "Labor Relations in the Public Sector in the United States," *International Labour Review*, vol. 109, no. 3 (1974), pp. 201-202.

[185] Ibid., p. 202.

[186] Kenneth Bullock, "Official Time as a Form of Union Security in Federal Sector Labor-Management Issues," *The Air Force Law Review*, vol. 59 (2007), pp. 169-173.

[187] Executive Order 10988, "Employee-Management Cooperation in the Federal Service," 27 *Federal Register* 551, January 17, 1962.

[188] Under majority exclusive recognition, once a union is recognized as the exclusive unit representative, an agency can collectively bargain with only that union.

[189] Executive Order 11491, "Labor-management relations in the Federal Service," 34 *Federal Register* 17,605, October 29, 1969.

[190] 5 U.S.C. §7131 (a). CRS Report R41732, *Collective Bargaining and Employees in the Public Sector*, by Jon O. Shimabukuro.

[191] Louis C. LaBrecque, "Obama Order Creates Federal Labor Council; No Mandate to Bargain on Permissive Topics," *Daily Labor Report*, December 12, 2009, p. A-14. For additional information on the National Council on Federal Labor-Management Relations, see its website, http://www.lmrcouncil.gov/index.aspx.

[192] P.L. 96-191. In 2007, analysts at GAO voted to be represented by the International Federation of Professional and Technical Engineers (IFPTE). In February 2012, support employees at GAO also voted to be represented by IFPTE.

[193] U.S. General Accounting Office, *Labor-Management Relations: Tennessee Valley Authority Situation Needs to Improve*, GAO/GGD-91-129, September 1991, http://archive.gao.gov/ d18t9/145065.pdf.

[194] 39 U.S.C. §1201 et seq.

[195] 5 U.S.C. §7103(a)(3).

[196] 5 U.S.C. §7103(b)(1)(B).

[197] Executive Order 12171, "Exclusions from the Federal Labor-Management Relations Program," 3 C.F.R. §§1979 Comp., p. 458. Executive Order 13480, "Exclusions from the Federal Labor-Management Relations Program," 73 C.F.R. §234.

[198] 5 U.S.C. §1703(a)(2)(B). Although members of the uniformed services are broadly excluded from the statute's coverage, some members of the National Guard are protected under the statute. See, e.g., *Spence v. Holesinger*, 696 F.Supp. 398 (C.D. Ill. 1988).

[199] 5 U.S.C. §7103(a)(4).

[200] 5 U.S.C. §7101.

[201] 5 U.S.C. §5332. Employees at agencies excluded from the statute's coverage may be able to bargain over wages, depending on the statute that covers collective bargaining in their agency. See "Other Federal Workforce Labor-Relations Statutes and Policies," *supra*.

[202] 5 U.S.C. §7103(a)(14).

[203] 5 U.S.C. §7106(a).

[204] 5 U.S.C. §7106(b).

[205] 5 U.S.C. §7111.

[206] 5 U.S.C. §7114(a)(1).

[207] 5 U.S.C. §7112(a).

[208] Federal Labor Relations Authority, *A Guide to the Federal Service Labor-Management Relations Program* (2001), p. 6 (Hereafter cited as FLRA, *A Guide to the FLMRP*).

[209] A management official is an individual who has the duty or authority to determine or influence agency policy. 5 U.S.C. §7103(a)(11). A supervisor is an individual who has the authority to use independent judgment to take personnel actions, such as hiring, firing, or disciplining employees. 5 U.S.C. §7103(a)(10).

[210] FLRA, *A Guide to the FLMRP*, pp. 6-7.

[211] 5 U.S.C. §7111(d).

[212] See *Army & Air Force Exchange Service, Panama Area Exchange and ALF-CIO Local 907*, 7 F.L.R.A. 514 (1981). *For Buchanan Installation Club Management System and Congreso de Uniones Industriales de Puerto Rico*, 9 F.L.R.A. 143 (1982).

[213] See *Small Business Administration and AFGE*, 16 F.L.R.A. 180 (1984).

[214] 5 U.S.C. §7111 (b). The FLRA can dismiss applications for investigation under one of several election bar doctrines. Under these doctrines, the FLRA, generally, will dismiss an application for a specific amount of time after an election has been held or a previous application has been filed between the same bargaining unit and agency as in the current election or application before it. 5 C.F.R. §2422.12. Federal Labor Relations Authority Office of the General Counsel, *Representation Case Law Guide* (2000), pp. 128-129, http:// www.flra.gov/webfm_send/27.

[215] If a party disputes the status of an organization as a "labor organization" under the statute, it can do so for one of two reasons. A party can either assert that the union does not fall within the definition of "labor organization"

under the statute or that a union should not be given exclusive representative status when it is subject to corrupting influences. Federal Labor Relations Authority Office of General Counsel, *Representation Proceeding: Case Handling Manual* (2000), pp. 99-100, 263, 275-276, http://www.flra.gov/webfm_send/33.

[216] 5 C.F.R. §2422.16. FLRA, *A Guide to the FLMRP*, p. 13.

[217] 5 U.S.C. §7111.

[218] 5 C.F.R. §2422.26.

[219] 5 C.F.R. §2422.34.

[220] 5 U.S.C. §7113.

[221] Ibid. FLRA, *A Guide to the FLMRP*, p. 10.

[222] 5 U.S.C. §7111(b).

[223] 5 C.F.R. §2432.3(b).

[224] 5 U.S.C. §7116.

[225] 5 U.S.C. §7118.

[226] 5 U.S.C. §7116. FLRA, *A Guide to the FLMRP*, pp. 43-48.

[227] 5 U.S.C. §7116(a)(3). FLRA, *A Guide to the FLMRP*, p. 44.

[228] 5 U.S.C. §§7116, 7103(a)(12).

[229] FLRA, *A Guide to the FLMRP*, pp. 18-19, 45-47.

[230] 5 U.S.C. §7116. FLRA, *A Guide to the FLMRP*, pp. 44-46.

[231] 5 U.S.C. §7116(b)(4).

[232] For instance, an employer commits a ULP if it refuses to honor dues allotment authorizations for a representative submitted by employees pursuant to 5 U.S.C. §7115.

[233] FLRA, *A Guide to the FLMRP*, pp.47-48.

[234] 5 U.S.C. §§7104-7105.

[235] 5 U.S.C. §7104(f)(1). Although the Foreign Service falls outside of FSLMRS jurisdiction, the FLRA provides staff support to the Foreign Service Impasse Disputes Panel and the Foreign Service Labor Relations Board. Federal Labor Relations Authority, *Performance and Accountability Report: Fiscal Year 2011* (2011), pp. 3, 5, http://www.flra.gov/webfm_ send/542.

[236] 5 U.S.C. §7119(a).

[237] Federal Mediation & Conciliation Service, 2011 Annual Report, 2011, p. 9, http://fmcs.gov/ assets/files/ Public%20Documents/2011_Annual_Report.pdf.

[238] The Panel also assists in resolving agency-union disputes under the Federal Employees Flexible and Compressed Work Schedules Act. 5 U.S.C. §6161(c)(2)(A).

[239] 5 U.S.C. §7119.

[240] Ibid. FLRA, *A Guide to the FLMRP*, pp. 2-3.

[241] 5 U.S.C. §7123. Generally, parties cannot seek judicial review of the Authority's decision not to issue a ULP complaint, because it is not a final order under the statute. See *Rizzitelli v. FLRA*, 212 F.3d 710 (2nd Cir. 2000).

[242] See, e.g., *National Treasury Employees Union v. FLRA*, 732 F.2d 703 (9th Cir. 1984).

[243] Although direct review is unavailable, parties may have an indirect means to gain review of a Panel order. Courts may grant a review if a party does not comply with the Panel's order. Noncompliance is a ULP, which could be subject to the statute's provisions. See, e.g., *Council of Prison Locals v. Brewer*, 735 F.2d 1497 (D.C. 1984).

[244] FLRA, *A Guide to the FLMRP*, pp. 49-51.

[245] 5 C.F.R. §2423.2.

[246] FLRA, *A Guide to the FLMRP*, pp. 49-50.

[247] Ibid., p. 51.

[248] Federal Labor Relations Authority Office of General Counsel, "The Charge," in *Unfair Labor Practice Casehandling Manual* (2010), p. 14, http://www.flra.gov/webfm_send/497.

[249] FLRA, *A Guide to the FLMRP*, p. 22.

[250] Ibid., pp. 22-23.

[251] Ibid., pp. 22-27.

[252] 5 U.S.C. §7121.

[253] 5 U.S.C. §7121(c). FLRA, *A Guide to the FLMRP*, p. 32-33.

[254] The Authority cannot review awards for disputes involving a removal or demotion for unacceptable performance; serious adverse actions, such as a reduction in grade or pay; employment discrimination allegations; or personnel actions prohibited by statute. Awards for these matters can be appealed to U.S. federal courts. FLRA, *A Guide to the FLMRP*, pp. 38-39.

[255] 5 U.S.C. §7122.

[256] Although parties can agree on private arbitration, the agreement must first be approved by FSIP. FLRA, *A Guide to the FLMRP*, p. 28.

[257] 5 U.S.C. §7119(a).

[258] Ibid., pp. 29-30.

In: Labor Relations
Editors: A. Daniels and R. Hoffman

ISBN: 978-1-62257-420-9

Chapter 2

LABOR UNION CERTIFICATION PROCEDURES: USE OF SECRET BALLOTS AND CARD CHECKS*

Gerald Mayer

SUMMARY

The National Labor Relations Act of 1935 (NLRA) gives private sector workers the right to join or form a labor union and to bargain collectively over wages, hours, and other working conditions. An issue before Congress is whether to change the procedures under which a union is certified as the bargaining representative of a union chosen by a majority of workers.

Under current law, the National Labor Relations Board (NLRB) conducts a secret ballot election when a petition is filed requesting one. A petition can be filed by a union, worker, or employer. Workers or a union may request an election if at least 30% of workers have signed authorization cards (i.e., cards authorizing a union to represent them). The NLRA does not require secret ballot elections. An employer may voluntarily recognize a union if a majority of workers have signed authorization cards.

In recent Congresses, legislation has been introduced that, if enacted, would change current union certification procedures. The Employee Free Choice Act would require the NLRB to certify a union if a majority of employees sign authorization cards. The Secret Ballot Protection Act would make it an unfair labor practice for an employer to recognize or bargain with a union without a secret ballot election.

Proponents of both measures sometimes use similar language to support their positions. Employers argue that, under card check certification, workers may be pressured or coerced into signing authorization cards and may only hear the union's point of view. Unions argue that, during an election campaign, employers may pressure or coerce workers into voting against a union. Supporters of secret ballot elections argue that casting a secret ballot is private and confidential. Unions argue that, during an election campaign, employers have greater access to workers. Unions argue that card check certification is less costly than a

* This is an edited, reformatted and augmented version of the Congressional Research Service Publication, CRS Report for Congress RL32930, dated March 12, 2012.

secret ballot election. Employers maintain that unionization may be more costly to workers, because union members must pay dues and higher union wages may result in fewer union jobs.

Requiring card check certification may increase the level of unionization, while requiring secret ballot elections may decrease it. Research suggests that, where card check recognition is required, unions undertake more union drives and the union success rate is higher. The union success rate is also greater where card check recognition is combined with a neutrality agreement (i.e., an agreement where the employer agrees to remain neutral during a union organizing campaign).

To the extent that requiring secret ballot elections or requiring certification when a majority of employees sign authorization cards would affect the level of unionization, the economic effects may depend on how well labor markets fit the model of perfect competition. Requiring card check certification may improve worker benefits and reduce earnings inequality—if more workers are unionized. Requiring secret ballot elections may increase inequality in compensation—if fewer workers are unionized.

The National Labor Relations Act of 1935 (NLRA), as amended, gives private sector workers the right to join or form a labor union and to bargain collectively over wages, hours, and other conditions of employment.[1] The act also requires employers to bargain in good faith with a union chosen by a majority of employees. An issue before Congress is whether to change the procedures under which a union is certified as the bargaining representative of a union chosen by a majority of workers.

In recent Congresses, legislation has been introduced that, if enacted, would change current union certification procedures. This report begins by summarizing legislation introduced in the 112th and 111th Congresses. The report then reviews the rights and responsibilities of workers and employers under the NLRA and the different ways that workers may form or join a union. Next, the report analyzes the potential effects of changes in union certification procedures. Finally, the report considers whether there is an economic rationale for protecting the rights of workers to organize and bargain collectively.

LEGISLATIVE ACTIVITY

Several bills have been introduced in recent Congresses that would change union representation procedures.

112th Congress

In the 112th Congress, similar versions of the Secret Ballot Protection Act have been introduced in both the House and the Senate. Both the House (H.R. 972) and Senate (S. 217) versions of the legislation would make it an unfair labor practice for an employer to recognize or bargain with a union that has not been selected by a majority of employees in a secret ballot election conducted by the NLRB. Both bills would make it an unfair labor practice for a union to cause or attempt to cause an employer to recognize or bargain with a union that has not been chosen by a majority of employees in a secret ballot election.[2]

In addition to some differences in language, H.R. 972 includes conforming amendments that are not in S. 217. Also, S. 217 includes a section that is not in H.R. 972. Section 4(b) of S. 217 states that "Nothing in this Act (or the amendments made by this Act) shall be construed to limit or otherwise diminish the remedial authority of the National Labor Relations Board." With this provision, the NLRB should, for example, be able to issue a bargaining order as a remedy to employer unfair labor practices. The NLRB may issue a bargaining order without holding a secret ballot election. For more information on bargaining orders, see the section on "Bargaining Orders" later in this report.

H.R. 972 was introduced by Representative David Roe and referred to the House Committee on Education and the Workforce. S. 217 was introduced by Senator Jim DeMint. The bill was referred to the Senate Committee on Health,
Education, Labor, and Pensions (HELP). The House version of the Secret Ballot Protection Act is also included in H.R. 3487, the Job Creation Act of 2011. H.R. 3487 was introduced by Representative Vern Buchanan.

111th Congress

In the 111th Congress, the Employee Free Choice Act (EFCA) was introduced in both the House and Senate. H.R. 1409 would require the National Labor Relations Board (NLRB) to certify a union if a majority of employees in a bargaining unit sign authorization cards designating the union as their bargaining representative.[3] If less than a majority, but at least 30%, of employees sign authorization cards, a secret ballot election may be held. (See the section on "Secret Ballot Elections" later in this report.)

H.R. 1409 would also establish a timetable for reaching a first contract agreement. Within 10 days after receiving a request to begin bargaining (or a longer period if agreed to by both the union and employer), the employer and union must meet to negotiate an initial contract agreement. If the employer and union cannot reach an agreement within 90 days after bargaining has begun (or a longer period if agreed to by both parties), either party may request mediation by the Federal Mediation and Conciliation Service (FMCS). If an agreement cannot be reached within 30 days through mediation (or a longer period if agreed to by both parties), the FMCS would refer the dispute to binding arbitration. The arbitration decision would be binding on both the employer and union for two years, unless the parties agree to amend it. The legislation would increase the penalties for employer violations of certain unfair labor practices committed during a union organizing campaign or during negotiation of a first contract. H.R. 1409 was introduced by Representative George Miller and was referred to the House Committee on Education and Labor.

In the Senate, the Employee Free Choice Act of 2009, S. 560, was introduced by Senator Edward Kennedy. The bill was referred to the Committee on Health, Education, Labor, and Pensions (HELP).[4]

In the 111th Congress, similar versions of the Secret Ballot Protection Act were introduced in both the House and Senate. H.R. 1176, the Secret Ballot Protection Act, would make it an unfair labor practice for an employer to recognize or bargain with a union that has not been selected by a majority of employees in a secret ballot election conducted by the NLRB.[5] It would also be an unfair labor practice for a union to cause or attempt to cause an employer to recognize or bargain with a union that has not been chosen by a majority of employees in a secret ballot election. H.R. 1176 was introduced by Representative John Kline and was referred to the House Committee on Education and Labor.

In the Senate, the Secret Ballot Protection Act of 2009, S. 478, was introduced by Senator Jim DeMint and was placed on the Senate Legislative Calendar.[6]

The National Labor Relations Modernization Act, H.R. 1355, was introduced by Representative Joe Sestak. For employers with 20 or more employees, the bill would create a timetable for reaching a first contract agreement. Within 10 days after receiving a request to begin bargaining (or a longer period if agreed to by both parties), the employer and union must meet to negotiate an initial contract. If the parties cannot reach an agreement within 120 days after bargaining begins (or a longer period if agreed to by both parties), either party may notify the FMCS of a dispute and request the appointment of an arbitration panel to help mediate an agreement. If an agreement still cannot be reached within 120 days after the request for mediation (or a longer period if agreed to by both parties), the panel, within 30 days, must issue a decision that will be binding on both parties for 18 months, unless the parties agree to amend it. The bill would also allow unions greater access to employees before a secret ballot election. Within 30 days after the NLRB has directed a secret ballot election, the employer must notify the union of any intended campaign activities and allow the union equal access to employees to campaign in favor of unionization. Finally, the legislation would increase the penalties for employer violations of certain unfair labor practices committed during a union organizing campaign or during negotiation of a first contract. The bill was referred to the House Committee on Education and Labor.

THE NATIONAL LABOR RELATIONS ACT

The NLRA, as amended, provides the basic framework governing labor-management relations in the private sector.[7] The act begins by stating that the purpose of the law is to improve the bargaining power of workers:

> The inequality of bargaining power between employees ... and employers ... substantially burdens and affects the flow of commerce, and tends to aggravate recurrent business depressions by depressing wage rates and the purchasing power of wage earners ... and by preventing the stabilization of competitive wage rates and working conditions within and between industries....
>
> It is hereby declared to be the policy of the United States to eliminate the causes of certain substantial obstructions to the free flow of commerce and to mitigate and eliminate these obstructions when they have occurred by encouraging the practice and procedure of collective bargaining.... [8]

The NLRA gives workers the right to join or form a labor union and to bargain collectively over wages, hours, and other conditions of employment. Under the act, workers also have the right not to join a union. The act requires an employer to bargain in good faith with a union chosen by a majority of employees. To protect the rights of employers and workers, the act defines certain activities as unfair labor practices.[9]

The NLRA does not apply to railroads or airlines, federal, state, or local governments, agricultural workers, family domestic workers, supervisors, independent contractors, and others. The definition of "employee" in the NLRA does not exclude unauthorized workers. Thus, unauthorized workers can engage in union activities.[10]

National Labor Relations Board (NLRB)

The NLRA is administered and enforced by the NLRB, which is an independent federal agency that consists of a five-member board and a General Counsel. The board resolves objections and challenges to secret ballot elections, decides questions about the composition of bargaining units, and hears appeals of unfair labor practices.[11] The General Counsel's office conducts secret ballot elections, investigates complaints of unfair labor practices, and supervises the NLRB's regional and other field offices.[12]

Bargaining Units

A bargaining unit is a group of employees represented, or seeking representation, by a union. A bargaining unit is generally determined on the basis of a "community of interest" of the employees involved. Employees who have the same or similar interests with respect to wages, hours, and other working conditions may be grouped together into a bargaining unit. A bargaining unit may include the employees of one employer, one establishment, or one occupation or craft. A bargaining unit may include both professional and nonprofessional employees, provided a majority of professional employees vote to be members of the unit. Guards cannot be included in the same bargaining unit as other employees. A union and employer may agree on the appropriate bargaining unit. If not, the issue is settled by the NLRB.

Specialty Healthcare and Rehabilitation Center of Mobile

In August 2011, the board reviewed a case in which an employer argued that the group of employees petitioning to be represented by a union was not an appropriate bargaining unit.[13] In this case, certified nursing assistants (CNAs) at the Specialty Healthcare and Rehabilitation Center of Mobile, AL, petitioned to be represented by the United Steelworkers (USW). The NLRB Regional Director found that the petitioned-for unit of CNAs was an appropriate bargaining unit. However, the employer requested a review of the decision, contending that the appropriate bargaining unit should include all other nonprofessional service and maintenance employees.

The duties of the CNAs at the healthcare center typically consist of assisting residents with day-to-day functions such as dressing, grooming, and bathing. The CNAs also help move residents throughout the facility, accompany them to appointments outside the center, record vital signs, and monitor daily intake of food and liquids. The CNAs wear nursing uniforms, are directly supervised by licensed practical nurses, are part of the facility's nursing department, and work one of three eight-hour shifts. The CNAs are required to obtain and maintain certification from the state of Alabama.

The employer argued that other employees should be included with the CNAs in the bargaining unit. The other employees include resident activity assistants who design and lead resident activities, a staffing coordinator who prepares work schedules for employees, a maintenance assistant who is responsible for building upkeep, a medical records clerk who maintains residents' medical records, and cooks. These employees have similar educational requirements as the CNAs (e.g., a high school degree). The CNAs and service and maintenance employees also receive annual evaluations under the same system, are eligible for pay raises based on their evaluations, and are eligible for the same benefits, such as health and life insurance. Unlike the CNAs, the other employees are not part of the nursing department and are not required to work one of three eight-hour shifts.

The board voted in favor (3-1) of the CNAs, determining that the CNAs' petitioned-for bargaining unit was appropriate. The board agreed with the Regional Director's original conclusion that the CNAs shared a community of interest because of their "[d]istinct training, certification, supervision, uniforms, pay rates, work assignments, shifts, and work areas." The board also concluded that the employer had not shown that the CNAs shared an "overwhelming community of interest" with the other service and maintenance employees.[14]

Organizing Campaign Rules

Campaign rules differ for employers, employees, and union organizers. Rules also differ for soliciting union support (e.g., expressing support for a union or handing out authorization cards) and for distributing union literature. Because of exceptions to the basic rules, the rules that apply to a specific union organizing campaign may differ from the general rules described here.[15]

Employers

Employers may campaign against unionization.[16] Employers may require employees to attend meetings during work hours where management can give its position on unionization. These meetings are called "captive audience" meetings. Employers cannot hold a captive audience meeting during the 24-hour period before an election. Supervisors can give employees written information (including memos and letters) and hold individual meetings with employees.

Employees

During work hours, employees can campaign for union support from their coworkers in both work and nonwork areas (e.g., a coffee room or the company parking lot). But employees can only campaign on their own time (e.g., at lunchtime or during breaks). If an employer does not allow the distribution of literature in work areas, employees may only distribute union literature in nonwork areas. If an employer allows the distribution of other kinds of literature in work areas, employees may also distribute union literature in those areas.

An employer may prevent employees from using the employer's e-mail for union activities (e.g., organizing and bargaining), provided the employer does not allow employees to use their work e-mail to solicit support for other causes or organizations.[17] Conversely, if an employer allows employees to use their work e-mail to solicit support for other causes or organizations, employees may also use their work e-mail for union activities.[18]

Union Organizers

In general, union organizers cannot conduct an organizing campaign on company property. A union cannot reply to an employer's captive audience speech if the union has other means of reaching employees.[19] Nonemployee union organizers may be allowed in the workplace if the site is inaccessible (e.g., a logging camp or remote hotel) or if the employer allows nonemployees to solicit on company property. Union organizers may meet with employees on union property. They may hand out literature or solicit support on public property (e.g., on public sidewalks outside of a business. Organizers may also contact employees at home by phone or mail or may visit employees at home.[20] Under a neutrality agreement (described later in this report), an employer may allow organizers onto company property.

Unfair Labor Practices

To protect the rights of both employees and employers, the NLRA defines certain activities as unfair labor practices.

Employers

Although employers have the right to campaign against unionization, they cannot interfere with, restrain, or coerce employees in their right to form or join a union. An employer cannot threaten employees with the loss of their jobs or benefits if they vote for a union or join a union. An employer cannot threaten to close a plant should employees choose to be represented by a union. An employer cannot raise wages to discourage workers from joining or forming a union. An employer cannot discriminate against employees with respect to the conditions of employment (e.g., fire, demote, or give unfavorable work assignments) because of union activities. An employer must bargain in good faith with respect to wages, hours, and other working conditions.[21]

Unions

Employees have the right to organize and bargain collectively. But a union cannot restrain or coerce employees to join or not join a union. A union cannot threaten employees with the loss of their jobs if they do not support unionization. A union cannot cause an employer to discriminate against employees with respect to the conditions of employment.

A union must bargain in good faith with respect to wages, hours, and other working conditions. A union cannot boycott or strike an employer that is a customer of or supplier to an employer that the union is trying to organize.[22]

An unfair labor practice may be filed by an employee, employer, labor union, or any other person. After an unfair labor practice charge is filed, regional staff of the NLRB investigate to determine whether there is reason to believe that the act has been violated. If no violation is found, the charge is dismissed or withdrawn. If a charge has merit, the regional director first seeks a voluntary settlement. If this effort fails, the case is heard by an NLRB administrative law judge. Decisions by administrative law judges can be appealed to the five-member board.[23]

Remedies

The NLRA attempts to prevent and remedy unfair labor practices. The purpose of the act is not to punish employers, unions, or individuals who commit unfair labor practices.

The act allows the NLRB to issue cease-and-desist orders to stop unfair labor practices and to order remedies for violations of unfair labor practices. If an employer improperly fires an employee for engaging in union activities, the employer may be required to reinstate the employee (to their prior or equivalent job) with back pay. If a union causes a worker to be fired, the union may be responsible for the worker's back pay.[24]

In FY2011, $60.5 million in backpay or reimbursement of fees, dues, and fines was awarded.[25] Backpay can be awarded to workers who were fired, demoted, denied work, or were otherwise discriminated against for union activities.

Estimates of the number of workers who are illegally fired for union activities range from 1,000 to 3,000 a year, with more firings in the 1980s than in later years.[26] In a study of 400 NLRB election campaigns conducted in 1998 and 1999, Kate Bronfenbrenner concluded that workers are fired for union activities in 25% of union campaigns.[27]

Figure 1 shows the trend in the number of unfair labor practice charges filed from FY1970 to FY2010. During this period, the number of charges filed peaked at 44,063 in FY1980. The number stood at 22,177 in FY2011.[28] In FY2010, 37.0% of the unfair labor practice charges filed were found to have merit.[29]

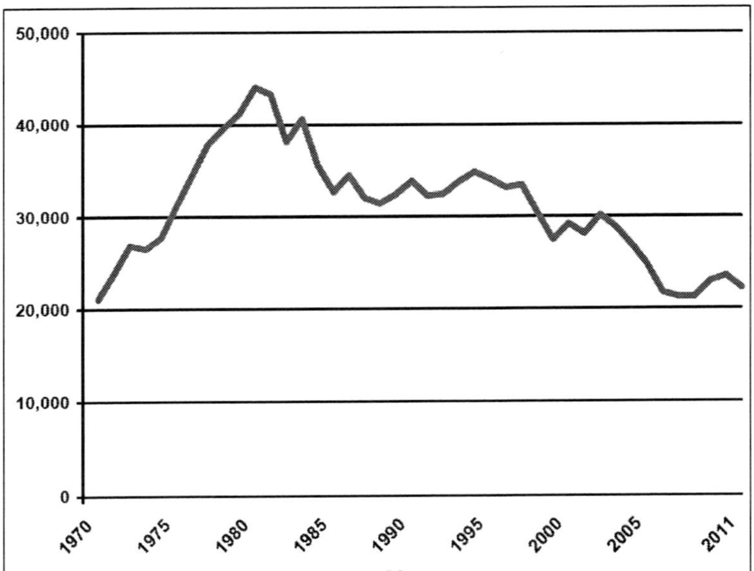

Sources: National Labor Relations Board, *Statistical Tables, FY2010*, Table 1, available at http://www.nlrb.gov/ node/3580. National Labor Relations Board, *Annual Report of the National Labor Relations Board*, various years, Chart 2.

Figure 1. Unfair Labor Practice Charges, FY1970-FY2011.

UNION CERTIFICATION AND RECOGNITION

Section 9(a) of NLRA states that a union may be "designated or selected for the purposes of collective bargaining by the *majority* of the employees" (emphasis added). Currently, there are three ways for employees to join or form a union. First, a union that is selected by a majority of employees in an election conducted by the NLRB is *certified* as the bargaining representative of employees in the bargaining unit. Second, an employer may voluntarily *recognize* a union if a majority of employees in a bargaining unit have signed authorization cards. Finally, the NLRB may order an employer to *recognize* and bargain with a union if a majority of employees have signed authorization cards and the employer has engaged in unfair labor practices that make a fair election unlikely.

A union must be certified through a secret ballot election or recognized by an employer before collective bargaining can begin. As discussed below under "Certification," a union that is certified as the result of a secret ballot election has certain advantages over a union that is recognized by an employer without an election.

Secret Ballot Elections

The NLRB conducts a secret ballot election when a petition is filed requesting one. A petition can be filed by a union, worker, or employer. Employees or a union may petition the NLRB for an election if at least 30% of employees have signed authorization cards. An employer may request an election if a union has claimed to represent a majority of its employees and has asked to bargain with the employer (and the union itself has not requested an election). An employer is not required to give a reason for requesting an election.[30] If a majority of employees voting (i.e., not a majority of employees in the bargaining unit) in an NLRB-conducted election choose to be represented by a union, the union is certified by the NLRB as the employees' bargaining representative.[31] The NLRA does not provide a timetable for holding an election. Certification of a union by the NLRB does not require that a union and employer reach an initial contract agreement.[32]

After a petition is filed requesting an election, the employer and union may agree on the time and place for the election and on the composition of the bargaining unit. If an agreement is not reached between the employer and union, a hearing may be held in the regional office of the NLRB. The regional director may then direct that an election be held. The regional director's decision may be appealed to the board.[33]

In a secret ballot election, employees choose whether to be represented by a labor union. If an election has more than one union on the ballot and no choice receives a majority of the vote, the two unions with the most votes face each other in a runoff election.[34]

The right of an individual to vote in an NLRB election may be challenged by either the employer or union. If the number of challenged ballots could affect the outcome of an election, the regional director determines whether the ballots should be counted. Either the employer or union may file objections to an election, claiming that the election or the conduct of one of the parties did not meet NLRB standards. A regional director's decision on challenges or objections may be appealed to the board.[35]

A union and employer may also agree to a secret ballot election conducted by a third party, such as an arbitrator, clergyman, or mediation board.[36]

The NLRB also conducts secret ballot elections to decertify a union that has previously been certified or recognized. A decertification petition may be filed by employees or a union acting on behalf of employees. A decertification petition must be signed by at least 30% of the employees in the bargaining unit represented by the union. Under what is called a "certification bar," a union that is certified after winning a secret ballot election is protected for a year from a decertification petition and from an election petition filed by another union. A secret ballot election is required for decertification.[37]

NLRB Changes in Representation Procedures

In June 2011, the NLRB published a Notice of Proposed Rulemaking (NPRM) in which it proposed a number of changes to current procedures for filing a petition requesting union representation, determining whether there is a question of union representation, conducting secret ballot elections, and resolving challenges and objections.[38] On December 22, 2011, the NLRB issued a final rule that makes selected changes to current representation procedures. The changes will take effect on April 30, 2012.[39]

The final rule gives hearing officers the discretion to limit pre-election hearings to matters "relevant to the existence of a question of representation." According to the NLRB, current regulations give parties the right to present evidence at pre-election hearings that are not related to the question of representation.[40] The rule also gives hearing officers the discretion to limit the filing and subject matter of legal briefs filed after a pre-election hearing.[41]

The final rule consolidates pre-election and post-election requests for review of decisions by regional directors. Currently, requests for review of pre-election decisions are filed before the election, while requests for review of post-election issues are filed after the election. Under the new rule, pre- and post-election requests for review will be filed after an election.[42]

Although the final rule consolidates pre-election and post-election requests for review, a party may request special permission for review of pre-election decisions. Under the final rule, the board will grant special permission to appeal pre-election rulings by hearing officers or regional directors in "extraordinary circumstances where it appears that the issue will otherwise evade review." According to the NLRB, current regulations do not provide a standard for the board to grant special permission for review.[43]

Currently, a regional director normally does not schedule an election until 25 days after the direction of an election. In part, the 25-day waiting period is intended to allow the board to consider requests for review of pre-election decisions. The final rule eliminates the 25-day waiting period.[44]

Finally, under the new rule requests for review by the board of decisions by regional directors on challenges and objections to elections will be discretionary. Currently, under a stipulated election agreement board review of post-election disputes is mandatory.[45] (In a stipulated election, the employer and union agree to an election, but either party may request board review of a regional director's or hearing officer's post-election decisions.[46])

Number of NLRB Elections

Table 1 shows the number of secret ballot elections conducted by the NLRB from FY1994 to FY2010. In FY2010, the NLRB conducted 1,823 elections. Unions won 62.3% of these elections, which was up from 46.6% in FY1994.[47]

Table 1. Number of Representation Elections Conducted by the NLRB, FY1994-FY2010

Fiscal Year	Number of Elections Conducted	Number of Elections Won by Unions	Percentage of Elections Won by Unions
2010	1,823	1,135	62.3%
2009	1,619	1,033	63.8%
2008	1,932	1,160	60.0%
2007	1,905	1,045	54.9%
2006	2,147	1,195	55.7%
2005	2,649	1,504	56.8%
2004	2,719	1,447	53.2%
2003	2,937	1,579	53.8%
2002	3,043	1,606	52.8%
2001	3,076	1,591	51.7%
2000	3,368	1,685	50.0%
1999	3,585	1,811	50.5%
1998	3,795	1,856	48.9%
1997	3,480	1,677	48.2%
1996	3,277	1,469	44.8%
1995	3,399	1,611	47.4%
1994	3,572	1,665	46.6%

Sources: National Labor Relations Board, *Statistical Tables, FY2010*, Table 13, available at http://www.nlrb.gov/node/3580. National Labor Relations Board, *Annual Report of the National Labor Relations Board,* various years, Chart 12, http://nlrb.gov/annual-reports.

Note: The number of elections conducted includes elections that resulted in a runoff or rerun.

In most elections conducted by the NLRB, the employer and union agree on the composition of the bargaining unit and on the time and place for an election. In FY2010, 89.3% of elections were based on consent or stipulated agreements between the two parties.[48]

First Contract Agreements Following Certification

The NLRB does not collect data on how long it takes for a union and employer to reach a first contract agreement after a union wins an NLRB election. Nor does the NLRB collect data on whether the parties reach a first contract agreement. However, a recent study estimated that, within two years of winning an NLRB election, a contract had not been reached in over two-fifths of cases. This is a higher percentage than found in estimates published in previous studies. Estimates from several studies are shown in **Table 2**. Although the NLRA does not provide a specific timetable for holding an election, most elections are held within two months of the filing of a petition. In FY2011, 91.7% of initial representation elections were conducted within 56 days of filing a petition. The median time to proceed to an election from the filing of a petition was 38 days.[49] In FY2011, post-election objections and/or challenges were filed in 115 cases. For objections and/or challenges that resulted in an investigative hearing (45 of 115) in FY2011, it took a median of 62 days to issue a decision or supplemental report; for those decisions and/or challenges that could be resolved without a hearing (70 of 115), it took a median of 21 days to issue a decision or supplemental report.[50]

Voluntary Card Check Recognition

The NLRA does not require secret ballot elections. An employer may voluntarily recognize a union when presented with authorization cards signed by a majority of employees in a bargaining unit. An employer may also enter into a card check agreement with a union before union organizers begin to collect signatures. A card check agreement between a union and employer may require the union to collect signatures from more than a majority (sometimes called a supermajority) of bargaining unit employees.[51] A neutral third party often checks, or validates, signatures on authorization cards. A collective bargaining contract may include a card check arrangement for unorganized (including new) branches, stores, or divisions of a company.

Table 2. First Contract Agreements Following Certification

Period Studied	Sample	A First Contract Agreement Was Reached	A First Contract Agreement Was Not Reached
October 1, 1999 to June 1, 2004[a]	First contract agreement after a union won an NLRB election.	In 56% of certifications, a contract was agreed to within two years of the election.	In 44% of certifications, a contract was not agreed to within two years of the election.
FY1986 to FY1993[b]	First contract agreement after a union won an NLRB election.	At least 56% of certifications resulted in a first contract. The actual percentage may be closer to two-thirds.	At most, 44% of certifications did not result in a first contract. The actual percentage may be closer to one-third.
1982 to 1986[c]	First contract agreement after a union won an NLRB election.	85% of service unions achieved a first contract agreement; 64% of manufacturing unions achieved a first contract.	15% of service unions did not reach a first contract agreement; 36% of manufacturing unions did not reach a first contract agreement.
April 1979 to March 1981[d]	First contract agreement after a union won an NLRB election. Sample included bargaining units of 100 or more employees.	63%	37%
1979 to 1980[e]	First contract agreement after a union won an NLRB election.	77%	33%
1970[f]	First contract agreement after a union won an NLRB election.	78%	22%
July 1, 1957 to June 30, 1962[g]	First contract agreement after a union won an NLRB election.	86%	14%

a. The estimate is based on 8,155 NLRB elections won by unions in cases closed between October 1, 1999 and June 1, 2004. Employers must bargain in good faith for one year after an NLRB election is won by a union. Therefore, the study used information from the FMCS for the period from October 1, 1999 to June 1, 2005. In recent years, the FMCS has attempted to contact the parties involved in first contract negotiations. John-Paul Ferguson, "The Eyes of the Needles: A Sequential Model of Union Organizing Drives, 1999-2004," *Industrial and Labor Relations Review*, vol. 62, October 2008, pp. 3-6.

b. The 56% estimate is based on 10,783 union elections certified by the NLRB and contract agreements in which the FMCS was involved. Other certifications may have resulted in a first contract agreement (e.g., where the FMCS was not contacted for help). Therefore, the actual percentage of certifications that resulted in a first contract may be closer to two-thirds. The estimates were calculated by the FMCS for the Commission on the Future of Worker-Management

Relations (the "Dunlop Commission"). U.S. Departments of Labor and Commerce, *Fact Finding Report: Commission on the Future of Worker-Management Relations*, May 1994, pp.73, 87, available at http://digitalcommons.ilr.cornell.edu/cgi/ viewcontent.cgi?article=1279&context=key_workplace.

c. The estimates are based on a survey of union organizers involved in 128 elections won by unions. Thomas F. Reed, "Union Attainment of First Contracts: Do Service Unions Possess a Competitive Advantage?," *Journal of Labor Research*, vol. 11, Fall 1990, pp. 428-430.

d. The estimates are based on a survey by the AFL-CIO of 271 elections won by unions. William N. Cooke, "The Failure to Negotiate First Contracts: Determinants and Policy Implications," *Industrial and Labor Relations Review*, vol. 38, January 1985, p. 164.

e. The estimates are based on a survey of unions that won 118 elections in Indiana during 1979 and 1980. The survey was conducted between June 1, 1982 and October 1, 1982. William N. Cooke, "The Failure to Negotiate First Contracts: Determinants and Policy Implications," *Industrial and Labor Relations Review*, vol. 38, January 1985, pp. 169-170.

f. The estimates are based on a 1975 survey by the AFL-CIO of 2,656 elections won by unions in 1970. The estimates are based on the number of responses, which was not reported. William N. Cooke, "The Failure to Negotiate First Contracts: Determinants and Policy Implications," *Industrial and Labor Relations Review*, vol. 38, January 1985, p. 164.

g. Paul Weiler, "Striking a New Balance: Freedom of Contract and the Prospects for Union Representation," *Harvard Law Review*, vol. 98, December 1984, pp. 353-355.

Under voluntary recognition, employees have 45 days to file a decertification petition or an election petition requesting representation by another union. After 45 days, an election petition cannot be filed for "a reasonable period of time." (See the section on "NLRB Review of Voluntary Recognition" later in this report.)

Neutrality Agreements

A card check arrangement may be combined with a neutrality agreement. Not all neutrality agreements are the same. However, in general, under a neutrality agreement an employer agrees to remain neutral during a union organizing campaign. The employer may agree not to attack or criticize the union, while the union may agree not to attack or criticize the employer. The agreement may allow managers to answer questions or provide factual information to employees. A neutrality agreement may give a union access to company property to meet with employees and distribute literature. An employer may also agree to give the union a list of employee names and addresses. A neutrality agreement may cover organizing drives at new branches of a company.[52]

Corporate Campaigns

To gain an agreement from an employer for a card check campaign—possibly combined with a neutrality agreement—unions sometimes engage in "corporate campaigns." A corporate campaign may include a call for consumers to boycott the employer; rallies and picketing; a public relations campaign (e.g., press releases, Internet postings, news conferences, or newspaper and television ads); charges that the employer has violated labor or other laws; public support from political, civic, and religious leaders; and other strategies.[53]

Bargaining Orders

The final way that a union may be recognized by an employer is through a bargaining order. The NLRB may order an employer to recognize and bargain with a union if a majority of employees have signed authorization cards and the employer has committed unfair labor practices that make it unlikely that a fair election can be held. A bargaining order may be issued without conducting a secret ballot election. An election may also be set aside because of employer unfair labor practices before the election.

According to Feldacker, "[h]ard and fast rules are not possible in determining the situations in which the Board will issue a bargaining order. Each case is based on the specific facts of the employer's violations."[54] Bargaining orders may be appealed to the U.S. Court of Appeals and to the U.S. Supreme Court.[55]

Certification Versus Recognition

A union that wins a secret ballot election is certified by the NLRB as the bargaining representative of employees in that bargaining unit. Voluntary recognition or a bargaining order do not result in certification by the NLRB. The Taft-Hartley Act of 1947 (P.L. 80-101) eliminated certification through any method other than an election conducted by the NLRB.[56]

Certification gives a union certain advantages. For instance, a union that is certified after winning a secret ballot election is protected for a year from a decertification petition and from an election petition requesting representation by another union (the "certification bar"). Under voluntary card check recognition, employees have 45 days to file a decertification petition or an election petition requesting to be represented by a different union (the "recognition bar").

The duration of an employer's duty to bargain also depends on whether a union has been certified by the board or has been recognized voluntarily by the employer. If a union wins an NLRB election (or under a bargaining order), the employer is required to bargain in good faith for a year. Under voluntary card check recognition, the employer is required to bargain with the union for "a reasonable period of time."[57]

Withdrawal of Recognition

Under certain circumstances, an employer may withdraw recognition of a union before a contract agreement has been reached. After one year, if an employer and a certified union have not reached a contract agreement, the employer may withdraw recognition of the union if both parties have engaged in good faith bargaining and the employer doubts, on the basis of objective information (e.g., a petition signed by a majority of employees and given to the employer), that a majority of employees no longer support the union. Under a voluntary recognition, if no contract agreement has been reached after a reasonable period of time, an employer may withdraw recognition if the employer has reasonable doubt on the basis of objective information that a majority of employees support the union.[58]

Joy Silk Doctrine

Before the Taft-Hartley Act of 1947, only a union or employee could request a secret ballot election.[59] Section 9(c) of the Taft-Hartley Act gave employers the right to request an election. Soon after Taft-Hartley was enacted, a U.S. Appeals court ruled that an employer's right to request an election was limited to instances where the employer had "good faith" doubt that the union was supported by a majority of employees. An employer had good faith doubt if he believed that signatures on authorization cards were obtained through misrepresentation or coercion.[60] An employer who did not have good faith doubt that the union was supported by a majority of employees was required to recognize the union or face a bargaining order for refusing to bargain with a union chosen by a majority of employees.[61] This approach was known as the "Joy Silk doctrine."[62]

By 1969, the board said that it had abandoned the Joy Silk doctrine. Thereafter, if a majority of employees signed authorization cards, an employer could voluntarily recognize the union or could insist on an election, either by requesting the union to file an election petition or by filing a petition himself.[63] In a 1974 ruling, the U.S. Supreme Court said that, if an employer insists on an election, the union must take the next step and file an election petition.[64]

Under EFCA, if a majority of employees sign authorization cards, it would be up to the union to request an election. Opponents of EFCA maintain that unions may not request secret ballot elections.

NLRB Review of Voluntary Recognition

In recent years, the NLRB has considered cases involving voluntary recognition.

The United Auto Workers (UAW) and the Dana and Metaldyne Corporations

In June 2004, the board voted 3-2 to review two cases where bargaining unit employees filed a decertification petition within weeks after the employer recognized a union under a card check agreement. In the first case, the United Auto Workers (UAW) and Metaldyne Corporation entered into a card check and neutrality agreement in September 2002. Metaldyne recognized the UAW as the bargaining representative of production and maintenance workers at its St. Marys, Pennsylvania plant in December 2003. In the second case, the UAW and Dana Corporation entered into a card check and neutrality agreement in August 2003. The company recognized the union at its Upper Sandusky, Ohio plant in December 2003.

In both the Dana and Metaldyne cases, the UAW and the employers entered into card check and neutrality agreements before signatures on authorization cards were collected. The signatures were validated by a neutral third party. In both cases, employees filed decertification petitions after the UAW was recognized by the employer, but before an agreement was reached on a contract. Regional NLRB directors dismissed both decertification petitions, saying that they were inconsistent with the board's "recognition bar" doctrine. Under this doctrine, following an employer's voluntary recognition of a union, employees or another union cannot file a petition for an election for a "reasonable period of time."

Employees at both Dana and Metaldyne Corporations petitioned the NLRB to review the dismissals. The employees were represented by the National Right to Work Legal Defense Foundation. The NLRB granted the request, saying that the issue was whether voluntary recognition should prevent employees from filing a decertification petition within a reasonable time in cases where an employer and union enter into a card check agreement.[65]

In September 2007, the board issued a decision in both cases. The board said that, following a voluntary recognition, employees have 45 days to file a petition to decertify the union. Similarly, a rival union has 45 days to file an election petition. The petitions must be signed by at least 30% of bargaining unit employees. Employees must also receive notice of the voluntary recognition and their right to petition for a decertification or representation election. If a petition is not filed within 45 days of notice of the voluntary recognition, an election petition cannot be filed during the recognition bar period (i.e., for a reasonable period of time).[66]

Lamons Gasket Company

On August 26, 2011, the board reversed its decision in the Dana and Metaldyne cases. In July 2003, Lamons Gasket and the United Steelworkers (USW) entered into a card check agreement. In November 2009, Lamons Gasket voluntarily recognized the USW as the sole representative of a unit of employees. Within 45 days following the voluntary recognition, a bargaining unit employee filed a petition for a decertification election, supported by authorization cards signed by at least 30% of employees. In a 3-1 decision, the board overruled the Dana and Metaldyne decisions and returned to the previously established rule that, following a voluntary recognition, an election petition is barred for a reasonable period of time. Additionally, the board defined a reasonable period of time as at least six months, but not more than a year, after the first bargaining session between the employer and union.[67]

The board also stated that, in determining whether a reasonable period of time has passed after a voluntary recognition, it would follow standards used in its decision in Lee Lumber and Building Material Corporation.[68]

Following the decision in Lamons Gasket, the Chairman of the House Committee on Education and the Workforce and the Chairman of the committee's Subcommittee on Health, Employment, Labor, and Pensions requested that the NLRB provide the committee with a list of cases in which an election petition was filed under the Dana decision and a list of cases that have been dismissed as a result of the decision in Lamons Gasket. The committee also requested a list of cases in which an election petition was filed under the Dana decision and an unfair labor practice charge was filed, a list of cases that have been dismissed as a result of the decision in Lamons Gasket and an unfair labor practice was filed, and the ballots in cases that were dismissed because of the decision in Lamons Gasket.[69]

Shaw's Supermarkets and the United Food and Commercial Workers (UFCW) Union

In another case involving voluntary card check recognition, the NLRB agreed to review a case where a union claimed that an employer had agreed to voluntary card check recognition at newly acquired stores. In December 2004, the board by a vote of 2-1 agreed to review a case involving Shaw's Supermarkets and the United Food and Commercial Workers Union (UFCW).[70]

In August 2003, Shaw's opened a new store in Mansfield, Massachusetts. A majority of workers at the new store signed authorization cards. The UFCW claimed that, under a clause in an existing bargaining contract, Shaw's had agreed to voluntary card check recognition at newly acquired stores.[71] Shaw's filed a petition requesting a secret ballot election.

In May 2004, an acting regional director of the NLRB dismissed Shaw's petition without a hearing. The board agreed to review the case and returned it to the regional office for a hearing. In its decision, the board said

> The issues in this case include (1) Whether the Employer clearly and unmistakably waived the right to a Board election; (2) if so, whether public policy reasons outweigh the Employer's private agreement not to have an election.

The board went on to say: "We do not resolve these issues at this stage. We merely hold that they are worthy of review."[72] After the hearing ordered by the board, a regional director, in March 2005, again dismissed Shaw's petition for an election.[73] In March 2006, the board again agreed to review the case.[74] As of November 24, 2008, the board has not issued a final decision.

NLRB Review of Withdrawal of Recognition

Once a union and employer enter into a collective bargaining agreement, election petitions are subject to a "contract bar." A contract of up to three years bars an election petition for the duration of the contract.[75] The election petition may be for a decertification election or for representation by another union.

In August 2007, the board issued a decision allowing an employer to withdraw recognition of a union after the third year of a longer-term contract. In January 1999, Shaw's Supermarkets entered into a five-year contract with the UFCW. After three years, a majority of employees signed a petition requesting a decertification election. Instead of going forward with a decertification election, Shaw's withdrew recognition of the union. The action was appealed to the NLRB.

Under current rules, neither the employer nor the incumbent union can initiate an election petition (requesting decertification or representation by another union) for the duration of a contract. Under a three-year "contract bar," employees or another union (but not the employer or existing union) can file an election petition after three years of a contract of more than three years. Thus, the General Counsel of the NLRB argued that Shaw's should not be allowed to withdraw recognition of the union during the term of the five-year contract. By a vote of 2-1 the board disagreed with the General Counsel. The majority members of the board concluded that Shaw's had acted properly when it withdrew recognition of the union. The majority said that the employer relied on evidence of a loss of majority support for the union (i.e., signatures of a majority of employees). The dissenting member said that the NLRB should have gone forward with a decertification election.[76]

Bargaining Impasses: Mediation and Arbitration

When a union and employer cannot reach a settlement on a collective bargaining agreement, the dispute is called an impasse.[77] An impasse may lead to a work stoppage.

Workers may strike or the employer may lock out employees.[78] Instead of resorting to a strike or lockout, a union and employer may use a neutral third party to help them reach a contract agreement. A neutral third party may be used to reach an agreement on either an initial or successor contract. The Employee Free Choice Act (EFCA) would establish mediation and arbitration procedures when an employer and union cannot reach an agreement on an initial contract. If a union and employer cannot reach a contract agreement, they may continue to negotiate or the impasse can go to mediation and then to binding arbitration. EFCA does not specify the type of arbitration that would be used. The legislative language of EFCA states that if an employer and union cannot reach an initial contract agreement following 30 days of mediation (or a longer period if agreed to by both parties), the FMCS "shall refer the dispute to an arbitration board established in accordance with such regulations as may be prescribed by the Service [i.e., the FMCS]." The arbitrator's decision would be binding on both parties.

Mediation

When mediation is used to resolve a collective bargaining impasse, a mediator tries to help the union and employer reach an agreement.[79] A mediator does not have the authority to impose a settlement on the parties. Instead, a mediator can help the two sides reach an agreement by defining the issues underlying the impasse, identifying alternative solutions, and suggesting areas where the parties can compromise.[80]

Arbitration

In arbitration, the union and employer each present their positions to an arbitrator who decides how the issues will be resolved. Arbitration can take different forms. In grievance or "rights" arbitration, an arbitrator resolves disputes over the terms and conditions of an existing collective bargaining agreement. In contract or "interest" arbitration, an arbitrator determines the terms and conditions of an initial or successor contract. Interest arbitration can take different forms: voluntary or compulsory, conventional or final-offer, and binding or nonbinding. In addition, in final-offer arbitration, the arbitrator may choose between the complete final offers of the employer and union (i.e., the entire package) or between the final offers from each side on each issue.

- *Voluntary versus compulsory.* In voluntary interest arbitration, the union and employer agree to use arbitration to resolve a bargaining impasse. With compulsory arbitration, the law requires the parties to use arbitration.
- *Conventional versus final-offer.* In conventional arbitration, the arbitrator is free to decide on a final contract agreement. The settlement may be a compromise between each side's final offer, or the arbitrator may choose the final offer from either one of the parties. With final-offer arbitration, the arbitrator must choose either the union's or the employer's final offer.
- *Package versus issue-by-issue arbitration.* In final-offer arbitration, the arbitrator may be required to choose the complete final offer (i.e., package) of either the union

or the employer. Alternatively, the arbitrator may be allowed to choose between the final offers from each side on each issue.[81]

- *Binding versus nonbinding*. In binding arbitration, the arbitrator's decision is imposed on both parties. With nonbinding arbitration, the parties may choose to accept or reject the decision of the arbitrator.[82]

The different forms of arbitration can be combined. For example, conventional arbitration may be voluntary or compulsory. Final-offer arbitration may be binding or nonbinding.

Med-Arb

Med-Arb combines the role of mediator and arbitrator.[83] As a mediator, a neutral third party tries to facilitate an agreement. If the parties cannot reach a settlement, the neutral party becomes the arbitrator and decides on a settlement. With Med-Arb, a neutral party's recommendations for a settlement may become the settlement that is imposed. Knowing this, the parties may be more willing to negotiate an agreement.[84]

Advantages and Disadvantages of Interest Arbitration in Resolving Bargaining Impasses

The use of interest arbitration to resolve bargaining impasses has occurred mainly in the public sector, where the right to strike is generally limited or prohibited. In the private sector, the legal right of employees to strike and of employers to lock out employees can encourage the parties to reach a contract agreement.[85] Nevertheless, in the private sector, a union and employer may voluntarily agree to use interest arbitration to settle bargaining impasses.[86]

The use of interest arbitration in contract negotiations may have both advantages and disadvantages. The main advantage is that it may deter or prevent a strike or lockout. The main disadvantages are that it may change negotiating behavior and may become the normal way to settle bargaining impasses.

Strike Impact

When a union and employer reach a bargaining impasse, they can resort to mediation or arbitration. But employers can also lock out employees or workers can go on strike. The main reason for using interest arbitration to resolve contract disputes is to avoid the use of strikes or lockouts. A strike over wages, hours, or working conditions is called an economic strike. Employers can permanently replace striking workers. Replaced workers can only be rehired when jobs become available.[87] Thus, a strike can impose costs on both workers and employers.

"Chilling" Effect

An adverse effect of interest arbitration is that it may have a "chilling" effect on negotiations. The availability of interest arbitration to resolve bargaining impasses may affect the willingness of the two sides to engage in serious bargaining. If either side believes that it can gain a better settlement through arbitration than through negotiation, it may not bargain seriously. If the parties expect an arbitrator to split the difference between their final offers, they may take extreme positions during negotiations and be unwilling to compromise.

"Narcotic" Effect

A second adverse effect of interest arbitration is that it may have a "narcotic" effect on contract negotiations. Interest arbitration may become habit-forming. If negotiations over a contract end with binding arbitration, the parties may come to rely on it and not engage in serious negotiations on future contracts.[88]

Possible Responses to the Chilling and Narcotic Effect of Arbitration

The binding arbitration provision in EFCA would apply only to first contracts. Therefore, the criticism that interest arbitration may become addictive and be used to resolve future bargaining impasses may not apply if EFCA were enacted. On the other hand, if EFCA were enacted, having used arbitration once, a union and employer may voluntarily agree to use interest arbitration to resolve bargaining impasses on future contracts.

A common criticism of conventional arbitration is that it may prevent the parties from engaging in serious negotiations. Each side may take an extreme position and may not make the kinds of compromises needed for a negotiated settlement.[89] One proposal for dealing with the chilling effect of conventional arbitration is to require final-offer arbitration. The argument for using final-offer arbitration is that, if an arbitrator is limited to selecting the last offer of either the union or employer, each side may be more willing to make an offer that it believes will be acceptable to the arbitrator. If both parties are more willing to compromise, they may also reach a contract settlement on their own.[90]

Under final-offer arbitration, the arbitrator could be restricted to choosing between the complete final offer of either the union or employer. Alternatively, the arbitrator could be allowed to choose between the final offers of each party on each issue.[91] The latter approach would give an arbitrator greater discretion in fashioning the terms of an agreement and may also encourage the parties to bargain and make concessions on each issue.[92]

Potential Effects of Changes in Union Certification Procedures

Changes in union certification procedures may affect the level of unionization in the United States.[93] This section summarizes the most common arguments made in favor of requiring secret ballot elections and the most common arguments made in support of card check certification. The section also reviews research on the effects of different union certification procedures on union success rates.

The most common arguments made by the proponents of requiring card check certification and the proponents of requiring secret ballot elections are summarized in Table 3.[94]

Proponents of each view sometimes use similar language in support of their positions. Employers argue that, under card check certification, employees may be pressured or coerced into signing authorization cards and that employees may only hear the union's point of view. On the other hand, unions argue that during an election campaign, employers may pressure or coerce employees into voting against a union. Proponents of secret ballot elections argue that unlike signing an authorization card, casting a secret ballot is private and confidential. Unions argue that during an election campaign, employers have greater access to employees (e.g., captive audience meetings and access to employees on company property). Unions argue that card check certification is less costly than a secret ballot election. But employers maintain that unionization may be more costly to employees, because union members must pay dues and higher union wages may result in fewer union jobs.

Table 3. Common Arguments Made by Proponents of Requiring Card Check Certification and Requiring Secret Ballots

Proponents of Requiring Card Check Certification	Proponents of Requiring Secret Ballot Elections
Card check certification requires signatures from more than 50% of bargaining unit employees. A secret ballot election is decided by a majority of workers voting.	Casting a secret ballot is private and confidential. A secret ballot election is conducted by the NLRB. Under card check certification, authorization cards are controlled by the union.
During a secret ballot campaign, the employer has greater access to employees.	Under card check certification, employees may only hear the union's point of view.
Because of potential employer pressure or intimidation during a secret ballot election, some workers may feel coerced into voting against a union.	Because of potential union pressure or intimidation, some workers may feel coerced into signing authorization cards.
Employer objections can delay a secret ballot election.	Most secret ballot elections are held soon after a petition is filed.
Allegations against a union for unfair labor practices can be addressed under existing law. Existing remedies do not deter employer violations of unfair labor practices.	Allegations against an employer for unfair labor practices can be addressed under existing law. Existing remedies do not deter union violations of unfair labor practices.
Card check certification is less costly for both the union and employer. If secret ballot elections were required, the NLRB would have to devote more resources to conducting elections.	Union members must pay union dues. Unionization may result in fewer union jobs.
Neutrality agreements and card check certification may lead to more cooperative labor-management relations.	An employer may be pressured by a corporate campaign into accepting a neutrality agreements and card check certification. If an employer accepts a neutrality agreement, employees who do not want a union may hesitate to speak out.

Source: Table compiled by CRS.

Research Findings

Little research has been done comparing the effects of requiring card check certification versus the effects of requiring secret ballot elections. The research that exists, however, suggests that changes in union recognition procedures could affect the level of unionization in the United States. Research suggests that the union success rate is greater with card check certification than with secret ballots. Unions also undertake more unionization drives under card check certification. The union success rate under card check certification is greater when a card check campaign is combined with a neutrality agreement.

Evidence from Canada suggests that the union success rate is higher under automatic card check recognition than under secret ballots. In Canada, each of the 10 provinces has laws governing union recognition.[95] In 1976, all 10 provinces allowed card check recognition. Beginning with Nova Scotia in 1977, five provinces currently require secret ballot elections.[96] British Columbia changed from card check recognition to requiring secret ballot elections in 1984, repealed mandatory voting in 1993, and restored mandatory voting in 2001.[97] Under mandatory voting a union must receive a majority of votes in a secret ballot election to be recognized as the bargaining agent. Under card check recognition, a union is automatically recognized if the number of employees who sign authorization cards meets a minimum threshold. In general, a union is automatically recognized if more than 50% to 65% of employees, depending on the province, sign authorization cards.[98]

A study of the union success rate under mandatory voting and automatic card check recognition concluded that the union success rate in Canada is nine percentage points higher under card check recognition than under secret ballots. The study examined 171 union organizing campaigns between 1978 and 1996 in nine provinces.[99]

In the province of British Columbia, union recognition based on card checks was allowed until 1984. From 1984 through 1992, union certification required a secret ballot election. Card checks were again allowed beginning in 1993. (As noted above, mandatory voting resumed in 2001.) The union success rate fell almost 19 percentage points (from 93.1% to 74.5%) after mandatory voting was adopted in 1984 and increased by about the same amount when card check recognition was reinstated in 1993. In addition, during the period when mandatory voting was in effect, there were about 50% fewer attempts to organize workers. After 1993, the number of union organizing drives did not return to their pre-1984 levels.[100]

In the province of Ontario, card check recognition was allowed before 1995. Since November 1995, secret balloting is required. A study of 3,564 certification applications before and after the switch to secret ballots found that the certification rate was higher with the use of card checks. After the change to secret ballots, the union success rate fell from 72.7% to 64.3%. On the other hand, under secret balloting, larger bargaining units were organized. The average size of units certified under secret balloting was 63.1 workers, compared to an average of 36.3 employees under card check recognition. The average size of the bargaining units where organizing drives were held was also larger after secret balloting was initiated; 63.1 workers versus 39.7 workers under card check recognition. Under card check recognition, a union was certified if 55% of employees signed cards. Under secret balloting, elections are normally held within five working days after the date of an application. The study included both private and public sector employers, but excluded the construction industry.[101]

A study based on unionization in Canada concluded that each one percentage point increase in unionization raised the short-term unemployment rate by 0.30 to 0.35 percentage points. The study was based in union membership data in the 10 Canadian provinces over the period from 1976 to 1997.[102]

Evidence also suggests that card check recognition may be more successful under a neutrality agreement. A study of union organizing drives in the United States concluded that union success rates are higher when a card check agreement is combined with a neutrality agreement. The study examined 57 card check agreements involving 294 organizing drives.

Unions had a success rate of 78.2% in drives where card check recognition was combined with a neutrality agreement and a 62.5% success rate in cases where there was only a card check agreement.[103]

The union success rate may be higher under card check recognition because, in part, employers have less of an opportunity to campaign against unionization. Unions may initiate more organizing drives under card check recognition because a card check campaign costs less than a secret ballot election. A secret ballot election may take longer than a card check campaign and employer opposition may be greater (requiring a union to expend more resources).[104] Unions may have a higher success rate when card check recognition is combined with a neutrality agreement because there may be less employer opposition to unionization under a neutrality agreement. (Some research has concluded that management opposition is a key factor affecting union success rates in NLRB conducted elections.)[105]

Requiring card check certification if a majority of employees sign authorization cards may increase the union success rate. Whether or not requiring card check certification would reverse the decline in private sector unionization in the United States is not certain. Shrinking employment in unionized firms and decertifications may offset any increase in union membership due to requiring card check recognition. In addition, requiring card check recognition may increase employer opposition during the collection of authorization cards.

Public Opinion

According to an annual Gallup poll, Americans are generally supportive of unions. The latest poll, from August 2008, concluded that 59% of Americans approve, while 31% disapprove, of unions.[106]

According to a March 2009 Gallup poll, 53% of Americans favor a law that would make it easier for labor unions to organize; 39% of those polled said they opposed such a law; and 8% said they had no opinion. Of those polled, 34% said they were following news about EFCA either "very closely" or "somewhat closely"; 65% said they were following news about the bill "not too closely' or "not at all." Of those who have been following the bill very closely, 58% opposed the legislation. On the other hand, of those not following the bill at all, 58% favored the legislation.[107]

According to a poll from Rasmussen Reports, also from March 2009, 33% of respondents agreed that Congress should change the law to make it easier for workers to form or join a union; 40% disagreed and 27% were not sure. Sixty-one percent of respondents agreed when asked the following question: "Under current law, if enough workers express interest in forming a union, a secret ballot is held. Is it fair to require a secret ballot to determine if workers want to form a union?" Thirty-two percent of respondents agreed to the following question: "Some people believe that a secret ballot vote is not necessary and that a union should be formed whenever a majority of workers sign a card saying they want one. If a majority of a company's workers sign a card saying they want to form a union, is it fair to form a union without having a vote?" At the same time, 57% of respondents thought that it is "very difficult" or "somewhat difficult" to form a union.[108]

Two other surveys provide information about secret ballot elections and card check recognition.[109] According to a March 2006 survey conducted for the Center for Union Facts (a business group), 75% of 1,000 persons surveyed said that they believe that a secret ballot election is the most fair and democratic way for employees to decide whether or not to join a union. By contrast, 12% of respondents said that card check recognition is the most fair and democratic way to form a union.[110] According to a 2005 survey conducted by American Rights at Work (a labor group), 22% of 430 workers who had gone through a union organizing campaign said that they experienced a "great deal" of pressure from management. By contrast, 6% of workers said that they experienced a great deal of union pressure. Among workers who signed authorization cards in the presence of a union organizer, 5% said that the presence of the organizer made them feel pressure to sign the cards.[111]

SMALL BUSINESS

The NLRA does not include a statutory exemption for small businesses. However, the NLRB does not certify bargaining units of only one employee. Nor does it assert jurisdiction over employers with annual revenues or sales below certain standards.

Size of Bargaining Unit

The board does not certify a bargaining unit that consists of only one employee. The principle of collective bargaining presupposes that there is more than one employee who wants to bargain collectively.[112]

Jurisdictional Standards

The NLRB has statutory jurisdiction over employers whose operations affect interstate commerce. Thus, the board can certify the results of an election where the employer's operations affect commerce.[113] However, in addition to this statutory requirement, the NLRB has established administrative standards that an employer must meet before the board will assert jurisdiction over a question of union representation. These jurisdictional standards are generally based on an employer's annual sales or gross revenue. For example, a retail business must have annual sales of at least $500,000 before the board will assert jurisdiction. Hotels and motels must have at least $500,000 in gross revenues. A nonretail business must have either $50,000 in annual direct or indirect sales to buyers in other states or make $50,000 in direct or indirect purchases from sellers in other states. Private colleges and symphony orchestras must have at least $1 million in annual revenue.[114] These standards have been in effect since August 1, 1959.

The board's ability to establish jurisdictional standards was codified by the Labor-Management Reporting and Disclosure Act of 1959, which added Section 14(c)(1) to the NLRA (29 U.S.C. 164(c)(1)). In part, Section 14(c)(1) states:

> The Board, in its discretion, may ... decline to assert jurisdiction over any labor dispute involving any class or category of employers, where, in the opinion of the Board, the effect of such labor dispute on commerce is not sufficiently substantial to warrant the exercise of its jurisdiction: Provided, That the Board shall not decline to assert

> jurisdiction over any labor dispute over which it would assert jurisdiction under the standards prevailing upon August 1, 1959.

In other words, the board *must* assert jurisdiction over a labor dispute where the employer meets the jurisdictional standards that were in effect on August 1, 1959 (provided the employer's operations affect commerce). But the board *may* decline to assert jurisdiction over a labor dispute that does not have a substantial effect on interstate commerce. Thus, for the purposes of EFCA, it is not certain that the board would not certify the results of a majority card check if the employer did not meet the current jurisdictional standards (because the statute says that the board may, as opposed to must, decline to assert jurisdiction).

If EFCA were enacted and the board did not assert jurisdiction over smaller employers, employees at these companies may be able to unionize through other means. An employer could voluntarily recognize a union if a majority of employees sign authorization cards or a secret ballot election could be supervised by a third party other than the NLRB. In addition, Section 14(c)(2) of the NLRA (29 U.S.C. 164(c)(2)) states, in part:

> Nothing in this subchapter shall be deemed to prevent or bar any agency or the courts of any State or Territory ... from assuming and asserting jurisdiction over labor disputes over which the Board declines ... to assert jurisdiction.

Thus, if the NLRB does not assert jurisdiction over a successful card check campaign at a small business, a state labor agency may assert jurisdiction.

A report by the Government Accountability Office (GAO) estimated that, in February 2001, because of the jurisdictional standards, 5 million employees of small employers do not have collective bargaining rights under the NLRA (excluding supervisors and managers who are excluded by statute from coverage under the NLRA).[115] If more recent data were used, the 5 million estimate could be higher or lower today. Because the dollar amounts for the jurisdictional standards are not adjusted for inflation, employers who met the standards in 1959 would probably not meet them today. On the other hand, there are more businesses today, many of which would meet the standards.

Is There an Economic Rationale for Protecting the Rights of Workers to Organize and Bargain Collectively?

The NLRA gives private sector workers the right to organize and bargain collectively over wages, hours, and other working conditions. It also requires employers to bargain in good faith with a union chosen by a majority of employees. The act says that the purpose of the law is to improve the bargaining power of workers. This section considers whether there is an economic rationale for protecting the rights of workers to organize and bargain collectively.

Government Intervention in Labor Markets

Governments may intervene in labor markets for a number of reasons. One of these reasons is to improve competition.[116] According to standard economic theory, competitive markets generally result in the most efficient allocation of resources, where resources consist of individuals with different skills, capital goods (i.e., buildings and equipment and associated technology), and natural resources. In turn, an efficient allocation of resources generally results in greater total output and consumer satisfaction.

In competitive labor markets workers are paid according to the value of their contribution to output. Under perfect competition, wages include compensation for unfavorable working conditions. The latter theory, called the "theory of compensating wage differentials," recognizes that individuals differ in their preferences or tolerance for different working conditions—such as health and safety conditions, hours worked, holidays and annual leave, and job security.[117]

If labor markets do *not* fit the model of perfect competition, increasing the bargaining power of workers may raise wages, improve benefits (e.g., for health care and retirement), and improve working conditions to levels that would exist under competitive conditions. In labor markets where a firm is the only employer (called a monopsony) unionization could, within limits, increase both wages and employment.[118]

On the other hand, increasing the bargaining power of employees in competitive labor markets may result in a misallocation of resources—and reduce total economic output and consumer satisfaction. In competitive labor markets, higher union wages may reduce employment for union workers below the levels that would exist in the absence of unionization.[119] If unions lower employment in the unionized sector, they may increase the supply of workers to employers in the nonunion sector, lowering the relative wages of nonunion workers.[120]

It is difficult, however, to determine the competitiveness of labor markets. First, identifying the appropriate labor market may be difficult. Labor markets can be local (e.g., for unskilled labor), regional, national, or international (e.g., for managerial and professional workers). Second, measuring the competitiveness of labor markets is difficult. Finally, labor markets may change over time because of demographic, economic, technological, or other changes.[121]

Distribution of Earnings

A second reason governments may intervene in labor markets is to reduce earnings inequality.[122] Competitive labor markets may allocate resources efficiently, but they may result in a distribution of earnings that some policymakers find unacceptable. Unionization may be a means of reducing earnings inequality. Some economists argue that, during a recession, greater earnings equality may increase aggregate demand and, therefore, reduce unemployment.

Collective Voice

Finally, some economists maintain that unions give workers a "voice" in the workplace. According to this argument, unions provide workers an additional way to communicate with management. For instance, instead of expressing their dissatisfaction with an employer by quitting, workers can use dispute resolution or formal grievance procedures to resolve issues relating to pay, working conditions, or other matters.[123]

Conclusion

The economic impact of requiring card check certification or secret ballot elections may rest on the desired objectives of policymakers.

By bargaining collectively, unionized workers may obtain higher wages, improved benefits, and better working conditions than if each worker bargained individually.[124] But, depending on how well labor markets fit the model of perfect competition, collective bargaining may improve or harm the allocation of resources (i.e., economic efficiency). If labor markets are competitive, increasing the bargaining power of workers may reduce economic output and consumer satisfaction, but may increase equality. On the other hand, if labor markets are not competitive, increasing the bargaining power of workers may improve the allocation of resources as well as increase equality.[125]

By requiring card check certification, the number of organizing campaigns and the union success rate may increase. Conversely, by requiring secret ballot elections, the number of organizing drives and the union success rate may decline. Thus, compared with existing recognition procedures, requiring secret ballot elections may lower the level of unionization, whereas requiring card check certification may raise it. Accordingly, depending on the competitive-ness of labor markets, requiring card check certification may either improve or harm economic efficiency. Similarly, requiring secret ballot elections may either improve or harm efficiency. If either change were enacted, it may be difficult, however, to predict or measure the size of the effects.

Regardless of the competitiveness of labor markets, requiring secret ballot elections may increase earnings inequality—if fewer workers are unionized. Requiring card check certification may reduce inequality—if more workers are unionized. Again, the size of the effects may be difficult to predict or measure.

End Notes

[1] The NLRA is also known as the Wagner Act, after Senator Robert Wagner of New York who sponsored the bill in the U.S. Senate. Representative William Connery of Massachusetts sponsored the bill in the U.S. House of Representatives.

[2] On November 2, 2010, voters in four states approved amendments to their state constitutions that supporters claim would preserve workers' rights to a secret ballot election. The four states were Arizona, South Carolina, South Dakota, and Utah. (Bureau of National Affairs, "Voters in Four States Approve Preemptive Strikes at EFCA," *Daily Labor Report*, no. 212, November 3, 2010.) On May 6, 2011, the National Labor Relations Board (NLRB) filed suit against the state of Arizona. The suit alleges that the amendment to Arizona's constitution is preempted by the NLRA. In addition, on June 16, 2011, the Governor of Tennessee signed legislation that

would require secret ballot elections to be used to determine if a majority of employees want to be represented by a union.

[3] This section uses terms and refers to agencies (e.g., certification, recognition, bargaining unit, unfair labor practices, National Labor Relations Board (NLRB), and Federal Mediation and Conciliation Service (FMCS)) that are described later in this report.

An authorization card may serve more than one purpose. A single-purpose card authorizes the union to represent the employee signing the card. A dual-purpose card designates the union as the employees' bargaining representative and requests an election. The NLRB may not issue a bargaining order (see "Bargaining Orders" later in this report) if a union uses dual-purpose cards. Dual-purpose cards could indicate that a majority of employees want an election, but not that a majority of employees want to be represented by a union. Commerce Clearing House, *Labor Law Reporter: Labor Relations* (Chicago: CCH Inc., 2007), ¶ 3042. Bruce S. Feldacker, *Labor Guide to Labor Law*, 3rd ed.(Englewood Cliffs, N.J.: Prentice Hall, 1990), p. 72. (Hereafter cited as Feldacker, *Labor Guide to Labor Law*.)

[4] The Employee Free Choice Act was also introduced in the 108th, 109th, and 110th Congresses. For more information on the act, see CRS Report RS21887, The Employee Free Choice Act, by Jon O. Shimabukuro. Legislation that would require card check recognition was introduced in Congress as early as the 95th Congress (1977-1978). Early in the 95thCongress, Representative Frank Thompson Jr. introduced H.R. 77, the Labor Reform Act of 1977. H.R. 77 would have required the NLRB to certify a union as the exclusive bargaining representative of employees in a bargaining unit if55% of the employees signed authorization cards. No hearings were held and no action was taken on the bill. Later in the 95th Congress, President Jimmy Carter sent to Congress proposals to amend the NLRA. H.R. 8410/S. 1883, which was also called the Labor Reform Act of 1977, was introduced in the House by Representative Frank Thompson Jr. and in the Senate by Senators Harrison Williams Jr. and Jacob Javits. H.R. 8410/S. 1883 would have created timetables for holding representation elections. The bill passed the House. In the Senate, the Senate Human Resources Committee reported a bill (renumbered as S. 2467). The measure was filibustered on the Senate floor. After six cloture votes, the bill was returned to committee for changes. The committee did not report another bill.

[5] The Secret Ballot Protection Act was also introduced in the 108th, 109th, and 110th Congresses.

[6] H.R. 1176 and S. 478 are not identical. Section 4(b) of S. 478 states that "Nothing in this Act (or the amendments made by this Act) shall be construed to limit or otherwise diminish the remedial authority of the National Labor Relations Board." With this provision, the NLRB should, for example, be able to issue a bargaining order as a remedy to an employer for unfair labor practices. See the section on "Bargaining Orders" later in this report.

[7] More specifically, the NLRA applies to employers engaged in interstate commerce. 29 U.S.C. §152(6).

[8] 29 U.S.C. §151. Many economists argue that there is not an inequality of bargaining power between employers and employees. For example, see Morgan O. Reynolds, *Power and Privilege: Labor Unions in America*, New York: Universe Books, 1984, pp. 59-62; and Morgan O. Reynolds, "The Myth of Labor's Inequality of Bargaining Power," *Journal of Labor Research*, vol. 12, spring 1991, pp. 168-183. The argument that workers and employers have equal bargaining power is generally based on the premise that labor markets fit the economic model of perfect competition. See the section later in this report on whether there is an economic rationale for protecting the rights of workers to organize and bargain collectively.

[9] National Labor Relations Board, *Basic Guide to the National Labor Relations Act* (Washington: U.S. Govt. Print. Off., 1997), pp. 1, 17, available at https://www.nlrb.gov/sites/default/ files/documents/224/basicguide.pdf.. (Hereafter cited as NLRB, *Basic Guide to the NLRA*.)

The Labor Management Relations Act of 1947 (P.L. 80-101, commonly called the Taft-Hartley Act) amended the NLRA to add language that employees have the right to refrain from joining a union, unless a collective bargaining agreement with a union security agreement is in effect. A union security agreement may require bargaining unit employees to join the union after being hired (i.e., a union shop) or, if the employee is not required to join the union, to pay a representation fee to the union (i.e., an agency shop). Under Section 14(b) of the Taft-Hartley Act, states may enact right-to-work laws, which do not allow contracts to include a union security agreement. Michael Ballot, Laurie Lichter-Heath, Thomas Kail, and Ruth Wang, *Labor-Management Relations in a Changing Environment*, New York: John Wiley and Sons, Inc., 1992, pp. 265-268. (Hereafter cited as Ballot et al., *Labor-Management Relations in a Changing Environment.*)

[10] NLRB, *Basic Guide to the NLRA*, p. 37.

In a 1984 decision (Sure-Tan, Inc. v. NLRB, 467 U.S. 883), the U.S. Supreme Court ruled that the definition of employee in the NLRA does not exclude unauthorized workers. Thus, unauthorized workers can engage in union organizing and collective bargaining, can vote in NLRB elections, and are protected from unfair labor practices. But, the Supreme Court has also ruled that unauthorized workers cannot be awarded backpay as the result of violations of unfair labor practices. See CRS Report RS21186, *Hoffman Plastic Compounds v. NLRB and Backpay Awards to Undocumented Aliens*, by Jon O. Shimabukuro.

[11] NLRB, *Basic Guide to the NLRA*, p. 7. Feldacker, *Labor Guide to Labor Law*, pp. 39-44.

[12] NLRB, *Basic Guide to the NLRA*, p. 33. William N. Cooke, *Union Organizing and Public Policy: Failure to Secure First Contracts* (Kalamazoo, MI: W.E. Upjohn Institute, 1985), p. 85.

[13] National Labor Relations Board, *Specialty Healthcare and Rehabilitation Center of Mobile and United Steelworkers, District 9*, 356 NLRB No. 56 (2011), pp. 8-13, available at http:// nlrb.gov/case/15-RC-008773#casedetails.

[14] The CNAs voted for union representation. United Steel Workers, District 9, http://www.usw. org/.

[15] Unless noted otherwise, this section is based on Stephen I. Schlossberg and Judith A. Scott, *Organizing and the Law*, 4th ed., Washington: Bureau of National Affairs, 1991, pp. 45-55. (Hereafter cited as Schlossberg and Scott, *Organizing and the Law*.) James J. Brudney, *Neutrality Agreements and Card Check Recognition: Prospects for Changing Paradigms*, Public Law and Legal Theory Working Paper Series No. 28, November 2004, p. 8, available at http://law.bepress.com/cgi/viewcontent.cgi?article=1002&context=osulwps. (Hereafter cited as Brudney, *Neutrality Agreements and Card Check Recognition*.) Feldacker, *Labor Guide to Labor Law*, pp. 74-79.

[16] The Taft-Hartley Act of 1947 amended the NLRA to add Section 8(c), which gives employers and unions the right to express their views on unionization, provided such "expression contains no threat of reprisal or force or promise of benefit." For a legal history of this provision, see Kate E. Andrias, "A Robust Public Debate: Realizing Free Speech in Workplace Representation Elections, *Yale Law Journal*, vol. 112, June 2003, pp. 2419-2432.

[17] In a December 2007 decision, the board ruled that an employer's e-mail system is the employer's property and that employees do not have a statutory right to use their work e-mail for union activities. National Labor Relations Board, *The Guard Publishing Company d/b/a The Register-Guard and Eugene Newspaper Guild, CWA Local 37194*, 351 NLRB 1110, pp. 1110, 1114, 1116 (2007), available at.http://www.nlrb.gov/case/36-CA-008743.

[18] National Labor Relations Board, Office of the General Counsel, *Report on Case Developments*, May 15, 2008, available at https://www.nlrb.gov/publications/general-counsel-memos?memo_date=2008..

[19] Comment, "Labor Law Reform: The Regulation of Free Speech and Equal Access in NLRB Representation Elections," *University of Pennsylvania Law Review*, vol. 127, January 1979, p. 768.

[20] Under what is known as the "Excelsior" rule, within seven days after the NLRB has directed that a representation election be held or after a union and employer have agreed to hold an election, an employer must provide the regional director of the NLRB a list of the names and addresses of employees eligible to vote in the election. This list is made available to all parties. National Labor Relations Board, Office of the General Counsel, *An Outline of Law and Procedures in Representation Cases*, (Washington: U.S. GPO, April 2002) p. 251. U.S. Departments of Labor and Commerce, *Fact Finding Report: Commission on the Future of Worker-Management Relations*, May 1994, p. 68, available at http://digitalcommons.ilr. cornell.edu/cgi/ viewcontent.cgi?article=1279&context=key_workplace. The latter report is popularly called the "Dunlop report," after former Secretary of Labor John T. Dunlop, who chaired the commission. (Hereafter cited as John T. Dunlop, *Fact Finding Report: Commission on the Future of Worker-Management Relations*.)

[21] NLRB, *Basic Guide to the NLRA,* pp. 14-22.

[22] Ibid., pp. 23-32.

[23] National Labor Relations Board, *Annual Report of the National Labor Relations Board, for the Fiscal Year Ended September 30, 2009* (Washington: U.S. Govt. Print. Off., February 24, 2010), p. 4, http://www.nlrb.gov/sites/ default/ files/documents/119/nlrb2009.pdf. (Hereafter cited as NLRB, *Annual Report, Fiscal Year 2009*.) NLRB, *Basic Guide to the NLRA*, p. 36.

[24] 29 U.S.C. §160(c). NLRB, *Basic Guide to the NLRA*, p. 38.

The amount of backpay awarded is "net backpay" plus interest. Net backpay is the amount of compensation (i.e., wages plus benefits) that a worker would have received if he or she had not been unlawfully fired less the amount of compensation received (less the expenses from looking for work) from other work during the backpay period. If a discharged employee is able to work but does not look for work, compensation that he or she could have received from work may be deducted from gross backpay. National Labor Relations Board, *NLRB Casehandling Manual, Part 3, Compliance Proceedings*, §10536, available at http://www.nlrb.gov/sites/default/files/documents/44/compliancemanual.pdf.

In a May 2007 memorandum, the General Counsel of the NLRB directed that interest on net backpay should be compounded interest. Previously, interest on backpay was simple interest. Office of the General Counsel, *Seeking Compound Interest on Board Monetary Remedies*, Memorandum GC 07-07, May 2, 2007, available at http://www.nlrb.gov/ publications/general-counsel-memos.

In a September 2007 decision, the board ruled that if a worker who is fired for union activities does not start to look for work within two weeks of being fired, backpay does not begin to accrue until the worker starts to look for work. *Grosvenor Resort*, 350 NLRB 1197, p. 1199 (2007), available at http://www.nlrb.gov/case/12-CA-018190.

[25] In FY2010, NLRB collected $86.6 million in backpay. National Labor Relations Board, General Counsel, *Summary of Operations: Fiscal Year 2011*, Memorandum GC 12-03, March 8, 2012, available at

http://www.nlrb.gov/publications/general-counsel-memos. (Hereafter cited as NLRB, *Summary of Operations: FY2011.*)

[26] John Schmitt and Ben Zipperer, *Dropping the Ax: Illegal Firings During Union Election Campaigns, 1951-2007*, Center for Economic and Policy Research, March 2009, p. 10, available at http://www.cepr.net/documents/publications/dropping-the-ax-2009-03.pdf. John T. Dunlop, *Fact Finding Report: Commission on the Future of Worker-Management Relations*, pp. 69-70, 84.
For a critique of the study by Schmitt and Zipperer, see U.S. Chamber of Commerce, Labor, Immigration and Employee Benefits Division, *Responding to Union Rhetoric: The Reality of the American Workplace*, 2009, available at http://www.uschamber.com/sites/default/ files/reports/0908_unionstudies_coercion.pdf. (Hereafter cited as U.S. Chamber of Commerce, *Responding to Union Rhetoric: The Reality of the American Workplace*.)

[27] Kate Bronfenbrenner, *Uneasy Terrain: The Impact of Capital Mobility on Workers, Wages and Union Organizing*, U.S. Trade Deficit Review Commission, 2000, p. 743, available at http://digitalcommons.ilr.cornell.edu/cgi/viewcontent.cgi?article=1002&context=reports.
For a critique of this study, see U.S. Chamber of Commerce, *Responding to Union Rhetoric: The Reality of the American Workplace.*

[28] National Labor Relations Board, *Statistical Tables, FY2010*, Table 1, available at http://www. nlrb.gov/node/3580.

[29] NLRB, *Summary of Operations: FY2011.*

[30] U.S. Supreme Court, "National Labor Relations Board v. Gissel Packing Co., Inc.," *United States Reports*, vol. 395 (Washington: U.S. Govt. Print. Off., 1969), pp. 593-594, 609. (Hereafter cited as U.S. Supreme Court, *NLRB v. Gissel Packing*.) In *NLRB v. Gissel Packing*, the U.S. Supreme Court consolidated four NLRB cases. In each case, a majority of employees signed authorization cards. The employer refused to bargain, arguing that authorization cards are inherently unreliable. The NLRB concluded that the employers committed unfair labor practices that made a fair election unlikely and ordered the employers to bargain with the respective unions. U.S. Supreme Court, *NLRB v. Gissel Packing*, pp. 575-595.

[31] 29 U.S.C. §159(c). NLRB, *Annual Report, Fiscal Year 2009*, p. 29. National Labor Relations Board, *The NLRB: What it is, What it Does, National Labor Relations Board*, p. 3, available at http://www.nlrb.gov. U.S. Supreme Court, *NLRB v. Gissel Packing*, pp. 593-594, 609. NLRB, *Basic Guide to the NLRA,* p. 8.

[32] Some evidence indicates that within three years of winning an election, approximately one-fourth of unions have not reached a first contract with the employer. Thomas F. Reed, "Union Attainment of First Contracts: Do Service Unions Possess a Competitive Advantage?" *Journal of Labor Research*, vol. 11, fall 1990, pp., 426, 430. William N. Cooke, "The Failure to Negotiate First Contacts: Determinants and Policy Implications," *Industrial and Labor Relations Review*, vol. 38, January 1985, p. 170.

[33] NLRB, *Basic Guide to the NLRA*, pp. 8-9. National Labor Relations Board, *NLRB Rules and Regulations*, §102.67, available at http://ecfr.gpoaccess.gov/cgi/t/text/text-idx?c=ecfr&sid= 14fc6dc47b3466d9d515 edc 695d76cef&rgn=div8&view=text&node=29:2.1.1.3.3.25.8& idno=29.

[34] NLRB, *Basic Guide to the NLRA*, p. 36.

[35] NLRB, *Annual Report, Fiscal Year 2009*, pp. 4, 82, 85. 29 C.F.R. §102.69(a).

[36] Schlossberg and Scott, *Organizing and the Law,* p. 176.

[37] NLRB, *Annual Report, Fiscal Year 2009*, p. 29. National Labor Relations Board, *The National Labor Relations Board and YOU: Representation Cases*, p. 2, available at http://www.nlrb. gov.Feldacker, *Labor Guide to Labor Law*, p. 57. House, Committee on Education and the Workforce, Subcommittee on Employer-Employee Relations, H.R. 4343, *Secret Ballot Protection Act of 2004*, hearings, 108th Congress, second session, Serial No. 108-70, September 2004, Washington: U.S. Govt. Print. Off., p. 11. (Hereafter cited as House Education and the Workforce, *H.R. 4343, Secret Ballot Protection Act of 2004*.)

[38] National Labor Relations Board, "Representation Case Procedures," *Federal Register*, vol. 76, June 22, 2011, pp. 36812-36847.

[39] National Labor Relations Board, "Representation Case Procedures," *Federal Register*, vol. 76, December 22, 2011,pp. 80138-80189.

[40] Ibid. pp. 80141, 80185 (§102.66(a)).

[41] Ibid. p. 80185 (§102.66(d)).

[42] Ibid. p. 80177.

[43] Ibid. pp. 80162, 80172-80173, 80184 (§102.65(c)).

[44] Ibid. p. 80177.

[45] Ibid. pp. 80158-80159, 80162, 80184 (§102.65(c)).

[46] Ibid. p. 80139. National Labor Relations Board, *Casehandling Manual, Part Two: Representation Proceedings*, Section 11084, August 2007, available at http://www.nlrb.gov/ sites/default/files/documents/44/chm2.pdf.

[47] National Labor Relations Board, *Statistical Tables, FY2010*, Table 13, available at http://www. nlrb.gov/node/3580.

[48] Ibid., Table 11A.

[49] NLRB, *Summary of Operations: FY2011.*

[50] NLRB, *Summary of Operations: FY2010.*

[51] One study of card check agreements found that, under some agreements, a union needed signatures from at least 65% of bargaining unit employees. Adrienne E. Eaton and Jill Kriesky, "Union Organizing Under Neutrality and Card Check Agreements," *Industrial and Labor Relations Review*, vol. 55, October 2001, p. 48. (Hereafter cited as Eaton and Kriesky, *Union Organizing Under Neutrality and Card Check Agreements*.)

[52] Eaton and Kriesky, *Union Organizing Under Neutrality and Card Check Agreements*, pp. 47-48. Charles I. Cohen, "Neutrality Agreements: Will the NRLB Sanction Its Own Obsolescence?" *The Labor Lawyer*, vol. 16, fall 2000, pp.203-204. Brudney, *Neutrality Agreements and Card Check Recognition*, pp. 5-6.

It has been argued that, under the NLRA, neutrality and card check agreements, may be unlawful. See Arch Stokes, Robert L. Murphy, Paul E. Wagner, and David S. Sherwyn, "Neutrality Agreements: How Unions Organize New Hotels Without an Employee Ballot," *Cornell Hotel and Restaurant Administration Quarterly*, vol. 42, October-November 2001, pp. 91-94. A counter argument can be found in Brudney, *Neutrality Agreements and Card Check Recognition*, pp. 28-53.

[53] A union may engage in a corporate campaign to achieve other objectives, e.g., a contract agreement. Charles R. Perry, *Union Corporate Campaigns* (Philadelphia: Industrial Research Unit, Wharton School, University of Pennsylvania, 1987), pp. 1-8, 37-53.

For different views on corporate campaigns, see U.S. Congress, House Committee on Education and the Workforce, Subcommittee on Workforce Protections, *Compulsory Union Dues and Corporate Campaigns*, hearings, 107th Cong., 2nd sess., July 23, 2002, Serial No. 107-74 (Washington: GPO, 2002). For a discussion of corporate campaigns published by the U.S. Chamber of Commerce, see Jarol B. Manheim, *Trends in Union Corporate Campaigns: A Briefing Book* (Washington: U.S. Chamber of Commerce, 2005), available at http://www.uschamber.com/sites/default/files/reports/union_booklet_final_small.pdf.

[54] Feldacker, *Labor Guide to Labor Law*, pp. 90-91.

[55] Daniel Quinn Mills, *Labor-Management Relations*, 5th ed., New York: McGraw-Hill, Inc., 1994, pp. 213-217. (Hereafter cited as Mills, *Labor-Management Relations*.)

[56] When enacted in 1935, Section 9(c) of the NLRA (P.L. 74-198) stated that whenever a question of employee representation arises the NLRB "may take a secret ballot of employees, or utilize any other suitable method to ascertain such representatives." Alternative methods of selection could include authorization cards, petitions, employee testimony, affidavits of union membership, participation in a strike, or acceptance of strike benefits. Whichever method was used, if a majority of employees chose to be represented by a union, the union would be certified by the NLRB. During the five years after the NLRA was enacted, the NLRB issued 897 certifications after an election and 272 certifications (or 23.3% of the total) without an election. According to Becker, from 1935 to 1939:

> Certification depended upon proof presented at a trial-like hearing rather than the outcome of an election. An employee or union filed a petition requesting certification, the Board investigated, and, if it discovered "a question" concerning representation, held a hearing. At the hearing, if the union offered sufficient evidence that employees had "already chosen" to be represented, the Board would certify the union without an election.

By 1939, the NLRB only certified unions that had been chosen by a secret ballot election. This approach was written into law by the Taft-Hartley Act. The act amended Section 9(c) to say that the board "shall direct an election by secret ballot and shall certify the results thereof." The words "or utilize any other suitable method to ascertain such representatives" were removed. National Labor Relations Board, *Legislative History of the National Labor Relations Act of 1935* (Washington: U.S. Govt. Print. Off., 1949), p. 3274. National Labor Relations Board, *Legislative History of the Labor Management Relations Act, 1947* (Washington: U.S. Govt. Print. Off., 1985), p. 1670. Craig Becker, "Democracy in the Workplace: Union Representation Elections and Federal Labor Law," *Minnesota Law Review*, vol. 77, 1992, pp. 507-510. Alan Roberts McFarland and Wayne S. Bishop, *Union Authorization Cards and the NLRB: A Study of Congressional Intent, Administrative Policy, and Judicial Review* (Philadelphia: University of Pennsylvania, 1969), pp. 12-14, 50. William B. Gould IV, *A Primer on American Labor Law*, 4th ed. (Cambridge, MA: MIT Press, 2004), p. 89.

[57] Feldacker, *Labor Guide to Labor Law*, pp. 57, 139-140.

[58] Feldacker, *Labor Guide to Labor Law*, p. 140.

[59] Marie C. Grossman, "Labor Law—Employer's Duty to Bargain—Authorization Cards," *Case Western Reserve Law Review*, vol. 21, 1970, p. 308.

[60] McFarland and Bishop, *Union Authorization Cards and the NLRB,* p. 55.

[61] Michael Eugene Earwood and Herbert C. Ehrhardt, "Labor Law—Employer's Duty to Bargain on the Basis of Authorization Cards—Union Has the Burden of Seeking an NLRB Election," *Mississippi Law Journal*, vol. 46, 1975, p. 522. McFarland and Bishop, *Union Authorization Cards and the NLRB,* p. 55.

[62] Joy Silk Mills, Inc., 85 NLRB 1263 (1949).

[63] U.S. Supreme Court, *NLRB v. Gissel Packing*, pp. 591-592, 594.

[64] U.S. Supreme Court, "Linden Lumber Division, Summer & Co. v. National Labor Relations Board," *United States Reports*, vol. 419 (Washington: U.S. Govt. Print. Off., 1974), p. 310.

[65] National Labor Relations Board, *Order Granting Review*, 341 NLRB No. 150 (2004), available at http://www.nlrb.gov/cases-decisions/case-decisions/board-decisions.

[66] National Labor Relations Board, Dana Corporation and United Automobile, Aerospace, and Agricultural Implement Workers of America and Metaldyne Corporation and International Union, United Automobile, Aerospace, and Agricultural Implement Workers of America, 351 NLRB No. 28 (2007), pp. 1, 9-10, available at http://www.nlrb.gov/case/06-RD-001518#casedetails.

[67] National Labor Relations Board, Lamons Gasket Company and United Steel, Paper and Forestry, Rubber, Manufacturing, and Energy, Allied Industrial and Service Workers International Union, 357 NLRB No. 72, p. 10 (2011), available at http://nlrb.gov/case/15-RC-008773#casedetails.

[68] In the Lee Lumber decision, the board determined that factors used to determine whether a reasonable period of time has passed include

(1) whether the parties are bargaining for an initial contract; (2) the complexity of the issues being negotiated and of the parties' bargaining processes; (3) the amount of time elapsed since bargaining commenced and the number of bargaining sessions; (4) the amount of progress made in negotiations and how near the parties are to concluding an agreement; and (5) whether the parties are at impasse.

Lee Lumber & Building Materials Corp., 334 NLRB 399, p. 402 (2001), available at https://www.nlrb.gov/case/13-CA-029377.

[69] Letter from Representatives John Kline, Chairman of the House Committee on Education and the Workforce, and David Roe, Chairman of the Subcommittee on Health, Employment, Labor, and Pensions, to Mark Pearce, Chairman of the National Labor Relations Board, October 14, 2011, available at http://edworkforce.house.gov/UploadedFiles/10-14-11_Kline_Roe_NLRB_Dana_Letter.pdf.

[70] The NLRA (Section 3(b)) allows the board to delegate decisions to a group of three or more members.

[71] These clauses have been called "after-acquired stores" clauses, "additional stores" clauses, and "Kroger" clauses. The latter term is the result of NLRB and court decisions involving the Kroger Company.

[72] National Labor Relations Board, *Shaw's Supermarkets and United Food and Commercial Workers Union Local 791, AFL-CIO*, Case 1-RM-1267, December 8, 2004, pp. 1-3, available at http://www.nlrb.gov/case/01-RM-001267.

[73] National Labor Relations Board, *Shaw's Supermarkets and Local 791, United Food and Commercial Workers Union, AFL-CIO*, Case 1-RM-1267, available at http://www.nlrb.gov/ case/01-RM-001267.

[74] Bureau of National Affairs, "NLRB 2-1 Grants Shaw's Request for Review in Case Involving After-Acquired Store Clause," *Daily Labor Report*, no. 55, March 22, 2006, p. A-1.

[75] NLRB, *Basic Guide to the NLRA*, p. 10.

[76] National Labor Relations Board, *Shaw's Supermarkets*, 350 NLRB 585 (2007), pp. 585-87, 591, available athttp://www.nlrb.gov/cases-decisions/case-decisions/board-decisions.

[77] John A. Fossum, *Labor Relations: Development, Structure, and Process*, Boston: McGraw-Hill Irwin, 2002, p. 377.

[78] In a lockout, an employer closes the workplace to employees involved in a labor dispute. The workers are not allowed to work and are not paid. Mills, *Labor-Management Relations*, p. 436.

[79] Instead of mediation, an employer and union may use conciliation, where a conciliator helps the two sides negotiate. If the two parties do not want to negotiate face-to-face, a conciliator can communicate to each side the position of the other party. Ballot et al., *Labor-Management Relations in a Changing Environment*, p. 364.

[80] Mills, *Labor-Management Relations*, p. 449; Bruce E. Kaufman, *The Economics of Labor Markets*, 4th ed., Fort Worth: Dryden Press, 1994, p. 584-585 (Hereafter cited as Kaufman, *The Economics of Labor Markets*.); Federal Mediation and Conciliation Service, *2008 Annual Report*, p. 3, available at http://fmcs.gov/assets/files/annual%20reports/FY2008_ Annual_Report.pdf; Ballot et al., *Labor-Management Relations in a Changing Environment*, pp. 363-364.

[81] Harry C. Katz and Thomas A. Kochan, *An Introduction to Collective Bargaining and Industrial Relations*, Boston: McGraw-Hill Irwin, 2nd ed., 2000, p. 226. (Hereafter cited as Katz and Kochan, *An Introduction to Collective Bargaining and Industrial Relations.*)

[82] Mills, *Labor-Management Relations*, p. 455.

[83] Fact-finding is another form of dispute resolution. In fact-finding, a neutral third party prepares a report that identifies the areas of disagreement between the two parties and the positions of each side. A fact-finder may make recommendations for a settlement. Fact-finding can help negotiations by clarifying the facts in a dispute. The fact-finder's recommendations can serve as the basis of a settlement. Fact-finding may also subject negotiations to public scrutiny, encouraging both sides to adopt more moderate positions. (Kaufman, *The Economics of Labor Markets*, p. 585; Mills, *Labor-Management Relations*, pp. 317-318.) Fact-finding is rarely used in the private sector, except to resolve labor disputes under the Railway Labor Act (RLA) and the National Labor Relations Act (NLRA). Both statutes include emergency dispute provisions to resolve bargaining impasses. Ballot et al., *Labor-Management Relations in a Changing Environment*, pp. 366-368.

[84] Ballot et al., *Labor-Management Relations in a Changing Environment*, p. 365.

[85] Kaufman, *The Economics of Labor Markets*, p. 584; Katz and Kochan, *An Introduction to Collective Bargaining and Industrial Relations*, p. 225.

[86] An example of voluntary interest arbitration in the private sector occurred during three rounds of contract negotiations between the United Steelworkers of America (USW) and the major steel companies during the

1970s and early 1980s. The union and producers entered into an agreement, called the Experimental Negotiating Agreement (ENA), where the union and companies voluntarily agreed to submit certain unresolved contract issues to a neutral third party for binding arbitration. During the three rounds of negotiations, the two sides successfully negotiated all issues and arbitration was not used. The Postal Reorganization Act of 1970 extended collective bargaining rights to postal workers. In the case of a first contract, the act includes a provision for binding arbitration if an impasse lasts for more than 180 days after the start of bargaining. (J. Joseph Loewenberg, "Interest Arbitration: Past, Present, and Future," in *Labor Arbitration Under Fire*, ed. by James L. Stern and Joyce M. Najita, Ithaca, NY: Cornell University Press, 1997, pp. 112, 115-116. (Hereafter cited as Loewenberg, *Interest Arbitration: Past, Present, and Future*.)Section 1207(d) of Title 39 of the U.S. Code, relating to labor disputes in the Postal Service, states that, in the case of an initial contract agreement, the FMCS will appoint a mediator if the parties cannot reach an agreement within 90 days after collective bargaining has begun. The section goes on to state that "if the parties fail to reach agreement within 180 days after the commencement of collective bargaining, and if they have not agreed to another procedure for binding resolution, an arbitration board shall be established to provide conclusive and binding arbitration." The statute states that an arbitration board shall consist of three members: one representing the Postal Service, one representing the employees, and a neutral third member.

[87] In the case of an economic strike, employers may hire permanent replacement workers. When there are openings, strikers are entitled to be recalled to jobs for which they are qualified. National Labor Relations Board, *Basic Guide to the National Labor Relations Act*, available at http://www.nlrb.gov/ nlrb/shared_files/ brochures/basicguide.pdf, p. 4.

[88] Harry S. Farber, "Splitting-the-Difference in Interest Arbitration," *Industrial and Labor Relations Review*, vol. 35,October 1981, p. 70; Loewenberg, *Interest Arbitration: Past, Present, and Future*, pp. 117-118; Kaufman, *The Economics of Labor Markets*, p. 587; Ballot et al., *Labor-Management Relations in a Changing Environment*, p. 370.

[89] James R. Chelius and James B. Dworkin, "An Economic Analysis of Final-Offer Arbitration as a Conflict Resolution Device," *Journal of Conflict Resolution*, vol. 24, June 1980, pp. 293-294.

[90] Ballot et al., *Labor-Management Relations in a Changing Environment*, p. 371.

[91] Loewenberg, *Interest Arbitration: Past, Present, and Future*, pp. 117-118; Kaufman, *The Economics of Labor Markets*, pp. 587-588.

[92] Ballot et al., *Labor-Management Relations in a Changing Environment*, p. 371.

[93] For a discussion of union membership trends in the United States, see CRS Report RL32553, *Union Membership Trends in the United States*, by Gerald Mayer.

[94] The arguments for and against requiring card check certification and secret ballot elections are considered in House, Committee on Education and the Workforce, Subcommittee on Employer-Employee Relations, H.R. 4343, *Secret Ballot Protection Act of 2004*.

[95] Gary N. Chaison and Joseph B. Rose, "The Canadian Perspective on Workers' Rights to Form a Union and Bargain Collectively," Edited by Sheldon Friedman, Richard W. Hurd, Rudolph A. Oswald, and Ronald L. Seeber, in *Restoring the Promise of American Labor Law* (Ithaca, NY: ILR Press, 1994), p. 244.

[96] The five Canadian provinces that currently require secret ballot elections are Alberta, British Columbia, Newfoundland, Nova Scotia, and Ontario. Keith Godin, Milagros Palacios, Jason Clemens, Niels Veldhuis, and Amela Karabegovic, "An Empirical Comparison of Labour Relations Laws in Canada and the United States," *Centre for Labour Market States*, No. 2, May 2006, available at http://www.fraserinstitute. org/publicationdisplay.aspx?id=12808&
terms=An+Empirical+Comparison+of+Labour+Relations+Laws+in+Canada+and+the+United+States, p. 10. (Hereafter cited as Godin et al., *An Empirical Comparison of Labour Relations Laws in Canada and the United States*.) Susan Johnson, "The Impact of Mandatory Votes on the Canada-U.S. Union Density Gap: A Note," *Industrial Relations*, vol. 43, April 2004, p. 357.

[97] Beginning in 1993, British Columbia eliminated the requirement for secret ballot elections. Union certification occurred when at least 55% of employees signed authorization cards. Elections were held if 45% to 55% of employees signed authorization cards. Elections were held within ten days, or a longer period if the election was conducted by mail. Canada, Human Resources and Social Development, *Highlights of Major Developments in Labour Legislation (1992-1993)*, available at http://www.hrsdc.gc.ca/en/lp/spila/ clli/dllc/11_1992_ 1993.shtml. Beginning in 2001, secret ballot elections were required—when at least 45% of employees in a bargaining unit signed authorization cards. An election must be held within 10 days, or longer if the vote is conducted by mail. Canada, Human Resources and Social Development, *Highlights of Major Developments in Labour Legislation (2000-2001)*, available at http://www.hrsdc.gc.ca/ eng/labour/ labour_law/dllc/pdf/h00-01_e.pdf.

[98] Godin et al., *An Empirical Comparison of Labour Relations Laws in Canada and the United States*, p. 11.

[99] Susan Johnson, "Card Check or Mandatory Representation Vote? How the Type of Union Recognition Procedure Affects Union Certification Success," *Economic Journal*, vol. 112, pp. 355-359.

[100] The data are based on 6,550 private sector union drives from 1978 to 1998. The calculations of the union success rate are for the six years before 1984—when card check recognition was in effect, the nine years from 1984 to

1992when mandatory voting was in effect, and the six years from 1993 to 1998 after card check recognition was restored. Chris Riddell, "Union Certification Success Under Voting Versus Card-Check Procedures: Evidence from British Columbia, 1978-1998," *Industrial and Labor Relations Review*, vol. 57, July 2004, pp. 493-494, 506-507, 510.

[101] Sara Slinn, "An Empirical Analysis of the Effects of the Change from Card Check to Mandatory Vote Certification," *Social Science Research Network (SSRN)*, available at papers.ssrn.com, pp. 4-6, 16, 23.

[102] The study estimated the effect on the unemployment rate one year after an increase in union membership. Anne Layne-Farrar, "An Empirical Assessment of the Employee Free Choice Act: The Economic Implications," *Social Science Research Network (SSRN)*, available at papers.ssrn.com, pp. 20-22, 35.

[103] The success rate was measured as the percentage of organizing campaigns that resulted in union recognition. The results include some agreements in the public sector. Some of the agreements were with employers where a union represented other workers. Some of the agreements were with employers with whom the union had no existing bargaining relationship. Eaton and Kriesky, *Union Organizing Under Neutrality and Card Check Agreements*, pp. 45-48, 51-52.

Because the Employee Free Choice Act may increase the number of unionized workers, a report by the Institute for America's future argues that, if the legislation were enacted, 3.5 million more persons would have health insurance and 2.8 million more people would have pensions. Alex Carter and Eric Lotke, *The Employee Free Choice Act: Impact on Health Care and Pension Benefits*, Institute for America's Future, April 2007, http://www. americansunitedforchange.org/page/-/CAF/EFCA%20by%20IAF%20Minnesota% 20Report.pdf.

[104] Robert J. Flanagan, "Has Management Strangled U.S. Unions?," *Journal of Labor Research*, vol. 26, winter 2005, p. 51.

[105] Richard B. Freeman and Morris M. Kleiner, "Employer Behavior in the Face of Union Organizing Drives," *Industrial and Labor Relations Review*, vol. 43, April 1990, p. 351.

[106] The results of the poll are based on telephone interviews with 1,009 adults ages 18 and older. Jeffrey M. Jones, "Americans Remain Broadly Supportive of Labor Unions," December 1, 2008, available at http://www.gallup.com/poll/112717/Americans-Remain-Broadly-Supportive-Labor-Unions.aspx.

[107] The results of the poll are based on telephone interviews with 1,024 adults ages 18 or older. Lydia Saad, "Majority Receptive to Law Making Union Organizing Easier," Gallup, Inc., March 17, 2009, available athttp://www.gallup.com/poll/116863/Majority-Receptive-Law-Making-Union-Organizing-Easier.aspx.

[108] The results of the Rasmussen poll are based on an automated survey of 1,000 adults. Rasmussen Reports, *61% Say Secret Ballot Is Fair Way To Vote For A Union*, March 17, 2009, available at http://www. Rasmussen-reports.com.

[109] For information on the two surveys, see Bureau of National Affairs, *Two Surveys Reach Different Conclusions on Benefits of Card Checks, NLRB Elections*, no. 55, March 22, 2006, p. A-5.

[110] The survey was conducted by the Opinion Research Corporation (a social and marketing research firm). Center for Union Facts, *Everyone (Including Union Leaders) Prefers Real Elections*, accessed February 14, 2012, available at http://www.unionfacts.com/the-problem/everyone-including-union-leaders-prefers-real-elections.

[111] The survey was prepared by two university professors and conducted by the Eagleton Research Center at Rutgers University. American Rights at Work, *Fact Over Fiction: Opposition to Card Check Doesn't Add Up*, March 2006, available at http://www. americanrightsatwork.org/ dmdocuments/ ARAWReports/ IBFact OverFictFinal.pdf.

[112] National Labor Relations Board, "Appropriate Unit: General Principles," *Outline of Law and Procedure in Representation Cases*, Chapter 12, p. 130, available at http://www.nlrb.gov/ sites/default/files/ documents/ 44/rc_outline_2008_full.pdf.

[113] Although a business may not sell directly to consumers in another state or buy from businesses in another state, its operations my nevertheless affect commerce. For example, the operations of a manufacturer that sells all of its goods to a retailer in the same state may affect commerce if that retailer sells to consumers in another state. NLRB, *Basic Guide to the NLRA*, p. 33.

[114] NLRB, *Basic Guide to the NLRA*, pp. 33-34. National Labor Relations Board, "Jurisdiction," *Outline of Law and Procedure in Representation Cases*, Chapter 1, pp. 1-15, available at http://www.nlrb.gov/sites/ default/ files/documents/44/rc_outline_2008_full.pdf.

[115] U.S. Government Accountability Office, *Collective Bargaining Rights: Information on the Number of Workers with and Without Bargaining Rights*, GAO-02-835, September 2002, pp. 11-12, 26-27 available at http://www.gao.gov/new.items/d02835.pdf.

[116] The following conditions are the general characteristics of a competitive labor market: (1) There are many employers and many workers. Each employer is small relative to the size of the market. (2) Employers and workers are free to enter or leave a labor market and can move freely from one market to another. (3) Employers do not organize to lower wages and workers do not organize to raise wages. Governments do not intervene in labor markets to regulate wages. (4) Employers and workers have equal access to labor market information. (5) Employers do not prefer one worker over another equally qualified worker. Workers do not prefer one employer over another employer who pays the same wage for the same kind of work. (6) Employers seek to maximize profits; workers seek to maximize satisfaction. Lloyd G. Reynolds, Stanley H. Masters, and

Colletta H. Moser, *Labor Economics and Labor Relations*, 11th ed. (Englewood Cliffs, N.J.: Prentice-Hall, 1998), pp. 16-21.

[117] Randall K. Filer, Daniel S. Hamermesh, and Albert E. Rees, *The Economics of Work and Pay*, 6th ed., New York: Harper Collins, 1996, pp. 376-390. Ronald G. Ehrenberg and Robert S. Smith, *Modern Labor Economics: Theory and Public Policy*, 7th ed. (Reading, MA: Addison-Wesley, 2000), pp. 251-259. (Hereafter cited as Ehrenberg and Smith, *Modern Labor Economics*.)

[118] Kaufman, *The Economics of Labor Markets*, pp. 277-280.

[119] In competitive labor markets, unions can offset the employment effect of higher wages by trying to persuade consumers to buy union-made goods (e.g., campaigns to "look for the union label"), limiting competition from foreign made goods (e.g., though tariffs or import quotas), or negotiating contracts that require more workers than would otherwise be needed. Kaufman, *The Economics of Labor Markets*, pp. 276-277. Ehrenberg and Smith, *Modern Labor Economics*, p. 493. Toke Aidt and Zafiris Tzannatos, *Unions and Collective Bargaining: Economic Effects in a Global Environment* (Washington: The World Bank, 2002), p. 27.

[120] If unions raise the wages of union workers and lower employment in the union sector, the supply of workers available to nonunion employers may increase, resulting in greater competition for jobs and lower wages for nonunion workers (the "spillover" effect). On the other hand, nonunion employers, in order to discourage workers from unionizing, may pay higher wages (the "threat" effect). Ehrenberg and Smith, *Modern Labor Economics*, pp. 504-508.

[121] Kaufman argues that labor markets in the United States have become more competitive since World War II. Bruce E. Kaufman, "Labor's Inequality of Bargaining Power: Changes over Time and Implications for Public Policy," *Journal of Labor Research*, vol. 10, summer 1989, pp. 292-293.

[122] Governments may also intervene in private markets to produce "public" goods (e.g., national defense) or correct instances where the market price of a good does not fully reflect its social costs or benefits—called, respectively, negative and positive "externalities." Air and water pollution are frequently cited as examples of negative externalities; home maintenance and improvements are often cited as examples of positive externalities.

[123] Richard B. Freeman and James L. Medoff, "The Two Faces of Unionism," *Public Interest*, no. 57, fall 1979, pp. 70-73. Richard B. Freeman, "The Exit-Voice Tradeoff in the Labor Market: Unionism, Job Tenure, Quits, and Separations," *Quarterly Journal of Economics*, vol. 94, June 1980, pp. 644-645.

[124] Bargaining between employers and workers includes the right of workers to strike (in the private sector) and the right of employers to lock out employees.

[125] The results of research on the wage differential between union and nonunion workers vary. But, in general, most studies find that, after controlling for individual, job, and labor market characteristics, the wages of union workers are in the range of 10% to 30% higher than the wages of nonunion workers. Although the evidence is not conclusive, some studies have concluded that unions reduce earnings inequality in the overall economy. CRS Report RL32553, *Union Membership Trends in the United States*, by Gerald Mayer.

In: Labor Relations
Editors: A. Daniels and R. Hoffman

ISBN: 978-1-62257-420-9

Chapter 3

THE EMPLOYEE FREE CHOICE ACT*

Jon O. Shimabukuro

SUMMARY

This report discusses legislative attempts to amend the National Labor Relations Act ("NLRA") to allow for union certification without an election, based on signed employee authorizations. The Employee Free Choice Act ("EFCA"), introduced in the 111th Congress as H.R. 1409 and S. 560, would have allowed union certification based on signed authorizations, provided a process for the bargaining of an initial agreement, and prescribed new penalties for certain unfair labor practices. This report reviews the current process for selecting a bargaining representative under the NLRA, and discusses the role of the Federal Mediation and Conciliation Service in resolving bargaining disputes under that act. The EFCA has been introduced in the past four Congresses. During the 110th Congress, the measure was passed by a vote of 241-185 in the House. In the Senate, proponents of the EFCA fell nine votes short of the 60 votes needed to limit debate and proceed to final consideration of the measure. The EFCA is widely expected to be reintroduced in the 112th Congress.

Legislation that would allow a union to become the exclusive bargaining representative of a unit of employees without an election has been introduced in the past four Congresses.[1] The Employee Free Choice Act ("EFCA" or "the act"), introduced in the 111th Congress as H.R. 1409 and S. 560, would have amended the National Labor Relations Act ("NLRA") to allow union certification based on signed employee authorizations, provided a process for the bargaining of an initial agreement, and prescribed new penalties for certain unfair labor practices. Labor officials indicated that the EFCA was "the most important work we'll be doing, because it's a key to succeeding on everything else."[2]

This report reviews the current process for selecting a bargaining representative under the NLRA, and examines how the EFCA would have altered that process. In addition, this report discusses the other changes proposed by the act. Some of these changes had been previously

---

* This is an edited, reformatted and augmented version of the Congressional Research Service Publication, CRS Report for Congress RS21887, dated January 12, 2011.

suggested in other past measures. For example, legislation that would have established a process for the bargaining of an initial agreement was first introduced in the 105th Congress.[3]

Union Certification without Election

The EFCA would have amended the NLRA to allow an individual or labor organization to be certified as the exclusive representative of a bargaining unit without an election. The act would have required the National Labor Relations Board ("the Board") to conduct an investigation whenever a petition was filed by "an employee or group of employees or any individual or labor organi-zation acting in their behalf," that alleged that a majority of employees in a bargaining unit wished to be represented by an individual or labor organization for the purpose of collective bargaining. If the Board found that a majority of employees in the unit signed authorizations designating the individual or labor organization as their bargaining representative, it would certify such individual or labor organization as the representative.

Currently, a labor organization usually becomes the exclusive represen-tative for a bargaining unit following an election. Under existing law, the Board conducts an investigation following the filing of a petition that alleges that a substantial number of employees wish to be represented for collective bargaining and that the employer declines to recognize their representative as the exclusive representative for the bargaining unit.[4] To constitute a "substantial number of employees," at least 30 percent of the employees must indicate support for representation.[5] A representation hearing will be conducted if the parties cannot voluntarily resolve the details of an election.[6] Based on the record of such a hearing, the Board will direct an election by secret ballot and certify the results.[7]

Although a labor organization that has obtained signed authorizations from a majority of employees in a bargaining unit may request to be recognized voluntarily by an employer as the exclusive representative of employees in the unit, few employers engage in such voluntary recognition.[8] In *NLRB v. Gissel Packing Co.*, the U.S. Supreme Court confirmed that signed authorization cards from a majority of employees could give rise to bargaining obligations under section 8(a)(5) of the NLRA.[9] Section 8(a)(5) indicates that it shall be an unfair labor practice for an employer to refuse to bargain collectively with the representatives of his employees subject to the provisions of section 9(a) of the NLRA.[10] Section 9(a) provides that representatives "designated or selected for the purposes of collective bargaining by a majority of the employees" in an appropriate bargaining unit "shall be the exclusive representatives of all the employees in such unit for the purposes of collective bargaining."[11] Because section 9(a) refers to exclusive representatives "designated or selected" by a majority of employees without specifying how the representatives must be chosen, it was understood that the showing of majority support through signed authorization cards could give rise to a duty to bargain.

The *Gissel* Court also noted, however, that an employer is not obligated to accept the authorization cards as proof of majority status, and could insist on an election.[12] Moreover, the Court maintained that an employer is not required to justify his insistence on an election by making his own investigation of employee sentiment or by providing affirmative reasons for doubting the majority status.[13] In a subsequent case, *Linden Lumber v. NLRB*, the Court further concluded that a union with authorization cards purporting to represent a majority of the employees, which is denied recognition by the employer, has the burden of invoking the Board's election procedure.[14]

Labor organizations contend that employers decline voluntary recognition based on authorization cards because they want to discourage support for representation in the period before an election is held.[15] During this period, it is believed that employers often hire anti-union consultants, terminate pro-union employees, and conduct captive-audience meetings where employees are exposed to the employer's views against representation.[16] Proponents of the EFCA maintained that certification based on a majority of signed authorizations would eliminate this misconduct.

In FY2008, the median time to proceed to an election from the filing of a representation petition was 38 days.[17] According to the Board, in FY2008, 95.1% of all initial representation elections were conducted within 56 days of the filing of a petition.[18]

Those who have opposed the certification process proposed by the EFCA expressed concern for a union's possible use of coercive and intimidating tactics to obtain signatures.[19] They have also feared the increased possibility of forged signatures on authorization cards.[20] Consistent with those concerns, another measure would have made it an unfair labor practice for an employer to recognize or bargain with a labor organization that was not selected through an election. The Secret Ballot Protection Act, introduced in the 111th Congress as H.R. 1176 and S. 478, stated the following in its findings: "[T]he right of employees to choose by secret ballot is the only method that ensures a choice free of coercion, intimidation, irregularity, or illegality."[21]

Role of the Federal Mediation and Conciliation Service

In addition to providing for union certification without an election, the EFCA would have amended the NLRA to allow for the involvement of the Federal Mediation and Conciliation Service ("FMCS") during the negotiation of an initial agreement following certification or recognition of a labor organization.[22] If, after 90 days of bargaining or such additional period as the parties agreed upon, the parties failed to reach an agreement, the act would have permitted either party to notify the FMCS and request mediation. If, after 30 days from the date mediation was requested or such additional period agreed upon by the parties, the FMCS was unable to bring the parties to agreement, the FMCS would have referred the dispute to an arbitration board that would render a binding decision.

Under existing law, the FMCS may provide mediation and conciliation services upon its own motion or upon the request of one or more of the parties to the dispute whenever "in its judgment such dispute threatens to cause a substantial interruption of commerce."[23] Where state or other conciliation services are available to the parties, the FMCS is directed to "avoid attempting to mediate disputes which would have only a minor effect on interstate commerce."[24] Existing law does not distinguish between initial agreements and other agreements negotiated by the parties. Moreover, the NLRA does not provide for the use of binding arbitration to resolve disputes.

Proponents of the EFCA have argued that legislation is needed to promote the prompt negotiation of initial collective bargaining agreements.[25] In 32 percent of all cases, the employer and the union reportedly fail to reach agreement within the first two years following an election.[26] Some have observed, however, that the availability of binding arbitration under the EFCA discouraged support for the legislation from the business community. Under the act, employers would have been faced with the possibility of having to accept what could have been viewed as unfavorable terms and conditions by the arbitration board. Under existing law, the employer does not have to accept such terms and conditions. The employer may decline unfavorable proposals with the hope that the union may change its position to avert a strike. If binding arbitration was required, the employer would lose that bargaining leverage.

PENALTIES UNDER THE NLRA

The EFCA would have amended the NLRA to impose new penalties for specified existing unfair labor practices. For example, if the Board found that an employer discriminated against an employee with respect to his hiring, tenure, or any term or condition of employment to encourage or discourage membership in a labor organization either while employees of the employer were seeking representation by a labor organization or during the period after a labor organization was recognized as a unit's exclusive representative, but before the first collective bargaining agreement was executed, the Board would have been permitted to award employee back pay and 2 times that amount as liquidated damages.[27]

The EFCA would have also imposed a civil penalty for certain willful and repeated unfair labor practices. Any employer who willfully and repeatedly

> (a) interferes with, restrains, or coerces an employee in the exercise of his right to organize, or
>
> (b) discriminates against an employee with respect to his hiring, tenure, or any term or condition of employment to encourage or discourage membership in a labor organization

either while employees of the employer were seeking representation by a labor organization or during the period after a labor organization had been recognized as a unit's exclusive representative, but before the first collective bargaining agreement has been executed, would have been subject to a civil penalty not to exceed $20,000 for each violation. The exact amount of the penalty would have been determined by the Board based on the gravity of the unfair labor practice and its impact on the charging party, on others seeking to exercise rights guaranteed by the NLRA, or on the public interest.[28]

Under existing law, the Board may order any person committing an unfair labor practice to cease and desist from such misconduct.[29] The Board may also take such affirmative action, including reinstatement with back pay, as will effectuate the policies of the NLRA.[30] Section 12 of the NLRA provides that any person who willfully resists, prevents, impedes, or interferes with any member of the Board or any of its agents or agencies in the performance of their duties under the act shall be punished by a fine of not more than $5,000 or by imprisonment for not more than one year, or both.[31] However, no specific penalty currently exists for the kind of willful and repeated misconduct described in the EFCA.

SMALL BUSINESSES AND THE EFCA

In 1959, Congress amended the NLRA to provide relief for small employers and their employees who occupied a so-called "no man's land" in labor-management relations. The Board, confronted with a rising backlog of cases, maintained a practice of declining jurisdiction in industries with revenue less than a certain dollar volume of business. This practice effectively excluded a significant number of smaller enterprises from coverage under the NLRA.[32] At the same time, in a series of cases, the Court concluded that parties denied coverage under the NLRA could not have their disputes settled by a state labor agency or in state court.[33] The House, in considering changes to the NLRA, noted, "Since, therefore, the excluded parties have neither Federal nor State remedies available to them, they are said to be in the 'no man's land.'"[34]

Congress responded to concerns over the "no man's land" for small employers and their employees by amending section 14 of the NLRA to add a new subsection (c). Section 14(c) states the following:

> (1) The Board, in its discretion, may, by rule of decision or by published rules adopted pursuant to the Administrative Procedure Act, decline to assert jurisdiction over any labor dispute involving any class or category of employers, where, in the opinion of the Board, the effect of such labor dispute on commerce is not sufficiently substantial to warrant the exercise of its jurisdiction: *Provided*, That the Board shall not decline to assert jurisdiction over any labor dispute over which it would assert jurisdiction under the standards prevailing upon August 1, 1959.
>
> (2) Nothing in this Act shall be deemed to prevent or bar any agency or the courts of any State or Territory (including the Commonwealth of Puerto Rico, Guam, and the Virgin Islands), from assuming and asserting jurisdiction over labor disputes over which the Board declines, pursuant to paragraph (1) of this subsection, to assert jurisdiction.[35]

By enacting section 14(c)(1), Congress appeared to endorse the Board's practice of declining jurisdiction over smaller employers.[36] At the same time, however, Congress prevented the Board from refusing to assert jurisdiction over employers that met the jurisdictional standards in effect on August 1, 1959. These standards were established for 10 types of enterprises and, in general, continue to apply.[37] If the Board declines jurisdiction over a labor dispute in accordance with one of the standards, section 14(c)(2) authorizes a state or territorial agency or court to assert jurisdiction.

The jurisdictional standards that arguably have the broadest application are those for retail and non-retail enterprises. Pursuant to its standards for retail enterprises, the Board will assert jurisdiction if such an enterprise has an annual gross volume of business of at least $500,000 and has some business, greater than de minimis, across state lines. Under its standards for non-retail enterprises, the Board will assert jurisdiction if such an enterprise has a direct or indirect inflow or outflow of goods or services across state lines of at least $50,000.[38] The EFCA would not have amended section 14(c) of the NLRA and did not specifically address the treatment of small employers. Opponents of the EFCA argued that the impact of the measure on small businesses could be significant given the financial thresholds in the jurisdictional standards for retail and non-retail enterprises.[39] Some maintained that the thresholds are so low that many businesses that are likely perceived as "small businesses" would have become subject to the EFCA.[40] Others argued, however, that the vast majority of small businesses are too small to have to worry about unionizing.[41]

PAST LEGISLATIVE ALTERNATIVES

While the EFCA received significant attention for the changes it would have made to the NLRA, some observed that other past measures proposed similar, but arguably less dramatic, amendments to the labor statute. Some of these measures, for example, would have required an expedited election, but not automatic certification, if a specified percentage of employees signed authorization cards. Other measures would have permitted automatic certification only if 75% of employees in an appropriate bargaining unit signed authorization cards.

The Labor Relations Representative Amendment Act, introduced by Senator Paul Simon in the 103rd and 104th Congresses, would have required the Board to direct an expedited election to be held within 30 days after the receipt of signed authorization cards from 60% of employees in an appropriate unit.[42] Under the measure, an expedited election could not be delayed for any reason or purpose.

Similarly, the Right to Organize Act of 2001, introduced by Senator Paul D. Wellstone in the 107th Congress, contemplated an expedited election, but would have required the Board to direct such an election to be held within 14 days after the receipt of signed authorization cards from 60% of the employees in an appropriate unit.[43]

The National Labor Relations Fair Elections Act, introduced by Representative Major R. Owens in the 101st, 102nd, and 103rd Congresses, would have permitted the certification of an individual or labor organization as the exclusive representative of a bargaining unit without an election if 75% of the employees in an appropriate unit signed authorization cards.[44] If authorization cards were signed only by a majority of employees, the measure provided for an expedited election. Within 7 days after the filing of the representation petition and the receipt of the authorization cards, the Board would have been required to direct an election to be held no later than 15 days after the petition was filed.

The National Labor Relations Fair Elections Act would have also established a schedule for all other representation elections. Under the measure, such elections would have been required to occur no later than 45 days after the filing of a petition, unless the Board determined that the proceeding "present[ed] issues of exceptional novelty or complexity.[45] When such issues were involved, the election could occur no later than 75 days after the filing of the petition.

Past efforts to amend the NLRA to allow for expedited elections may prove instructive if, as widely expected, the EFCA is reintroduced in the 112th Congress. Opponents of the measure who maintained that it undermines the sanctity of the secret ballot election may support efforts to expedite elections under the NLRA rather than allow for the automatic certification of a union.[46]

End Notes

[1] H.R. 1409, 111th Cong. (2009); S. 560, 111th Cong. (2009); H.R. 800, 110th Cong. (2007); S. 1041, 110th Cong. (2007); H.R. 1696, 109th Cong. (2005); S. 842, 109th Cong. (2005); H.R. 3619, 108th Cong. (2003); S. 1925, 108th Cong. (2003).

[2] *See* Dale Russakoff, "Labor to Push Agenda in Congress It Helped Elect," *Wash. Post*, December 8, 2006, at A13.

[3] *See* S. 2389, 105th Cong. (1998).

[4] 29 U.S.C. § 159(c)(1).

[5] *See* 29 C.F.R. § 101.18(a).

[6] 29 U.S.C. § 159(c)(4).

[7] *But see* 29 U.S.C. § 159(c)(3) ("No election shall be directed in any bargaining unit or any subdivision within which in the preceding twelve-month period, a valid election shall have been held."). In addition, an election will be denied for a bargaining unit where such unit is already covered by a valid collective bargaining agreement. The so-called "contract bar" to an election operates when there is a written bargaining agreement that has been properly signed by the parties, is binding on the parties, and is of a definite duration.

[8] *See* Stephen I. Schlossberg and Judith A. Scott, Organizing and the Law 173 (1991).

[9] 395 U.S. 575 (1969).

[10] 29 U.S.C. § 158(a)(5).

[11] 29 U.S.C. § 159(a).

[12] *Gissel*, 395 U.S. at 609.

[13] *Id.*

[14] 419 U.S. 301 (1974).

[15] *See* Steven Greenhouse, "Unions, Bruised in Direct Battles With Companies, Try a Roundabout Tactic," *N.Y. Times*, March 10, 1997, at B7.

[16] *See Witnesses at House Hearing Discuss Merits of Elections Versus Card-Check Recognition*, Daily Lab. Rep. (BNA), April 23, 2004, at A-7.

[17] Memorandum from Ronald Meisburg, General Counsel, National Labor Relations Board, to All Employees of the Office of General Counsel, National Labor Relations Board (Oct. 29, 2008), *available at* http://www.nlrb.gov/shared_files/GC%20Memo/2009/GC%2009-03% 20Summary%20of%20Operations%20FY%2008.pdf.

[18] *Id.*

[19] *Witnesses at House Hearing Discuss Merits of Elections Versus Card-Check Recognition*, *supra* note 16.

[20] *Id.*

[21] H.R. 1176, 111th Cong. § 2(2) (2009); S. 478, 111th Cong. § 2(2) (2009).

[22] H.R. 1409, 111th Cong. § 3 (2009); S. 560, 111th Cong. § 3 (2009).

[23] 29 U.S.C. § 173(b).

[24] *Id.*

[25] *Witnesses at House Hearing Discuss Merits of Elections Versus Card-Check Recognition*, *supra* note 16.

[26] *Id.*

[27] H.R. 1409, 111th Cong. § 4(b) (2009); S. 560, 111th Cong. § 4(b) (2009).

[28] *Id.*

[29] 29 U.S.C. 160(c).

[30] *Id.*

[31] 29 U.S.C. § 162.

[32] *See* S. Rep. No. 187, at 25 (1959), *reprinted in* 1959 U.S.C.C.A.N. 2318, 2341.

[33] *See Guss v. Utah Labor Relations Board*, 353 U.S. 1 (1957); *Amalgamated Meat Cutters, et al. v. Fairlawn Meats, Inc.*, 353 U.S. 20 (1957); *San Diego Building Trades Council v. Garmon*, 353 U.S. 26 (1957).

[34] S. Rep. No. 187, *supra* note 32, at 25.

[35] 29 U.S.C. § 164(c)(1).

[36] The Developing Labor Law 2223 (John E. Higgins, Jr., et al. eds., 2006).

[37] *See Leedom v. Fitch Sanitarium, Inc.*, 294 F.2d 251, 255-56 (D.C. Cir. 1961) (identifying jurisdictional standards in effect on August 1, 1959, for the following: non-retail enterprises; office buildings; public utilities; newspapers and communications systems; retail enterprises; hotels; transportation enterprises, links, and channels of interstate commerce; transit systems; taxicabs; and national defense enterprises). Since 1959, the Board has established additional jurisdictional standards for other enterprises, including apartment houses and art museums. See Nat'l Lab. Rel. Board, An Outline of Law and Procedure in Representation Cases 1-24 (2005) (discussing jurisdictional standards).

[38] *See* Nat'l Lab. Rel. Board, An Outline of Law and Procedure in Representation Cases 2 (2005) ("Direct outflow refers to goods shipped or services furnished by an employer directly outside the State. Indirect outflow refers to sales of goods or services within the State to users meeting any standard except solely an indirect inflow or indirect outflow standard.").

[39] *See* Matthew Bandyk, *Small Business Issues in The Ballot Box: The Employee Free Choice Act* (Oct. 31, 2008), *available at* http://www.usnews.com/articles/business/small-business-entrepreneurs/2008/10/31/small-business-issues-in-the-ballot-box-the-employee-free-choice-act.html; James Sherk, *EFCA Authorizes Government Control of 4 Million Small Businesses* (Mar. 12, 2009), at http://www.heritage.org/ Research/ Labor/wm2341.cfm.

[40] *See* Sherk, *supra* note 39.

[41] *See* Bandyk, *supra* note 39.

[42] S. 778, 104th Cong. (1995); S. 1529, 103rd Cong. (1993).

[43] S. 1102, 107th Cong. (2001). Other versions of the Right to Organize Act introduced in the 106th Congress did not include provisions for an expedited election.

[44] H.R. 689, 103rd Cong. (1993); H.R. 503, 102nd Cong. (1991); H.R. 4800, 101st Cong. (1990).

[45] H.R. 689, 103rd Cong. § 3 (1993); H.R. 503, 102nd Cong. § 3 (1991); H.R. 4800, 3 101st Cong. (1990).

[46] *See, e.g.*, 153 Cong. Rec. H2046 (daily ed. Mar. 1, 2007) (statement of Rep. Diaz-Balart) ("Now, I think we should work on expediting elections by the NLRB, and we should work to make sure elections for certification are as expedited as they are for decertification. That is another issue that I would like to work with my colleagues on. But I cannot support this legislation which goes to the heart of that most essential aspect of the right of human beings to express themselves in private, which is the secret ballot.").

In: Labor Relations
Editors: A. Daniels and R. Hoffman

ISBN: 978-1-62257-420-9

Chapter 4

COLLECTIVE BARGAINING AND EMPLOYEES IN THE PUBLIC SECTOR*

Jon O. Shimabukuro

SUMMARY

Faced with distressed state budgets and lower revenue, many governors and state legislatures have focused on the collective bargaining rights of public employees as a way to control expenses. Legislation that would limit such rights has reportedly been introduced in at least 22 states. In general, the sponsors of such legislation contend that unionized state and local employees enjoy unsustainable salaries and benefits as a result of collective bargaining.

According to the Bureau of Labor Statistics, 26.8% of all federal employees are members of a union. A slightly higher percentage of state employees—31.1%—are union members. At the local government level, 42.3% of employees are union members. Although all of these employees engage in some form of collective bargaining through their unions, the scope of such bargaining is generally different for federal and state and local workers. In addition, because the collective bargaining rights of state and local employees are defined by state law, other variations in bargaining may exist among these workers. Subjects that are negotiable in one state, for example, may not be negotiable in another state.

This report examines the collective bargaining rights of federal, state, and local workers. The report also discusses the constitutional concerns that may be raised by state legislation that attempts to invalidate existing collective bargaining agreements. In Michigan, the Local Government and School District Fiscal Accountability Act ("Fiscal Accountability Act") was adopted on March 16, 2011. Under the Fiscal Accountability Act, the governor may appoint an emergency manager if he determines that a local government financial emergency exists. The emergency manager would have broad powers to rectify the financial emergency, including the ability to reject, modify, or terminate one or more terms and conditions of an existing collective bargaining agreement. If the emergency manager were to reject, modify, or

* This is an edited, reformatted and augmented version of the Congressional Research Service Publication, CRS Report for Congress R41732, dated March 30, 2011.

terminate one or more terms and conditions of an existing agreement, constitutional concerns would likely be raised under the Contract Clause of the U.S. Constitution, which prohibits a state from passing any law "impairing the Obligation of Contracts."

Faced with distressed state budgets and lower revenue, many governors and state legislatures have focused on the collective bargaining rights of public employees as a way to control expenses. Legislation that would limit such rights has reportedly been introduced in at least 22 states.[1] In general, the sponsors of such legislation contend that unionized state and local employees enjoy unsustainable salaries and benefits as a result of collective bargaining. This report examines the collective bargaining rights of federal, state, and local workers, and discusses the constitutional concerns that may be raised by state legislation that attempts to invalidate existing collective bargaining agreements.

FEDERAL EMPLOYEES

According to the Bureau of Labor Statistics, 26.8% of all federal employees are members of a union.[2] A slightly higher percentage of state employees—31.1%—are union members.[3] While all of these employees engage in some form of collective bargaining through their unions, the scope of such bargaining is generally different for federal and state and local workers. In addition, because the collective bargaining rights of state and local employees are defined by state law, other variations in bargaining may exist among these workers. Subjects that are negotiable in one state, for example, may not be negotiable in another state.

Federal employees first obtained the right to engage in collective bargaining in 1962. Under Executive Order 10988, federal employees were permitted to "form, join and assist any employee organization or to refrain from such activity."[4] Once recognized as the exclusive representative of employees in an appropriate bargaining unit, an employee organization could negotiate an agreement that would cover all employees in that unit. Executive Order 11491, issued by President Nixon in 1969, further developed the framework for federal labor-management relations by establishing the Federal Labor Relations Council, a predecessor to the Federal Labor Relations Authority (FLRA), and the Federal Service Impasses Panel.[5] Executive Order 11491 also identified unfair labor practices that were prohibited for management and labor organizations.

In 1978, the right to engage in collective bargaining became recognized in statute. Title VII of the Civil Service Reform Act of 1978, commonly referred to as the "Federal Service Labor- Management Relations Statute" (FSLMRS), codified many of the concepts included in Executive Order 11491.[6] In addition to providing for the right to engage in collective bargaining, the FSLMRS also established the FLRA, which, among other duties, supervises union elections and resolves unfair labor practice complaints.

The FSLMRS states that "[e]ach employee shall have the right to form, join, or assist any labor organization, or to refrain from any such activity, freely and without fear of penalty or reprisal, and each employee shall be protected in the exercise of such right."[7] The right recognized by the FSLMRS includes the ability "to engage in collective bargaining with respect to conditions of employment through representatives chosen by employees."[8] The FSLMRS further defines the phrase "conditions of employment" to include personnel policies, practices, and matters that affect working conditions.[9] The term does not include, however, policies, practices, and matters "to the extent such matters are specifically provided for by Federal statute."[10] Thus, to the extent federal law provides for pay, health coverage, retirement benefits, and other items, such subjects are not negotiable.[11]

In addition, the FSLMRS identifies management rights that are generally not negotiable, except with regard to the procedures that will be used to implement an agency's proposals. Section 7106(a) of Title 5, U.S. Code, states, in relevant part:

[N]othing in this chapter shall affect the authority of any management official of any agency

(1) to determine the mission, budget, organization, number of employees, and internal security practices of the agency; and
(2) in accordance with applicable laws –
    (A) to hire, assign, direct, layoff, and retain employees in the agency, or to suspend, remove, reduce in grade or pay, or take other disciplinary action against such employees;
    (B) to assign work, to make determinations with respect to contracting out, and to determine the personnel by which agency operations shall be conducted;
    (C) with respect to filling positions, to make selections for appointments from –
        (i) among properly ranked and certified candidates for promotion; or
        (ii) any other appropriate source; and
    (D) to take whatever actions may be necessary to carry out the agency mission during emergencies.

Courts have noted that Section 7106 ensures that the collective bargaining system established by the FSLMRS does not "undermine the effectiveness of government through unwarranted intrusion on management prerogatives."[12] At the same time, however, the FSLMRS and Section 7106 "establish a balance between the nonnegotiable substantive rights of management and the negotiable procedures to be followed when management exercises its substantive rights."[13]

STATE AND LOCAL EMPLOYEES

Legislation authorizing collective bargaining for state and local government employees was first adopted during the 1950s. In 1959, Wisconsin became the first state to enact legislation granting organizational, represen-tation, and bargaining rights to municipal employees.[14] By the end of 1967, legislation authorizing some form of collective bargaining for state and/or local employees had been adopted in 21 states.[15] State laws governing collective bargaining for state and local workers are generally not identical. Rather, they exist on a continuum, with some prohibiting bargaining altogether and others providing comprehensive collective bargaining rights for various employees.

In two states, North Carolina and Virginia, the execution of a collective bargaining agreement is prohibited. Under North Carolina law, any agreement between a public employer and a labor organization acting as a bargaining agent for public employees is "declared to be against public policy of the State, illegal, unlawful, void and of no effect."[16] Under Virginia law, a public employer is prohibited from recognizing any labor organization as a bargaining agent of any public employees and may not "collectively bargain or enter into any collective bargaining contract" with such an organization.[17]

In at least 31 states, public employees appear to have the right to engage in some form of collective bargaining.[18] In general, this right includes the ability to negotiate wages, hours, and other conditions of employment. In at least five states, however, the negotiation of retirement or health benefits appears to be limited by state law. In Hawaii, for example, "[e]xcluded from the subjects of negotiations are ... benefits of but not contributions to the Hawaii employer-union health benefits trust fund ... and retirement benefits except as provided in [the optional retirement system of the University of Hawaii]."[19] Similarly, under Iowa law, all "retirement systems" are excluded from the scope of negotiations.[20]

Apart from the 31 aforementioned states, 11 additional states seem to provide a right to engage in collective bargaining, but limit that right to only certain specified employees.[21] In Wyoming, for example, only firefighters appear to have the right to engage in collective bargaining: "The firefighters in any city, town or county shall have the right to bargain collectively with their respective cities, towns or counties and to be represented by a bargaining agent in such collective bargaining as to wages, rates of pay, working conditions and all other terms and conditions of employment."[22]

Recent Collective Bargaining Legislation

On March 11, 2011, Wisconsin Governor Scott Walker signed Senate Bill/Assembly Bill 11, the so-called "Budget Repair Bill." The Budget Repair Bill amends the state's Municipal Employment Relations Act and State Employment Relations Act to permit only the negotiation of total base wages for general municipal and state employees.[23] With the measure's enactment, only public safety employees will be permitted to negotiate over wages, hours, and working conditions.[24]

While the enactment of the Budget Repair Bill received widespread attention, similar measures have also been introduced and approved by other state legislatures. In Michigan, for example, the Local Government and School District Fiscal Accountability Act ("Fiscal Accountability Act") was adopted on March 16, 2011.[25] Under the Fiscal Accountability Act, the governor may appoint an emergency manager if he determines that a local government financial emergency exists.[26] The emergency manager would have broad powers to rectify the financial emergency, including the ability to reject, modify, or terminate one or more terms and conditions of an existing collective bargaining agreement. Section 19(1)(k) of the Fiscal Accountability Act states, in relevant part,

> An emergency manager may take 1 or more of the following additional actions with respect to a local government which is in receivership, notwithstanding any charter provision to the contrary: ... After meeting and conferring with the appropriate bargaining representative and, if in the emergency manager's sole discretion and judgment, a prompt and satisfactory resolution is unlikely to be obtained, reject, modify, or terminate 1 or more terms and conditions of an existing collective bargaining agreement.

If the emergency manager were to reject, modify, or terminate one or more terms and conditions of an existing agreement, constitutional concerns would likely be raised under the

Contract Clause of the U.S. Constitution.[27] The Contract Clause states, "No State shall ... pass any ... Law impairing the Obligation of Contracts." The U.S. Supreme Court has maintained that the Contract Clause "limits the power of the States to modify their own contracts as well as to regulate those between private parties."[28] At the same time, however, the Court has indicated that the Contract Clause "does not prohibit the States from repealing or amending statutes generally, or from enacting legislation with retroactive effects."[29]

The Supreme Court has identified three factors that must be considered to determine whether a state law violates the Contract Clause.[30] The threshold inquiry is whether the state law has substantially impaired the contractual relationship.[31] While what constitutes a "substantial" contract impairment is not entirely certain, it appears that an impairment is substantial if "the right abridged was one that induced the parties to contract in the first place ... or ... was one on which there had been reasonable and especial reliance."[32] The Court has indicated that it is not necessary to have a "total destruction" of contractual expectations to find a substantial impairment.[33]

If it is determined that a state law constitutes a substantial impairment, a reviewing court will likely next consider whether the state has a significant and legitimate public purpose for the law.[34] In *Energy Reserves Group v. Kansas Power and Light Co.*, a 1983 case involving the Contract Clause and the Kansas Natural Gas Price Protection Act, the Court observed that "remedying ... a broad and general social or economic problem" can be a significant and legitimate public purpose.[35] The Court in *Energy Reserves Group* also indicated that the public purpose does not have to be associated with an emergency or temporary situation.[36]

In *U.S. Trust Company of New York v. New Jersey*, a 1977 case involving a New Jersey statute that repealed a statutory bond covenant that limited the ability of the Port Authority of New York and New Jersey to subsidize rail passenger transportation, the Court found mass transportation, energy conservation, and environmental protection to be goals "that are important and of legitimate public concern."[37]

The final factor that would be considered as part of a Contract Clause analysis, as established by the Court, is whether the state law is reasonable and necessary to serve the public purpose.[38] To determine whether a state law is "reasonable," a reviewing court will likely consider the circumstances surrounding the law. If circumstances have changed significantly since a contract was first executed, a court is probably more likely to find the state law to be reasonable. In *U.S. Trust*, the Court concluded that the New Jersey law was not reasonable in light of the surrounding circumstances. The Court maintained that the bond covenant was adopted with full knowledge of the concerns that would later lead to the enactment of the state law. The Court observed,

> [T]hese concerns were not unknown in 1962, and the subsequent changes were of degree and not of kind. We cannot say that these changes caused the covenant to have a substantially different impact in 1974 than when it was adopted in 1962. And we cannot conclude that the repeal was reasonable in the light of changed circumstances.[39]

With regard to whether a state law is "necessary," the Court in *U.S. Trust* explained that a determination should be based on two considerations. First, whether a less drastic modification of a contract could accomplish the state's purpose.[40] And, second, whether a state could achieve its goal by adopting alternative means, without contract modification.[41]

It is not entirely clear whether the Fiscal Accountability Act or a similar measure would satisfy all of the factors identified by the Court. The Fiscal Accountability Act does appear, however, to have been drafted with the factors in mind. Section 19(1)(k) of the Michigan law states, in relevant part,

> The rejection, modification, or termination of 1 or more terms and conditions of an existing collective bargaining agreement under this subdivision is a legitimate exercise of the state's sovereign powers if the emergency manager and state treasurer determine that all of the following conditions are satisfied:
>
> (i) The financial emergency in the local government has created a circumstance in which it is reasonable and necessary for the state to intercede to serve a legitimate public purpose.
> (ii) Any plan involving the rejection, modification, or termination of 1 or more terms and conditions of an existing collective bargaining agreement is reasonable and necessary to deal with a broad, generalized economic problem.
> (iii) Any plan involving the rejection, modification, or termination of 1 or more terms and conditions of an existing collective bargaining agreement is directly related to and designed to address the financial emergency for the benefit of the public as a whole.
> (iv) Any plan involving the rejection, modification, or termination of 1 or more terms and conditions of an existing collective bargaining agreement is temporary and does not target specific classes of employees.

At the outset, it seems possible that a rejection, modification, or termination of at least some of the provisions of an existing collective bargaining agreement would be viewed as a substantial impairment. In *Baltimore Teachers Union v. Mayor and City Council of Baltimore*, a 1993 case involving a salary reduction plan that was implemented in response to budget shortfalls in Baltimore City, the U.S. Court of Appeals for the Fourth Circuit observed, "In the employment context, there likely is no right both more central to the contract's inducement and on the existence of which the parties more especially rely, than the right to compensation at the contractually specified level."[42] Ultimately, whether the Fiscal Accountability Act survives a possible challenge under the Contract Clause may not be known until an emergency manager identifies the terms and conditions to be rejected, modified, or terminated, and it becomes clear that no alternatives were available to accomplish the state's purpose.

As states continue to explore legislative solutions to resolve their budget issues, the Contract Clause may act to forestall measures that repudiate a state's contractual obligations. Indeed, the facts involved with a particular law, such as the nature of a state's fiscal crisis and the existence of alternative solutions, will most likely inform whether there is a violation of the Contract Clause. The Supreme Court's willingness, however, to find remedying a broad and general economic problem as constituting a significant and legitimate public purpose may suggest to states facing economic hardship that a carefully considered state law could survive constitutional challenge.

End Notes

[1] Ryan Haggerty et al., State of the Unions: After Defeat in Wisconsin, Battle Lines Drawn Across Nation, Chi. Trib., Mar. 11, 2011, at 1.
[2] *See* News Release, Bureau of Lab. Stat., Union Members – 2010 (Jan. 21, 2011), *available at* http://www.bls.gov/news.release/pdf/union2.pdf.
[3] *Id.* The Bureau of Labor Statistics further reports that 42.3% of local government employees are union members.
[4] Exec. Order No. 10988, 27 Fed. Reg. 551 (Jan. 17, 1962).
[5] Exec. Order No. 11491, 34 Fed. Reg. 17,605 (Oct. 29, 1969).
[6] P.L. 95-454, tit. VII, 92 Stat. 1111, 1191-1218 (1978).
[7] 5 U.S.C. § 7102.
[8] 5 U.S.C. § 7102(2).
[9] 5 U.S.C. § 7103(a)(14).
[10] 5 U.S.C. § 7103(a)(14)(C).
[11] *See, e.g.*, 5 U.S.C. § 5332(a)(1) ("The General Schedule, the symbol for which is 'GS', is the basic pay schedule for positions to which this subchapter applies. Each employee to whom this subchapter applies is entitled to basic pay in accordance with the General Schedule."). The employees of at least seven agencies, however, are believed to have the ability to negotiate over pay. According to the U.S. Office of Personnel Management, employees of the Bonneville Power Administration, the Federal Aviation Administration, the Federal Deposit Insurance Corporation, the Office of Thrift Supervision, the Office of the Comptroller of the Currency, the Securities Exchange Commission, and the National Credit Union Administration may negotiate over wages. In addition, employees of the Department of Defense Domestic Dependent Elementary and Secondary Schools and white collar non-appropriated fund employees of the Department of Defense are also believed to have the ability to negotiate over pay. This authority appears to have been provided either by statute or by judicial or administrative decision. See U.S. Off. of Personnel Mgmt., Executive Branch Agencies With Bargaining Units That Have Authority to Negotiate Pay as of 01/05/2011 (on file with author).
[12] U.S. Dept. of Health and Human Services v. FLRA, 844 F.2d 1087, 1090 (4th Cir. 1988). See also Navy Charleston Naval Shipyard, Charleston, S.C. v. FLRA, 885 F.2d 185 (4th Cir. 1989).
[13] Veterans Admin. Med. Center. v. FLRA, 675 F.2d 260, 262 (11th Cir. 1982).
[14] *See* Joseph R. Grodin et al., Public Sector Employment: Cases and Materials 81 (2004).
[15] *Id.*
[16] N.C. Gen. Stat. § 95-98.
[17] Va. Code Ann. § 40.1-57.2.
[18] *See* Bureau of Nat'l Aff., *Public Sector Bargaining – State Laws*, *available at* http://laborandemploymentlaw.bna.com/lerc/2445/split_display.adp?fedfid=1480271&vname=lecbnlaw&fcn=1&wsn=501128000&fn=1480271&split =0 (last visited Mar. 18, 2011).
[19] Haw. Rev. Stat. § 89-9(d).
[20] Iowa Code § 20.9.
[21] *See* Bureau of Nat'l Aff., *supra* note 18.
[22] Wyo. Stat. Ann. § 27-10-102.
[23] *See* SB/AB 11, §§ 245, 314 (2011).
[24] *See* SB/AB 11, §§ 210, 262 (2011) (defining the term "collective bargaining").
[25] 2011 Mich. Pub. Act No. 4.
[26] 2011 Mich. Pub. Act No. 4, § 15(4).
[27] U.S. Const. art. I, § 10.
[28] U.S. Trust Company of New York v. New Jersey, 431 U.S. 1, 17 (1977).
[29] *Id.*
[30] *See* Energy Reserves Group v. Kansas Power and Light Co., 459 U.S. 400, 411-13 (1983); *U.S. Trust*, 431 U.S. at 17-23.
[31] *See Energy Reserves Group*, 459 U.S. at 411.
[32] *See* Baltimore Teachers Union v. Mayor and City Council of Baltimore, 6 F.3d 1012, 1017 (4th Cir. 1993).
[33] *U.S. Trust*, 431 U.S. at 26-27.
[34] *See Energy Reserves Group*, 459 U.S. at 411-12.
[35] *Id.*
[36] *Id.*
[37] *U.S. Trust*, 431 U.S. at 28.
[38] *See Energy Reserves Group*, 459 U.S. at 411-12. See also *U.S. Trust*, 431 U.S. at 22.
[39] *U.S. Trust*, 431 U.S. at 32.
[40] *U.S. Trust*, 431 U.S. at 29-30.
[41] *Id.*
[42] *Baltimore Teachers Union*, 6 F.3d at 1018.

In: Labor Relations
Editors: A. Daniels and R. Hoffman
ISBN: 978-1-62257-420-9

Chapter 5

BASIC GUIDE TO THE NATIONAL LABOR RELATIONS ACT*

National Labor Relations Board

FOREWORD

The Regional Offices of the National Labor Relations Board have found that, more than six decades after its enactment, there is still a lack of basic information about the National Labor Relations Act. Staff members have expressed a need for a simply stated explanation of the Act to which anyone could be referred for guidance. To meet this demand, the basic law under the Act has been set forth in this pamphlet in a nontechnical way so that those who may be affected by it can better understand what their rights and obligations are.

Any effort to state basic principles of law in a simple way is a challenging and unenviable task. This is especially true about labor law, a relatively complex field of law. Anyone reading this booklet must bear in mind several cautions.

First, it must be emphasized that the Office of the General Counsel does not issue advisory opinions and this material cannot be considered as an official statement of law. It represents the view of the Office of the General Counsel as of the date of publication only. It is important to note that the law changes and advances. In fact, it is the duty of the Agency to keep its decisions abreast of changing conditions, yet within the basic statute. Accordingly, with the passage of time no one can rely on these statements as absolute until and unless a check has been made to see whether the law may have been changed substantially or specifically.

Furthermore, these are broad general principles only and countless subprinciples and detailed rules are not included. Only by evaluation of specific fact situations in the light of current principles and with the aid of expert advice would a person be in a position to know definitely where the proposed conduct may fit under the statute. No basic primer or text can

* This is an edited, reformatted and augmented version of the Office of the General Counsel, National Labor Relations Board, dated 1997.

constitute legal advice in particular fact situations. This effort to improve basic education about the statute should not be considered as such. Many areas of the statute remain untested. Legal advisers and other experts can find the total body of "Board law" reported in other Agency publications.

One other caution: This material does not deal with questions arising under other labor laws, but only with the National Labor Relations Act. Laws administered by other Government agencies, such as the Labor-Management Reporting and Disclosure Act of 1959, the Employee Retirement Income Security Act, the Occupational Safety and Health Act, the Railway Labor Act, the Fair Labor Standards, Walsh-Healey and Davis-Bacon Acts, Title VII of the Civil Rights Act of 1964, Americans with Disabilities Act, the Federal Mine Safety and Health Act, and the Veterans' Preference Act, are not treated herein.

Lastly, this material does not reflect the view of the National Labor Relations Board as the adjudicating agency that in the end will decide each case as it comes before it.

It is hoped that with this cautionary note this booklet may be helpful to those in need of a better basic understanding of the National Labor Relations Act.

Summary of the Act

Purpose of the Act

It is in the national interest of the United States to maintain full production in its economy. Industrial strife among employees, employers, and labor organizations interferes with full production and is contrary to our national interest. Experience has shown that labor disputes can be lessened if the parties involved recognize the legitimate rights of each in their relations with one another. To establish these rights under law, Congress enacted the National Labor Relations Act. Its purpose is to define and protect the rights of employees and employers, to encourage collective bargaining, and to eliminate certain practices on the part of labor and management that are harmful to the general welfare.

What the Act Provides

The National Labor Relations Act states and defines the rights of employees to organize and to bargain collectively with their employers through representatives of their own choosing or not to do so. To ensure that employees can freely choose their own representatives for the purpose of collective bargaining, or choose not to be represented, the Act establishes a procedure by which they can exercise their choice at a secret-ballot election conducted by the National Labor Relations Board. Further, to protect the rights of employees and employers, and to prevent labor disputes that would adversely affect the rights of the public, Congress has defined certain practices of employers and unions as unfair labor practices.

How the Act Is Enforced

The law is administered and enforced principally by the National Labor Relations Board and the General Counsel acting through 52 regional and other field offices located in major cities in various sections of the country. The General Counsel and the staff of the Regional Offices investigate and prosecute unfair labor practice cases and conduct elections to determine employee representatives. The five-member Board decides cases involving charges of unfair labor practices and determines representation election questions that come to it from the Regional Offices.

How This Material Is Organized

The rights of employees, including the rights to self-organization and collective bargaining that are protected by Section 7 of the Act, are presented first in this guide. The Act's provisions concerning the requirements for union-security agreements are covered in the same section, which also includes a discussion of the right to strike and the right to picket. The obligations of collective bargaining and the Act's provisions for the selection of employee representatives are treated in the next section. Unfair labor practices of employers and of labor organizations are then presented in separate sections. The final section, entitled "How the Act Is Enforced," sets forth the organization of the NLRB; its authority and limitations; its procedures and powers in representation matters, in unfair labor practice cases, and in certain special proceedings under the Act; and the Act's provisions concerning enforcement of the Board's orders.

The Rights of Employees

The Section 7 Rights

The rights of employees are set forth principally in Section 7 of the Act, which provides as follows:

> Sec. 7. Employees shall have the right to self-organization, to form, join, or assist labor organizations, to bargain collectively through representatives of their own choosing, and to engage in other concerted activities for the purpose of collective bargaining or other mutual aid or protection, and shall also have the right to refrain from any or all of such activities except to the extent that such right may be affected by an agreement requiring membership in a labor organization as a condition of employment as authorized in section 8(a)(3).

Examples of Section 7 rights

Examples of the rights protected by this section are the following:

- Forming or attempting to form a union among the employees of a company.
- Joining a union whether the union is recognized by the employer or not.

- Assisting a union to organize the employees of an employer.
- Going out on strike to secure better working conditions.
- Refraining from activity on behalf of a union.

Union Security

The Act permits, under certain conditions, a union and an employer to make an agreement, called a union-security agreement, that requires employees to make certain payments to the union in order to retain their jobs. A union-security agreement cannot require that applicants for employment be members of the union in order to be hired, and such an agreement cannot require employees to join or maintain membership in the union in order to retain their jobs. Under a union-security agreement, individuals choosing to be dues-paying nonmembers may be required, as may employees who actually join the union, to pay full initiation fees and dues within a certain period of time (a "grace period") after the collective-bargaining contract takes effect or after a new employee is hired. However, the most that can be required of nonmembers who inform the union that they object to the use of their payments for nonrepresentational purposes is that they pay their share of the union's costs relating to representational activities (such as collective bargaining, contract administration, and grievance adjustment).

Union-security agreements

The grace period, after which the union-security agreement becomes effective, cannot be less than 30 days except in the building and construction industry. The Act allows a shorter grace period of 7 full days in the building and construction industry (Section 8(f). A union-security agreement that provides a shorter grace period than the law allows is invalid, and any employee discharged because he or she has not complied with such an agreement is entitled to reinstatement.

Requirements for union-security agreements

Under a union-security agreement, employees who have religious objections to becoming members of a union or to supporting a union financially may be exempt from paying union dues and initiation fees. These employees may, however, be required to make contributions to a nonreligious, nonlabor tax exempt organization instead of making payments to a union. Unions representing such employees may also charge them the reasonable cost of any grievances processed at the employees' request.

Prehire agreements in the construction industry

For a union-security agreement to be valid, it must meet all the following requirements:

1. The union must not have been assisted or controlled by the employer (see Section 8(a)(2) under "Unfair Labor Practices of Employers" on pp. 14–15).
2. The union must be the majority representative of the employees in the appropriate collective-bargaining unit covered by such agreement when made.
3. The union's authority to make such an agreement must not have been revoked within the previous 12 months by the employees in a Board election.
4. The agreement must provide for the appropriate grace period.

Section 8(f) of the Act allows an employer engaged primarily in the building and construction industry to sign a union-security agreement with a union without the union's having been designated as the representative of its employees as otherwise required by the Act. The agreement can be made before the employer has hired any employees for a project and will apply to them when they are hired. As noted above, however, the union-security provisions of a collective-bargaining contract in the building and construction industry may become effective with respect to new employees after 7 full days. If the agreement is made while employees are on the job, it must allow existing employees the same 7-day grace period to comply. As with any other union-security agreement, the union involved must be free from employer assistance or control.

Collective-bargaining contracts in the building and construction industry can include, as stated in Section 8(f), the following additional provisions:

1. A requirement that the employer notify the union concerning job openings.
2. A provision that gives the union an opportunity to refer qualified applicants for such jobs.
3. Job qualification standards based on training or experience.
4. A provision for priority in hiring based on length of service with the employer, in the industry, or in the particular geographic area.

These four hiring provisions may lawfully be included in collective-bargaining contracts which cover employees in other industries as well.

Finally, pursuant to Section 14(b) of the Act, individual States may prohibit, and some States have prohibited, certain forms of union-security agreements.

The Right to Strike

Section 7 of the Act states in part, "Employees shall have the right. . . to engage in other concerted activities for the purpose of collective bargaining or other mutual aid or protection." Strikes are included among the concerted activities protected for employees by this section. Section 13 also concerns the right to strike. It reads as follows:

> Nothing in this Act, except as specifically provided for herein, shall be construed so as either to interfere with or impede or diminish in any way the right to strike, or to affect the limitations or qualifications on that right.

It is clear from a reading of these two provisions that: the law not only guarantees the right of employees to strike, but also places limitations and qualifications on the exercise of that right. See for example, restrictions on strikes in health care institutions, page 32.

Lawful and Unlawful Strikes

The lawfulness of a strike may depend on the object, or purpose, of the strike, on its timing, or on the conduct of the strikers. The object, or objects, of a strike and whether the objects are lawful are matters that are not always easy to determine. Such issues often have to be decided by the National Labor Relations Board. The consequences can be severe to striking employees and struck employers, involving as they do questions of reinstatement and backpay.

It must be emphasized that the following is only a brief outline. A detailed analysis of the law concerning strikes, and application of the law to all the factual situations that can arise in connection with strikes, is beyond the scope of this material. Employees and employers who anticipate being involved in strike action should proceed cautiously and on the basis of competent advice.

Strikes for a Lawful Object

Employees who strike for a lawful object fall into two classes "economic strikers" and "unfair labor practice strikers." Both classes continue as employees, but unfair labor practice strikers have greater rights of reinstatement to their jobs.

Economic Strikers Defined

If the object of a strike is to obtain from the employer some economic concession such as higher wages, shorter hours, or better working conditions, the striking employees are called economic strikers. They retain their status as employees and cannot be discharged, but they can be replaced by their employer. If the employer has hired bona fide permanent replacements who are filling the jobs of the economic strikers when the strikers apply unconditionally to go back to work, the strikers are not entitled to reinstatement at that time. However, if the strikers do not obtain regular and substantially equivalent employment, they are entitled to be recalled to jobs for which they are qualified when openings in such jobs occur if they, or their bargaining representative, have made an unconditional request for their reinstatement.

Unfair Labor Practice Strikers Defined

Employees who strike to protest an unfair labor practice committed by their employer are called unfair labor practice strikers. Such strikers can be neither discharged nor permanently replaced. When the strike ends, unfair labor practice strikers, absent serious misconduct on their part, are entitled to have their jobs back even if employees hired to do their work have to be discharged.

If the Board finds that economic strikers or unfair labor practice strikers who have made an unconditional request for reinstatement have been unlawfully denied reinstatement by their employer, the Board may award such strikers backpay starting at the time they should have been reinstated.

Strikes Unlawful Because of Purpose

A strike may be unlawful because an object, or purpose, of the strike is unlawful. A strike in support of a union unfair labor practice, or one that would cause an employer to commit an unfair labor practice, may be a strike for an unlawful object. For example, it is an unfair labor practice for an employer to discharge an employee for failure to make certain lawful payments to the union when there is no union-security agreement in effect (Section 8(a)(3). A strike to compel an employer to do this would be a strike for an unlawful object and, therefore, an unlawful strike. Strikes of this nature will be discussed in connection with the various unfair labor practices in a later section of this guide.

Furthermore, Section 8(b)(4) of the Act prohibits strikes for certain objects even though the objects are not necessarily unlawful if achieved by other means. An example of this would be a strike to compel Employer A to cease doing business with Employer B. It is not unlawful for Employer A voluntarily to stop doing business with Employer B, nor is it unlawful for a union merely to request that it do so. It is, however, unlawful for the union to strike with an object of forcing the employer to do so. These points will be covered in more detail in the explanation of Section 8(b)(4). In any event, employees who participate in an unlawful strike may be discharged and are not entitled to reinstatement.

Strikes Unlawful Because of Timing—Effect of No-Strike Contract

A strike that violates a no-strike provision of a contract is not protected by the Act, and the striking employees can be discharged or otherwise disciplined, unless the strike is called to protest certain kinds of unfair labor practices committed by the employer. It should be noted that not all refusals to work are considered strikes and thus violations of no-strike provisions. A walkout because of conditions abnormally dangerous to health, such as a defective ventilation system in a spray-painting shop, has been held not to violate a no-strike provision.

Same—Strikes at End of Contract Period

Section 8(d) provides that when either party desires to terminate or change an existing contract, it must comply with certain conditions. If these requirements are not met, a strike to terminate or change a contract is unlawful and participating strikers lose their status as employees of the employer engaged in the labor dispute. If the strike was caused by the unfair labor practice of the employer, however, the strikers are classified as unfair labor practice strikers and their status is not affected by failure to follow the required procedure.

Strikes Unlawful Because of Misconduct of Strikers

Strikers who engage in serious misconduct in the course of a strike may be refused reinstatement to their former jobs. This applies to both economic strikers and unfair labor practice strikers. Serious misconduct has been held to include, among other things, violence and threats of violence. The U.S. Supreme Court has ruled that a "sitdown" strike, when employees simply stay in the plant and refuse to work, thus depriving the owner of property, is not protected by the law. Examples of serious misconduct that could cause the employees involved to lose their right to reinstatement are:

- Strikers physically blocking persons from entering or leaving a struck plant.
- Strikers threatening violence against nonstriking employees.
- Strikers attacking management representatives.

The Right to Picket

Likewise the right to picket is subject to limitations and qualifications. As with the right to strike, picketing can be prohibited because of its object or its timing, or misconduct on the picket line. In addition, Section 8(b)(7) declares it to be an unfair labor practice for a union to picket for certain objects whether the picketing accompanies a strike or not. This will be covered in more detail in the section on union unfair labor practices.

Collective Bargaining and Representation of Employees

Collective bargaining is one of the keystones of the Act. Section 1 of the Act declares that the policy of the United States is to be carried out "by encouraging the practice and procedure of collective bargaining and by protecting the exercise by workers of full freedom of association, self-organization, and designation of representatives of their own choosing, for the purpose of negotiating the terms and conditions of their employment or other mutual aid or protection."

Collective Bargaining

Collective bargaining is defined in the Act. Section 8(d) requires an employer and the representative of its employees to meet at reasonable times, to confer in good faith about certain matters, and to put into writing any agreement reached if requested by either party. The parties must confer in good faith with respect to wages, hours, and other terms or conditions of employment, the negotiation of an agreement, or any question arising under an agreement.

Duty to Bargain Imposed on Both Employer and Union

These obligations are imposed equally on the employer and the representative of its employees. It is an unfair labor practice for either party to refuse to bargain collectively with the other. The obligation does not, however, compel either party to agree to a proposal by the other, nor does it require either party to make a concession to the other .

Section 8(d) provides further that when a collective-bargaining agreement is in effect no party to the contract shall end or change the contract unless the party wishing to end or change it takes the following steps:

Bargaining Steps to End or Change a Contract

1. The party must notify the other party to the contract in writing about the proposed termination or modification 60 days before the date on which the contract is scheduled to expire. If the contract is not scheduled to expire on any particular date, the notice in writing must be served 60 days before the time when it is proposed that the termination or modification take effect.

2. The party must offer to meet and confer with the other party for the purpose of negotiating a new contract or a contract containing the proposed changes.
3. The party must, within 30 days after the notice to the party, notify the Federal Mediation and Conciliation Service of the existence of a dispute if no agreement has been reached by that time. Said party must also notify at the same time any State or Territorial mediation or conciliation agency in the State or Territory where the dispute occurred.
4. The party must continue in full force and effect, without resorting to strike or lockout, all the terms and conditions of the existing contract until 60 days after the notice to the other party was given or until the date the contract is scheduled to expire, whichever is later.

(In the case of a health care institution, the requirement in paragraphs 1 and 4 is 90 days, and in paragraph 3 is 60 days. In addition, there is a 30-day notice requirement to the agencies in paragraph 3 when a dispute arises in bargaining for an initial contract.)

When the Bargaining Steps Are Not Required

The requirements of paragraphs 2, 3, and 4, above, cease to apply if the NLRB issues a certificate showing that the employees' representative who is a party to the contract has been replaced by a different representative or has been voted out by the employees. Neither party is required to discuss or agree to any change of the provisions of the contract if the other party proposes that the change become effective before the provision could be reopened according to the terms of the contract.

As has been pointed out, any employee who engages in a strike within the notice period loses status as an employee of the struck employer. This loss of status ends, however, if and when that individual is reemployed by the same employer.

The Employee Representative

Section 9(a) provides that the employee representatives that have been "designated or selected for the purposes of collective bargaining by the majority of the employees in a unit appropriate for such purposes, shall be the exclusive representatives of all the employees in such unit for the purposes of collective bargaining."

What Is an Appropriate Bargaining Unit

A unit of employees is a group of two or more employees who share a community of interest and may reasonably be grouped together for purposes of collective bargaining. The determination of what is an appropriate unit for such purposes is, under the Act, left to the discretion of the NLRB. Section 9(b) states that the Board shall decide in each representation case whether, "in order to assure to employees the fullest freedom in exercising the rights guaranteed by this Act, the unit appropriate for the purposes of collective bargaining shall be the employer unit, craft unit, plant unit, or subdivision thereof."

This broad discretion is, however, limited by several other provisions of the Act. Section 9(b)(1) provides that the Board shall not approve as appropriate a unit that includes both professional and nonprofessional employees, unless a majority of the professional employees involved vote to be included in the mixed unit.

Section 9(b)(2) provides that the Board shall not hold a proposed craft unit to be inappropriate simply because a different unit was previously approved by the Board, unless a majority of the employees in the proposed craft unit vote against being represented separately.

Section 9(b)(3) prohibits the Board from including plant guards in the same unit with other employees. It also prohibits the Board from certifying a labor organization as the representative of a plant guard unit if the labor organization has members who are nonguard employees or if it is "affiliated directly or indirectly" with an organization that has members who are nonguard employees.

How the Appropriateness of a Unit Is Determined

Generally, the appropriateness of a bargaining unit is determined on the basis of a community of interest of the employees involved. Those who have the same or substantially similar interests concerning wages, hours, and working conditions are grouped together in a bargaining unit. In determining whether a proposed unit is appropriate, the following factors are also considered:

1. Any history of collective bargaining.
2. The desires of the employees concerned.
3. The extent to which the employees are organized. Section 9(c)(5) forbids the Board from giving this factor controlling weight.

Finally, with regard to units in the health care industry, the Board also is guided by Congress' concern about preventing disruptions in the delivery of health care services, and its directive to minimize the number of appropriate bargaining units.

Who Can or Cannot Be Included in a Unit

A unit may cover the employees in one plant of an employer, or it may cover employees in two or more plants of the same employer. In some industries in which employers are grouped together in voluntary associations, a unit may include employees of two or more employers in any number of locations. It should be noted that a bargaining unit can include only persons who are "employees" within the meaning of the Act. The Act excludes certain individuals, such as agricultural laborers, independent contractors, supervisors, and persons in managerial positions, from the meaning of "employees." None of these individuals can be included in a bargaining unit established by the Board. In addition, the Board, as a matter of policy, excludes from bargaining units employees who act in a confidential capacity to an employer's labor relations officials.

Duties of Bargaining Representative and Employer

Once an employee representative has been designated by a majority of the employees in an appropriate unit, the Act makes that representative the exclusive bargaining agent for all employees in the unit. As exclusive bargaining agent it has a duty to represent equally and fairly all employees in the unit without regard to their union membership or activities. Once a collective-bargaining representative has been designated or selected by its employees, it is illegal for an employer to bargain with individual employees, with a group of employees, or with another employee representative.

Section 9(a) provides that any individual employee or a group of employees shall have the right at any time to present grievances to their employer and to have such grievances adjusted without the intervention of the bargaining representative provided:

1. The adjustment is not inconsistent with the terms of any collective-bargaining agreement then in effect.
2. The bargaining representative has been given the opportunity to be present at such adjustment.

How a Bargaining Representative is Selected

The Act requires that an employer bargain with the representative selected by its employees. The most common method by which employees can select a bargaining representative is a secret-ballot representation election conducted by the Board.

Petition for Certification of Representatives

The NLRB can conduct such an election only when a petition has been filed requesting one. A petition for certification of representatives can be filed by an employee or a group of employees or any individual or labor organization acting on their behalf, or it can be filed by an employer. If filed by or on behalf of employees, the petition must be supported by a substantial number of employees who wish to be represented for collective bargaining and must state that their employer declines to recognize their representative. If filed by an employer, the petition must allege that one or more individuals or organizations have made a claim for recognition as the exclusive representative of the same group of employees.

Petition for Decertification Election

The Act also contains a provision whereby employees or someone acting on their behalf can file a petition seeking an election to determine if the employees wish to retain the individual or labor organization currently acting as their bargaining representative, whether the representative has been certified or voluntarily recognized by the employer. This is called a decertification election.

Union-Security Deauthorization

Provision is also made for the Board to determine by secret ballot whether the employees covered by a union-security agreement desire to withdraw the authority of their representative to continue the agreement. This is called a union-security deauthorization election and can be brought about by the filing of a petition signed by 30 percent or more of the employees covered by the agreement.

If you will refer to the "Types of Cases" on pages 18 and 19, you may find it easier to understand the differences between the six types of petitions that can be filed under the Act.

Purpose of Investigation and Hearing

The same petition form is used for any kind of Board election. When the petition is filed, the NLRB must investigate the petition, hold a hearing if necessary, and direct an election if it finds that a question of representation exists. The purpose of the investigation is to determine, among other things, the following:

1. Whether the Board has jurisdiction to conduct an election.
2. Whether there is a sufficient showing of employee interest to justify an election.
3. Whether a question of representation exists.
4. Whether the election is sought in an appropriate unit of employees.
5. Whether the representative named in the petition is qualified.
6. Whether there are any barriers to an election in the form of existing contracts or prior elections.

Jurisdiction to Conduct an Election

The jurisdiction of the NLRB to direct and conduct an election is limited to those enterprises that affect commerce. (This is discussed in greater detail at pp. 33–36.) The other matters listed above will be discussed in turn.

Expedited Elections under Section 8(b)(7)(C)

First, however, It should be noted that Section 8(b)(7)(C) provides, among other things, that when a petition is filed within a reasonable period, not to exceed 30 days, after the commencement of recognitional or organizational picketing, the NLRB shall "forthwith" order an election and certify the results. This is so if the picketing is not within the protection of the second proviso to Section 8(b)(7)(C). When an election under Section (8)(b)(7)(C) is appropriate, neither a hearing nor a showing of interest is required, and the election is scheduled sooner than under the ordinary procedure.

Showing of Interest Required

Regarding the showing of interest, it is the policy to require that a petitioner requesting an election for either certification of representatives or decertification show that at least 30 percent of the employees favor an election. The Act also requires that a petition for a union-security deauthorization election be filed by 30 percent or more of the employees in the unit covered by the agreement for the NLRB to conduct an election for that purpose. The showing of interest must be exclusively by employees who are in the appropriate bargaining unit in which an election is sought.

Existence of Question of Representation

Section 9(c)(1) authorizes the NLRB to direct an election and certify the results thereof, provided the record shows that a question of representation exists. Petitions for certification of representatives present a question of representation if, among other things, they are based on a demand for recognition by the employee representative and a denial of recognition by the employer. The demand for recognition need not be made in any particular form; in fact, the filing of a petition by the representative itself is considered to be a demand for recognition. The NLRB has held that even a representative that is currently recognized by the employer can file a petition for certification and that such petition presents a question of representation provided the representative has not previously been certified.

A question of representation is also raised by a decertification petition that challenges the representative status of a bargaining agent previously certified or currently recognized by the employer. However, a decertification petition filed by a supervisor does not raise a valid question of representation and must be dismissed.

Who Can Qualify as Bargaining Representative

Section 2(4) of the Act provides that the employee representative for collective bargaining can be "any individual or labor organization." A supervisor or any other management representative may not be an employee representative. It is NLRB policy to direct an election and to issue a certification unless the proposed bargaining agent fails to qualify as a bona fide representative of the employees. In determining a union's qualifications as bargaining agent, it is the union's willingness to represent the employees rather than its constitution and bylaws that is the controlling factor. The NLRB's power to certify a labor organization as bargaining representative is limited by Section 9(b)(3) which prohibits certification of a union as the representative of a unit of plant guards if the union "admits to membership, or is affiliated directly or indirectly with an organization which admits to membership, employees other than guards."

Bars to Election

Existing Collective-Bargaining Contract

The NLRB has established the policy of not directing an election among employees presently covered by a valid collective-bargaining agreement except in accordance with certain rules. These rules, followed in determining whether or not an existing collective-bargaining contract will bar an election, are called the NLRB contract bar rules. Not every contract will bar an election. Examples of contracts that would not bar an election are:

- The contract is not in writing, or is not signed.
- The contract has not been ratified by the members or the union, if such is expressly required.
- The contract does not contain substantial terms or conditions of employment sufficient to stabilize the bargaining relationship.
- The contract can be terminated by either party at any time for any reason.
- The contract contains a clearly illegal union-security clause.
- The bargaining unit is not appropriate.
- The union that entered the contract with the employer is no longer in existence or is unable or unwilling to represent the employees.
- The contract discriminates between employees on racial grounds.
- The contract covers union members only.
- The contracting union is involved in a basic internal conflict at the highest levels with resulting unstabilizing confusion about the identity of the union.
- The employer's operations have changed substantially since the contract was executed.

Time Provisions

Under the NLRB rules a valid contract for a fixed period of 3 years or less will bar an election for the period covered by the contract. A contract for a fixed period of more than 3 years will bar an election sought by a contracting party during the life of the contract, but will act as a bar to an election sought by an outside party for only 3 years following its effective date. A contract of no fixed period will not act as a bar at all.

When a Petition Can Be Filed if There Is an Existing Contract

If there is no existing contract, a petition can bring about an election if it is filed before the day a contract is signed. If the petition is filed on the same day the contract is signed, the contract bars an election, provided the contract is effective immediately or retroactively and the employer has not been informed at the time of execution that a petition has been filed. Once the contract becomes effective as a bar to an election, no petition will be accepted until near the end of the period during which the contract is effective as a bar. Petitions filed not more than 90 days but over 60 days before the end of the contract-bar period will be accepted and can bring about an election. These time periods for filing petitions involving health care institutions are 120 and 90 days, respectively. Of course, a petition can be filed after the contract expires. However, the last 60 days of the contract-bar period is called an "insulated" period. During this time the parties to the existing contract are free to negotiate a new contract or to agree to extend the old one. If they reach agreement in this period. petitions will not be accepted until 90 days before the end of the new contract-bar period.

Effect of Certification

In addition to the contract-bar rules, the NLRB has established a rule that when a representative has been certified by the Board, the certification will ordinarily be binding for at least 1 year and a petition filed before the end of the certification year will be dismissed. In cases in which the certified representative and the employer enter a valid collective-bargaining contract during the year, the contract becomes controlling, and whether a petition for an election can be filed is determined by the Board's contract-bar rules.

Effect of Prior Election

Section 9(c)(3) prohibits the holding of an election in any collective-bargaining unit or subdivision thereof in which a valid election has been held during the preceding 12-month period. A new election may be held, however, in a larger unit, but not in the same unit or subdivision in which the previous election was held. For example, if all the production and maintenance employees in Company A, including draftsmen in the company's engineering office, are included in a collective-bargaining unit, an election among all the employees in the unit would bar another election among all the employees in the unit for 12 months. Similarly, an election among the draftsmen only would bar another election among the draftsmen for 12 months. However, an election among the draftsmen would not bar a later election during the 12-month period among all the production and maintenance employees including the draftsmen.

When a Petition Can Be Filed if There Has Been a Prior Election

It is the Board's interpretation that Section 9(c)(3) prohibits only the holding of an election during the 12-month period, but does not prohibit the filing of a petition. Accordingly, the NLRB will accept a petition filed not more than 60 days before the end of the 12-month period. The election cannot be held, of course, until after the 12-month period. If an election is held and a representative certified, that certification is binding for 1 year and a petition for another election in the same unit will be dismissed if it is filed during the 1-year period after the certification. If an election is held and no representative is certified, the election bars another election for 12 months. A petition for another election in the same unit can be filed not more than 60 days before the end of the 12-month period and the election can be held after the 12-month period expires.

The Representation Election

Section 9(c)(1) provides that if a question of representation exists, the NLRB must make its determination by means of a secret-ballot election. In a representation election employees are given a choice of one or more bargaining representatives or no representative at all. To be certified as the bargaining representative, an individual or a labor organization must receive a majority of the valid votes cast.

Consent-Election Agreements

An election may be held by agreement between the employer and the individual or labor organization claiming to represent the employees. In such an agreement the parties would state the time and place agreed on, the choices to be included on the ballot, and a method to determine who is eligible to vote. They would also authorize the NLRB Regional Director to conduct the election.

Who Determines Election Matters

If the parties are unable to reach an agreement, the Act authorizes the NLRB to order an election after a hearing. The Act also authorizes the Board to delegate to its Regional Directors the determination on matters concerning elections. Under this delegation of authority the Regional Directors can determine the appropriateness of the unit, direct an election, and certify the outcome. Upon the request of an interested party, the Board may review the action of a Regional Director, but such review does not stop the election process unless the Board so orders. The election details are left to the Regional Director. Such matters as who may vote, when the election will be held, and what standards of conduct will be imposed on the parties are decided in accordance with the Board's rules and its decisions.

Who May Vote in a Representation Election

To be entitled to vote, an employee must have worked in the unit during the eligibility period set by the Board and must be employed in the unit on the date of the election. Generally, the eligibility period is the employer's payroll period just before the date on which the election was directed. This requirement does not apply, however, to employees who are ill, on vacation, or temporarily laid off, or to employees in military service who appear in person at the polls. The NLRB rules take into consideration the fact that employment is typically irregular in certain industries. In such industries eligibility to vote is determined according to formulas designed to permit all employees who have a substantial continuing interest in their employment conditions to vote. Examples of these formulas, which differ from case to case, are:

- In one case, employees of a construction company were allowed to vote if they worked for the employer at least 65 days during the year before the "eligibility date" for the election.
- In another case longshoremen who worked at least 700 hours during a specified contract year, and at least 20 hours in each full month between the end of that year and the date on which the election was directed, were allowed to vote.
- Radio and television talent employees and musicians in the television film, motion picture, and recording industries have been held eligible to vote if they worked in the unit 2 or more days during the year before the date on which the election was directed.

When Strikers May Be Allowed to Vote

Section 9(c)(3) provides that economic strikers who have been replaced by bona fide permanent employees may be entitled to vote in "any election conducted within 12 months after the commencement of the strike." The permanent replacements are also eligible to vote at the same time. As a general proposition, a striker is considered to be an economic striker unless found by the NLRB to be on strike over unfair labor practices of the employer. Whether the economic striker is eligible to vote is determined on the facts of each case.

When Elections Are Held

Ordinarily, elections are held within 30 days after they are directed. Seasonal drops in employment or any change in operations that would prevent a normal work force from being present may cause a different election date to be set. Normally an election will not be conducted when unfair labor practice charges have been filed based on conduct of a nature which would have a tendency to interfere with the free choice of the employees in an election, except that, in certain cases, the Board may proceed to the election if the charging party so requests.

Conduct of Elections

NLRB elections are conducted in accordance with strict standards designed to give the employee voters an opportunity to freely indicate whether they wish to be represented for purposes of collective bargaining. Election details, such as time, place, and notice of an election, are left largely to the Regional Director who usually obtains the agreement of the parties on these matters.

Any party to an election who believes that the Board election standards were not met may, within 7 days after the tally of ballots has been furnished, file objections to the election with the Regional Director under whose supervision the election was held. In most cases, the Regional Director's rulings on these objections may be appealed to the Board for decision.

An election will be set aside if it was accompanied by conduct that the NLRB considers created an atmosphere of confusion or fear of reprisals and thus interfered with the employees' freedom of choice. In any particular case the NLRB does not attempt to determine whether the conduct actually interfered with the employees' expression of free choice, but rather asks whether the conduct tended to do so.

If it is reasonable to believe that the conduct would tend to interfere with the free expression of the employees' choice, the election may be set aside. Examples of conduct the Board considers to interfere with employee free choice are:

- Threats of loss of jobs or benefits by an employer or a union to influence the votes or union activities of employees.
- A grant of benefits or promise to grant benefits to influence the votes or union activities of employees.
- An employer firing employees to discourage or encourage their union activities or a union causing an employer to take such action.
- An employer or a union making campaign speeches to assembled groups of employees on company time within the 24-hour period before the election.
- The incitement of racial or religious prejudice by inflammatory campaign appeals made by either an employer or a union.
- Threats or the use of physical force or violence against employees by an employer or a union to influence their votes.
- The occurrence of extensive violence or trouble or widespread fear of job losses which prevents the holding of a fair election, whether caused by an employer or a union.

Unfair Labor Practices of Employers

The unfair labor practices of employers are listed in Section 8(a) of the Act; those of labor organizations in Section 8(b). Section 8(e) lists an unfair labor practice that can be committed only by an employer and a labor organization acting together. The "Types of Cases" chart at pages 18–19 may be helpful in getting to know the relationship between the various unfair labor practice sections of the Act.

Section 8(a)(1)—Interference with Section 7 Rights

Section 8(a)(1) forbids an employer "to interfere with, restrain, or coerce employees in the exercise of the rights guaranteed in section 7." Any prohibited interference by an employer with the rights of employees to organize, to form, join, or assist a labor organization, to bargain collectively, to engage in other concerted activities for mutual aid or protection, or to refrain from any or all of these activities, constitutes a violation of this section. This is a broad prohibition on employer interference, and an employer violates this section whenever it commits any of the other employer unfair labor practices. In consequence, whenever a violation of Section 8(a)(2), (3), (4), or (5) is committed a violation of Section 8(a)(1) is also found. This is called a "derivative violation" of Section 8(a)(1).

Examples of violations of Section 8(a)(1)

Employer conduct may, of course, independently violate Section 8(a)(1). Examples of such independent violations are:

- Threatening employees with loss of jobs or benefits if they should join or vote for a union.
- Threatening to close down the plant if a union should be organized in it.
- Questioning employees about their union activities or membership in such circumstances as will tend to restrain or coerce the employees.
- Spying on union gatherings, or pretending to spy.
- Granting wage increases deliberately timed to discourage employees from forming or joining a union.

Section 8(a)(2)—Domination or Illegal Assistance and Support of a Labor Organization

Section 8(a)(2) makes it unlawful for an employer "to dominate or interfere with the formation or administration of any labor organization or contribute financial or other support to it." This section not only outlaws "company unions" that are dominated by the employer, but also forbids an employer to contribute money to a union it favors or to give a union improper advantages that are denied to rival unions.

Domination

A labor organization is considered dominated within the meaning of this section if the employer has interfered with its formation and has assisted and supported its operation and activities to such an extent that it must be looked at as the employer's creation instead of the true bargaining representative of the employees. Such domination is the result of a combination of factors and has been found to exist where there is not only the factor of the employer getting the organization started, but also such other factors as the employer deciding how the organization will be set up and what it will do, or representatives of management actually taking part in the meetings and activities of the organization and trying to influence its actions and policies.

Illegal Assistance and Support

Certain lesser kinds of employer assistance to a union may constitute unlawful "interference" even if the union is not "dominated" by the employer. For example, an employer may not provide financial support to a union either by direct payments or indirect financial aid. (But an employer does not violate this prohibition by permitting employees to confer with it and/or the union regarding grievances or other union business during working hours without loss of pay.)

When rival unions are competing to organize an employer's employees, the employer is forbidden to give the union it favors privileges it denies to the other union. It is also forbidden to recognize either union once it knows that one of the unions has filed a valid petition with the Board requesting a representation election. When an employer and a union already have an established bargaining relationship, however, the employer is required to continue bargaining with the incumbent even though a rival union is attempting to organize the employees. In these circumstances, the rival's filing of a petition does not prevent continued dealing between the employer and the incumbent unless the incumbent has lost the support of a majority of the employees.

Examples of Violation of Section 8(a)(2)

An employer violates Section 8(a)(2) by:

- Taking an active part in organizing a union or a committee to represent employees.
- Bringing pressure on employees to support a union financially, except in the enforcement of a lawful union-security agreement.
- Allowing one of several unions, competing to represent employees, to solicit on company premises during working hours and denying other unions the same privilege.
- Soliciting and obtaining from employees and applicants for employment, during the hiring procedure, applications for union membership and signed authorizations for the check-off of union dues.

Remedy in Cases of Domination Differs from That in Cases of Illegal Assistance and Support

In remedying such unfair labor practices, the NLRB distinguishes between domination of a labor organization and conduct which amounts to no more than illegal assistance. When a union is found to be dominated by an employer, the Board has announced it will order the organization completely disestablished as a representative of employees. But, if the organization is found only to have been supported by employer assistance amounting to less than domination, the Board usually orders the employer to stop such support and to withhold recognition from the organization until such time as it has been certified by the Board as a bona fide representative of employees.

Section 8(a)(3)—Discrimination Against Employees

Section 8(a)(3) makes it an unfair labor practice for an employer to discriminate against employees "in regard to hire or tenure of employment or any term or condition of employment" for the purpose of encouraging or discouraging membership in a labor organization. In general, the Act makes it illegal for an employer to discriminate in employment because of an employee's union or other group, activity within the protection of the Act. A banding together of employees, even in the absence of a formal organization, may constitute a labor organization for purposes of Section 8(a)(3). It also prohibits discrimination because an employee has refrained from taking part in such union or group activity except where a valid union-security agreement is in effect. Discrimination within the meaning of the

Act would include such action as refusing to hire, discharging, demoting, assigning to a less desirable shift or job, or withholding benefits.

The Union Security Exception to Section 8(a)(3).

As previously noted, Section 8(a)(3) provides that an employee may be discharged for failing to make certain lawfully required payments to the exclusive bargaining representative under a lawful union-security agreement. For a fuller discussion of this issue, see pages 2–3, above.

Even when there is a valid union-security agreement in effect, an employer may not pay the union the dues and fees owed by its employees. The employer may, however, deduct these amounts from the wages of its employees and forward them to the union for each employee who has voluntarily signed a dues "checkoff" authorization. Such checkoff authorization may be made irrevocable for no more than a year. But employees may revoke their checkoff authorizations after a Board-conducted election in which the union's authority to maintain a union-security agreement has been withdrawn.

The Act Does Not Limit Employer's Right to Discharge for Economic Reasons

This section does not limit an employer's right to discharge, transfer, or layoff an employee for genuine economic reasons or for such good cause as disobedience or bad work. This right applies equally to employees who are active in support of a union and to those who are not.

In situations in which an employer disciplines an employee both because the employee has violated a work rule and because the employee has engaged in protected union activity, the discipline is unlawful unless the employer can show that the employee would have received the same discipline even if he or she had not engaged in the protected union activity.

An employer who is engaged in good-faith bargaining with a union may lock out the represented employees, sometimes even before impasse is reached in the negotiations, if it does so to further its position in bargaining. But a bargaining lockout may be unlawful if the employer is at that time unlawfully refusing to bargain or is bargaining in bad faith.

It is also unlawful if the employer's purpose in locking out its employees is to discourage them in their union loyalties and activities, that is, if the employer is motivated by hostility toward the union. Thus, a lockout to defeat a union's efforts to organize the employer's employees would violate the Act, as would the lockout of only those of its employees who are members of the union.

On the other hand, lockouts are lawful that are intended to prevent any unusual losses or safety hazards that would be caused by an anticipated "quickie" strike. And a whipsaw strike against one employer engaged in multiemployer bargaining justifies a lockout by any of the other employers who are party to the bargaining.

Examples of Violations of Section 8(a)(3)

Examples of illegal discrimination under Section 8(a)(3) include:

- Discharging employees because they urged other employees to join a union.
- Refusing to reinstate employees when jobs they are qualified for are open because they took part in a union's lawful strike.

- Granting of "superseniority" to those hired to replace employees engaged in a lawful strike.
- Demoting employees because they circulated a union petition among other employees asking the employer for an increase in pay.
- Discontinuing an operation at one plant and discharging the employees involved followed by opening the same operation at another plant with new employees because the employees at the first plant joined a union.
- Refusing to hire qualified applicants for jobs because they belong to a union. It would also be a violation if the qualified applicants were refused employment because they did not belong to a union, or because they belonged to one union rather than another.

Section 8(a)(4)—Discrimination for NLRB Activity

Section 8(a)(4) makes it an unfair labor practice for an employer "to discharge or otherwise discriminate against an employee because he has filed charges or given testimony under this Act."

This provision guards the right of employees to seek the protection of the Act by using the processes of the NLRB.

Like the previous section, it forbids an employer to discharge, layoff, or engage in other forms of discrimination in working conditions against employees who have filed charges with the NLRB, given affidavits to NLRB investigators, or testified at an NLRB hearing.

Violations of this section are in most cases also violations of Section 8(a)(3).

Examples of violations of Section 8(a)(4) are:

- Refusing to reinstate employees when jobs they are otherwise qualified for are open because they filed charges with the NLRB claiming their layoffs were based on union activity.
- Demoting employees because they testified at an NLRB hearing.

Section 8(a)(5)—Refusal to Bargain in Good Faith

Section 8(a)(5) makes it illegal for an employer to refuse to bargain in good faith about wages, hours, and other conditions of employment with the representative selected by a majority of the employees in a unit appropriate for collective bargaining.

A bargaining representative which seeks to enforce its right concerning an employer under this section must show that it has been designated by a majority of the employees, that the unit is appropriate, and that there has been both a demand that the employer bargain and a refusal by the employer to do so.

TYPES OF CASES

I. Charges of Unfair Labor Practices (C Cases)			
Charge Against Employer	**Charge Against Labor Organization**		
Section of the Act ***CA***	***Section of the Act*** ***CB***	***Section of the Act*** ***CC***	***Section of the Act*** ***CD***
8(a)(1) To interfere with, restrain, or coerce employees in exercise of their rights under Section 7 (to join or assist a labor organization or to refrain). *8(a)(2)* To dominate or interfere with the formation or administration of a labor organization or contribute financial or other support to it. *8(a)(3)* By discrimination in regard to hire or tenure of employment or any term or condition of employment to encourage or discourage membership in any labor organization. *8(a)(4)* To discharge or otherwise discriminate against employees because they have given testimony under the Act. *8(a)(5)* To refuse to bargain collectively with representatives of its employees.	*8(b)(1)(A)* To restrain or coerce employees in exercise of their rights under Section 7 (to join or assist a labor organization or to refrain). *8(b)(1)(B)* To restrain or coerce an employer in the selection of its representatives for collective bargaining or adjustment of grievances. *8(b)(2)* To cause or attempt to cause an employer to discriminate against an employee. *8(b)(3)* To refuse to bargain collectively with an employer. *8(b)(5)* To require or employees the payment of excessive or discriminatory fees for membership. *8(b)(6)* To cause or attempt to cause an employer to pay or agree to pay money or other thing of value for services which are not performed or not to be performed.	*8(b)(4)(i)* To engage in, or induce or encourage any individual employed by any person engaged in comm. erce or in an industry affecting commerce to engage in, a strike, work stoppage, or boycott, or *(ii)* to threaten, coerce, or restrain any person engaged in commerce or in an industry affecting commerce, where in either case an object is: *(A)* To force or require any employer or self-employed person to join any labor or employer organization or to enter into any agreement prohibited by Section 8(e) *(B)* To force or require any person to cease using, selling, handling, transporting, or otherwise dealing in the products of any other producer, processor, or manufacturer, or to cease doing business with any other person, or force or require any other employer to recognize or bargain with a labor organization as the representative of its employees unless such labor organization has been so certified. *(C)* To force or require any employer to recognize or bargain with a particular labor organization as the representative of its employees if another labor organization has been certified as the representative.	*8(b)(4)(i)* To engage in, or induce or encourage any individual employed by any person engaged in commerce or in an industry affecting commerce to engage in, a strike, work stoppage, or boycott, or *(ii)* to threaten, coerce, or restrain any person engaged in commerce or in an industry affecting commerce, where in either case an object is: *(D)* To force or require any employer to assign particular work to employees in a particular labor organization or in a particular trade, craft, or class rather than to employees in another trade, craft, or class, unless such employer is failing to conform to an appropriate Board order or certification. ***Section of the Act*** ***CG*** 8(g) To strike, picket, or otherwise concertedly refuse to work at any health care institution without notifying the institution and the Federal Mediation and Conciliation Service in writing 10 days prior to such action.
1. Charges of Unfair Labor Practices (C Cases)		**2. Petitions for Certification or Decertification of Representatives (R Cases)**	**3. Other Petitions**
Charge Against Labor Organization	**Charge Against Labor Organization and Employer**	**By or on Behalf of Employees**	**By or on Behalf of Employees**
Section of the Act ***CP***	***Section of the Act*** ***CE***	***Section of the Act*** ***RC***	***Section of the Act*** ***UD***
8(b)(7) To picket, or cause or threaten the picketing of, any employer where an object is to force or require an employer to recognize or bargain	*8(e)* To enter into any contract or agreement (any labor organization and any employer) whereby such employer ceases or refrains or	*9(c)(1)(A)(i)* Alleging that a substantial number of employees wish to be represented for collective bargaining and their employer declines to recognize their representative.*	*9(e)(1)* Alleging the employees (30 percent or more of an appropriate unit) wish to rescind an existing union security agreement.

1. Charges of Unfair Labor Practices (C Cases)		2. Petitions for Certification or Decertification of Representatives (R Cases)	3. Other Petitions
Charge Against Labor Organization	**Charge Against Labor Organization and Employer**	**By or on Behalf of Employees**	**By a Labor Organization or an Employer**
Section of the Act ***CP***	***Section of the Act*** ***CE***	***Section of the Act*** ***RD***	***Board Rules*** ***UC***
with a labor organization as the representative of its employees, or to force or require the employees of an employer to select such labor organization as their collective-bargaining representative, unless such labor organization is currently certified as the representative of such employees: *(A)* where the employer has lawfully recognized any other labor organization and a question concerning representation may not appropriately be raised under Section 9(c). (B) where within the preceding 12 months a valid election under Section 9(c) has been conducted, or *(C)* where picketing has been conducted without a petition under Section 9(c) being filed within a reasonable period of time not to exceed 30 days from the commencement of the picketing; except where the picketing is for the purpose of truthfully advising the public (including consumers) that an employer does not employ members of, or have a contract with, a labor organization, and it does not have an effect of interference with deliveries or services.	agrees to cease or refrain from handling or dealing in any product of any other employer, or to cease doing business with any other person.	*9(c)(1)(A)(ii)* Alleging that a substantial number of employees assert that the certified or currently recognized bargaining representative is no longer their representative.*	*Subpart C* Seeking clarification of an existing bargaining unit.
		By an Employer	***Board Rules*** ***AC***
		Section of the Act ***RM***	
		9(c)(1)(B) Alleging that one or more claims for recognition as exclusive bargaining representative have been received by the employer.*	*Subpart C* Seeking amendment of an outstanding certification of bargaining representative.
		*If an 8(b)(7) charge has been filed involving the same employer, these statements in RC, RD, and RM petitions are not required.	

Charges filed with the National Labor Relations Board are letter-coded and numbered. Unfair labor practice charges are classified as “C” cases and petitions for certification or decertification or representatives as “R” cases. This chart indicates the letter codes used for “C” cases, at left, and “R” cases, above, and also presents a summary of each section involved.

Required Subjects of Bargaining

The duty to bargain covers all matters concerning rates of pay, wages, hours of employment, or other conditions of employment.

These are called "mandatory" subjects of bargaining about which the employer, as well as the employees' representative, must bargain in good faith, although the law does not require "either party to agree to a proposal or require the making of a concession."

In addition to wages and hours of work, these mandatory subjects of bargaining include but are not limited to such matters as pensions for present employees, bonuses, group insurance, grievance procedures, safety practices, seniority, procedures for discharge, layoff, recall, or discipline, and union security.

Certain managerial decisions such as subcontracting, relocation, and other operational changes may not be mandatory subjects of bargaining, even though they affect employees' job security and working conditions. The issue of whether these decisions are mandatory subjects of bargaining depends on the employer's reasons for taking action. Even if the employer is not required to bargain about the decision itself, it must bargain about the decision's effects on unit employees. On "nonmandatory" subjects, that is, matters that are lawful but not related to "wages, hours, and other conditions of employment," the parties are free to bargain and to agree, but neither party may insist on bargaining on such subjects over the objection of the other party.

Duty to Bargain Defined

An employer who is required to bargain under this section must, as stated in Section 8(d), "meet at reasonable times and confer in good faith with respect to wages, hours, and other terms and conditions of employment, or the negotiation of an agreement or any question arising thereunder, and the execution of a written contract incorporating any agreement reached if requested by either party."

What Constitutes a Violation of Section 8(a)(5)

An employer, therefore, will be found to have violated Section 8(a)(5) if its conduct in bargaining, viewed in its entirety, indicates that the employer did not negotiate with a good faith intention to reach agreement. However, the employer's good faith is not at issue when its conduct constitutes an out-and-out refusal to bargain on a mandatory subject. For example, it is a violation for an employer, regardless of good faith, to refuse to bargain about a subject that it believes is not a mandatory subject of bargaining, when in fact it is.

Duty to Meet and Confer

The duty of an employer to meet and confer with the representative of its employees includes the duty to deal with whoever is designated by the employees' representative to carry on negotiations. An employer may not dictate to a union its selection of agents or representatives and the employer must, in general, recognize the designated agent.

Duty to Supply Information

The employer's duty to bargain includes the duty to supply, on request, information that is "relevant and necessary" to allow the employees' representative to bargain intelligently and effectively with respect to wages, hours, and other conditions of employment.

Multiemployer Bargaining

When there is a history of bargaining between a union and a number of employers acting jointly, the employees who are thus represented constitute a multiemployer bargaining unit. Once such a unit has been established, any of the participating employers—or the union—may retire from this multi-employer bargaining relationship only by mutual assent or by a timely submitted withdrawal. Withdrawal is considered timely if unequivocal notice of the withdrawal is given near the termination of a collective-bargaining agreement but before bargaining begins on the next agreement.

Duty to Refrain from Unilateral Action

Finally, the duty of an employer to bargain includes the duty to refrain from unilateral action, that is, taking action on its own with respect to matters concerning which it is required to bargain, and from making changes in terms and conditions of employment without consulting the employees' representative.

Duty of Successor Employers

An employer who purchases or otherwise acquires the operations of another may be obligated to recognize and bargain with the union that represented the employees before the business was transferred. In general, these bargaining obligations exist—and the purchaser is termed a successor employer—when there is a substantial continuity in the employing enterprise despite the sale and transfer of the business. Whether the purchaser is a successor employer is dependent on several factors, including the number of employees taken over by the purchasing employer, the similarity in operations and product of the two employers, the manner in which the purchaser integrates the purchased operations into its other operations, and the character of the bargaining relationship and agreement between the union and the original employer.

Examples of violations of Section 8(a)(5) are as follows:

- Refusing to meet with the employees' representative because the employees are out on strike.
- Insisting, until bargaining negotiations break down, on a contract provision that all employees will be polled by secret ballot before the union calls a strike.
- Refusing to supply the employees' representative with cost and other data concerning a group insurance plan covering the employees.
- Announcing a wage increase without consulting the employees' representative.
- Failing to bargain about the effects of a decision to close one of the employer's plants.

Section 8(e)—Entering a Hot Cargo Agreement

Section 8(e), added to the Act in 1959, makes it an unfair labor practice for any labor organization and any employer to enter into what is commonly called a "hot cargo" or "hot goods" agreement. It may also limit the restrict-ions that can be placed on the subcontracting of work by an employer. The typical hot cargo or hot goods clause in use before the 1959 amendment to the Act provided that employees would not be required by their employer to handle or work on goods or materials going to, or coming from, an employer designated by the union as "unfair." Such goods were said to be "hot cargo" thereby giving Section 8(e) its popular name. These clauses were most common in the construction and trucking industries.

What Is Prohibited

Section 8(e) forbids an employer and a labor organization to make an agreement whereby the employer agrees to stop doing business with any other employer and declares void and unenforceable any such agreement that is made. It should be noted that a strike or picketing, or any other union action, or the threat of it, to force an employer to agree to a hot cargo provision, or to force it to act in accordance with such a clause, has been held by the Board to be a violation of Section 8(b)(4). Exceptions are allowed in the construction and garment industries, and a union may seek, by contract, to keep within a bargaining unit work that is being done by the employees in the unit or to secure work that is "fairly claimable" in that unit.

Exceptions for Construction and Garment Industries

In the construction industry a union and an employer in the industry may agree to a provision that restricts the contracting or subcontracting of work to be done at the construction site. Such a clause contained in the agreement between the employer and the union typically provides that if work is subcontracted by the employer it must go to an employer who has an agree-ment with the union. A union in the construction industry may engage in a strike and picketing to obtain, but not to enforce, contractual restrictions of this nature. Similarly, in the garment industry an employer and a union can agree that work to be done on the goods or on the premises of a jobber or manufacturer, or work that is part of "an integrated process of production in the apparel and closing industry," can be subcontracted only to an employer who has an agreement with the union. This exception, unlike the previous one concerning the construction industry, allows a labor organization in the garment industry, not only to seek to obtain, but also to enforce, such a restriction on subcontracting by striking, picketing, or other lawful actions.

UNFAIR LABOR PRACTICES OF LABOR ORGANIZATIONS

Section 8(b)(1)(A)—Restraint and Coercion of Employees

Section 8(b)(1)(A) forbids a labor organization or its agents "to restrain or coerce employees in the exercise of the rights guaranteed in section 7." The section also provides that it is not intended to "impair the rights of a labor organization to prescribe its own rules" concerning membership in the labor organization.

Section 8(b)(1)(A) Compared with Section 8(a)(1)

Like Section 8(a)(1) , Section 8(b)(1)(A) is violated by conduct that independently restrains or coerces employees in the exercise of their Section 7 rights regardless of whether the conduct also violates other provisions of Section 8(b). But whereas employer violations of

Section 8(a)(2), (3), (4), and (5) are held to be violations of Section 8(a)(1) too, the Board has held, based on the intent of Congress when Section 8(b)(1)(A) was written, that violation of Section 8(b)(2) through (7) do not also "derivatively" violate Section 8(b)(1)(A). The Board does hold, however, that making or enforcing illegal union-security agreements or hiring agreements that condition employment on union membership not only violates Section 8(b)(2) but also Section 8(b)(1)(A), because such action restrains or coerces employees in their Section 7 rights.

Union conduct that is reasonably calculated to restrain or coerce employees in their Section 7 rights violates Section 8(b)(1)(A) whether it succeeds in actually restraining or coercing employees.

A union may violate Section 8(b)(1)(A) by coercive conduct of its officers or agents, of pickets on a picket line endorsed by the union, or of strikers who engage in coercion in the presence of union representatives who do not repudiate the conduct.

What Violates Section 8(b)(1)(A)

Unlawful coercion may consist of acts specifically directed at an employee such as physical assaults, threats of violence, and threats to affect an employee's job status. Coercion also includes other forms of pressure against employees such as acts of a union while representing employees as their exclusive bargaining agent (see Section 9(a), p. 8). A union that is a statutory bargaining representative owes a duty of fair representation to all the employees it represents. It may exercise a wide range of reasonable discretion in carrying out the representative function, but it violates Section 8(b)(1)(A) if, while acting as the employees' statutory bargaining representative, it takes or withholds action in connection with their employment because of their union activities or for any irrelevant or arbitrary reason such as an employee's race or sex.

Section 8(b)(1)(A) recognizes the right of unions to establish and enforce rules of membership and to control their internal affairs. This right is limited to union rules and discipline that affect the rights of employees as union members and that are not enforced by action affecting an employee's employment. Also, rules to be protected must be aimed at matters of legitimate concern to unions such as the encouragement of members to support a lawful strike or participation in union meetings. Rules that conflict with public policy, such as rules that limit a member's right to file unfair labor practice charges, are not protected. And a union may not fine a member for filing a decertification petition although it may expel that individual for doing so. A rule that prohibits a member from resigning from the union is unlawful. The union may not fine a former member for any protected conduct engaged in after he or she resigns.

Examples of Violations of Section 8(b)(1)(A)

Examples of restraint or coercion that violate Section 8(b)(1)(A) when done by a union or its agents include the following:

- Mass picketing in such numbers that nonstriking employees are physically barred from entering the plant.
- Acts of force or violence on the picket line, or in connection with a strike.
- Threats to do bodily injury to nonstriking employees.

- Threats to employees that they will lose their jobs unless they support the union's activities.
- Statement to employees who oppose the union that the employees will lose their jobs if the union wins a majority in the plant.
- Entering into an agreement with an employer that recognizes the union as exclusive bargaining representative when it has not been chosen by a majority of the employees.
- Fining or expelling members for crossing a picket line that is unlawful under the Act or that violates a no-strike agreement.
- Fining employees for crossing a picket line after they resigned from the union.
- Fining or expelling members for filing unfair labor practice charges with the Board or for participating in an investigation conducted by the Board.

The following are examples of restraint or coercion that violate Section 8(b)(1)(A) when done by a union that is the exclusive bargaining representative:

- Refusing to process a grievance in retaliation against an employee's criticism of union officers.
- Maintaining a seniority arrangement with an employer under which seniority is based on the employee's prior representation by the union elsewhere.
- Rejecting an application for referral to a job in a unit represented by the union based on the applicant's race or union activities.

Section 8(b)(1)(B)—Restraint and Coercion of Employers

Section 8(b)(1)(B) prohibits a labor organization from restraining or coercing an employer in the selection of a bargaining representative. The prohibition applies regardless of whether the labor organization is the majority representative of the employees in the bargaining unit. The prohibition extends to coercion applied by a union to a union member who is a representative of the employer in the adjustment of grievances. This section is violated by such conduct as the following:

Examples of Violations of Section 8(b)(1)(B)

- Insisting on meeting only with a company's owners and refusing to meet with the attorney the company has engaged to represent the company in contract negotiations, and threatening to strike to force the company to accept its demands.
- Striking members of an employer association that bargains with the union as the representative of the employers to compel the struck employers to sign individual contracts with the union.
- Insisting during contract negotiations that the employer agree to accept working conditions that will be established by a bargaining group to which it does not belong.
- Fining or expelling supervisors for the way they apply the bargaining contract while carrying out their supervisory functions or for crossing a picket line during a strike to perform their supervisory duties.

Section 8(b)(2)—Causing or Attempting to Cause Discrimination

Section 8(b)(2) makes it an unfair labor practice for a labor organization to cause an employer to discriminate against an employee in violation of Section 8(a)(3). As discussed earlier, Section 8(a)(3) prohibits an employer from discriminating against an employee in regard to wages, hours, and other conditions of employment for the purpose of encouraging or discouraging membership in a labor organization. It does allow, however, the making of union-security agreements under certain specified conditions. (See pp. 2–3, above.)

What Violates Section 8(b)(2)

A union violates Section 8(b)(2), for example, by demanding that an employer discriminate against employees because of their failure to make certain otherwise lawful payments to the union when there is no valid union-security agreement in effect. (See pp. 2–3, above.) The section can also be violated by agreements or arrangements with employers that unlawfully condition employment or job benefits on union membership, on the performance of union membership obligations, or on arbitrary grounds. Union conduct affecting an employee's employment in a way that is contrary to provisions of the bargaining contract may likewise be violative of the section. But union action that causes detriment to an individual employee in that individual's employment does not violate Section 8(b)(2) if it is consistent with nondiscriminatory provisions of a bargaining contract negotiated for the benefit of the total bargaining unit or if it is for some other legitimate purpose.

To find that a union caused an employer to discriminate, it is not necessary to show that any express demand was spoken. A union's conduct, accompanied by statements advising or suggesting that action is expected of an employer, may be enough to find a violation of this section if the union's action can be shown to be a causal factor in the employer's discrimination.

Illegal Hiring Hall Agreements and Practices

Contracts or informal arrangements with a union under which an employer gives preferential treatment to union members are violations of Section 8(b)(2). It is not unlawful for an employer and a union to enter into an agreement whereby the employer agrees to hire new employees exclusively through the union hiring hall so long as there is neither a provision in the agreement nor a practice in effect that discriminates against nonunion members in favor of union members or otherwise discriminates on the basis of union membership obligations. Both the agreement and the actual operation of the hiring hall must be nondiscriminatory: referrals must be made without reference to union membership or irrelevant or arbitrary considerations such as race. Referral standards or procedures, even if nondiscriminatory on their face, are unlawful when they continue previously discriminatory conditions of referral. However, a union may, in setting referral standards, consider legitimate aims such as sharing available work and easing the impact of local unemployment. It may also charge referral fees if the amount of the fee is reasonably related to the cost of operating the referral service.

Illegal Union-Security Agreements

Union-security agreements that require employees to make certain lawfully required payments to the union after they are hired are permitted by this section as previously discussed. Union-security agreements that do not meet all the requirements listed on page 2 will not support a discharge. A union that attempts to force an employer to enter into an illegal union-security agreement, or that enters into and keeps in effect such an agreement, violates Section 8(b)(2), as does a union that attempts to enforce such an illegal agreement by bringing about an employee's discharge. Even when a union-security provision of a bargaining contract meets all statutory requirements so that it is permitted by Section 8(a)(3), a union may not lawfully require the discharge of employees under the provision unless the employees had been informed of the union-security agreement and of their specific obligation under it. And a union violates Section 8(b)(2) if it tries to use the union-security provisions of a contract to collect payments other than those that lawfully may be required. (See pp. 2–3, above.) Assessments, fines, and penalties may not be enforced by application of a union-security agreement.

Examples of violations of Section 8(b)(2) are:

- Causing an employer to discharge employees because they circulated a petition urging a change in the union's method of selecting shop stewards.
- Causing an employer to discharge employees because they made speeches against a contract proposed by the union.
- Making a contract that requires an employer to hire only members of the union or employees "satisfactory" to the union.
- Causing an employer to reduce employees' seniority because they engaged in antiunion acts.
- Refusing referral or giving preference on the basis of race or union activities in making job referrals to units represented by the union.
- Seeking the discharge of an employee under a union-security agreement for failure to pay a fine levied by the union.

Section 8(b)(3)—Refusal to Bargain in Good Faith

Section 8(b)(3) makes it illegal for a labor organization to refuse to bargain in good faith with an employer about wages, hours, and other conditions of employment if it is the representative of that employer's employees. This section imposes on labor organizations the same duty to bargain in good faith that is imposed on employers by Section 8(a)(5). Both the labor organization and the employer are required to follow the procedure set out in Section 8(d) before terminating or changing an existing contract (see p. 6).

A labor organization that is the employees' representative must meet at reasonable times with the employer or his designated representative, must confer in good faith on matters pertaining to wages, hours, or other conditions of employment, or the negotiation of an agreement, or any question arising under an agreement, and must sign a written agreement if requested and if one is reached. The obligation does not require the labor organization or the employer to agree to a proposal by the other party or make a concession to the other party, but it does require bargaining with an open mind in an attempt to reach agreement. So, while a union may try in contract negotiations to establish wages and benefits comparable to those contained in other bargaining agreements in the area, it may not insist on such terms without giving the employer an opportunity to bargain about the terms. Likewise, a union may seek *voluntary* bargaining on nonmandatory subjects of bargaining (p. 20), such as a provision for an industry promotion fund, but may not *insist* on bargaining about such subjects or condition execution of a contract on the reaching of agreement on a nonmandatory subject.

When a union has been bargaining with a group of employers in a multiemployer bargaining unit, it may withdraw at any time from bargaining on that basis and bargain with one of the employers individually if the individual employer and the multiemployer group agree to the union's withdrawal. And even in the absence of employer consent, a union may withdraw from multiemployer bargaining by giving the employers unequivocal notice of its withdrawal near the expiration of the agreement but before bargaining on a new contract has begun.

Section 8(b)(3) not only requires that a union representative bargain in good faith with employers, but also requires that the union carry out its bargaining duty fairly with respect to the employees it represents. A union, therefore, violates Section 8(b)(3) if it negotiates a contract that conflicts with that duty, such as a contract with racially discriminatory provisions, or if it refuses to handle grievances under the contract for irrelevant or arbitrary reasons.

Examples of Violations of Section 8(b)(3)

Section 8(b)(3) is violated by any of the following:

- Insisting on the inclusion of illegal provisions in a contract, such as a closed shop or a discriminatory hiring hall.
- Refusing to negotiate on a proposal for a written contract.
- Striking against an employer who has bargained, and continues to bargain, on a multiemployer basis to compel it to bargain separately.
- Refusing to meet with the attorney designated by the employer as its representative in negotiations.
- Terminating an existing contract and striking for a new one without notifying the employer, the Federal Mediation and Conciliation Service, and the state mediation service, if any.
- Conditioning the execution of an agreement on inclusion of a nonmandatory provision such as a performance bond.
- Refusing to process a grievance because of the race, sex, or union activities of an employee for whom the union is the statutory bargaining representative.

Section 8(b)(4)—Prohibited Strikes and Boycotts

Section 8(b)(4) prohibits a labor organization from engaging in strikes or boycotts or taking other specified actions to accomplish certain purposes or "objects" as they are called in the Act. The proscribed action is listed in clauses (i) and (ii), the objects are described in subparagraphs (A) through (D). A union commits an unfair labor practice if it takes any of the kinds of action listed in clauses (i) and (ii) as a means of accomplishing any of the objects listed in the four subparagraphs.

Proscribed Action: Inducing or Encouraging a Strike Work Stoppage or Boycott

Clause (i) forbids a union to engage in a strike, or to induce or encourage a strike, work stoppage, or a refusal to perform services by "any individual employed by any person engaged in commerce or in an industry affecting commerce" for one of the objects listed in subparagraphs (A) through (D). The words "induce and encourage" are considered by the U. S. Supreme Court to be broad enough to include every form of influence or persuasion. For example, it has been held by the NLRB that a work stoppage on a picketed construction project was "induced" by a union through its business agents who, when they learned about the picketing, told the job stewards that they (the business agents) would not work behind the picket line. It was considered that this advice not only induced the stewards to leave the job, but caused them to pass the information on to their fellow employees, and that such conduct informed the other employees that they were expected not to work behind the picket line. The world "person" is defined in Section 2(1) as including "one or more individuals, labor organizations, partnerships, associations, corp-orations," and other legal persons. As so defined, the word "person" is broader than the word "employer." For example, a railroad company, although covered by the Railway Labor Act, is excluded from the definition of "employer" in the National Labor Relations Act and, therefore, neither the railroad company nor its employees are covered by the National Labor Relations Act. But a railroad company is a "person engaged in commerce" as defined above and, therefore, a labor organization is forbidden to "induce or encourage" individuals employed by a railroad company to engage in a strike, work stoppage, or boycott for any of the objects in subparagraphs (A) through (D).

Proscribed Action: Threats, Coercion, and Restraint

Clause (ii) makes it an unfair labor practice for a union to "threaten, coerce, or restrain any person engaged in commerce or in an industry affecting commerce" for any of the proscribed objects. Even though no direct threat is voiced by the union, there may nevertheless be coercion and restraint that violates this clause. For example, when a union picketed a construction job to bring about the removal of a nonunion subcontractor in violation of Section 8(b)(4)(B), the picketing induced employees of several other subcontractors to stop work. When the general contractor asked what could be done to stop the picketing, the union's business agent replied that the picketing would stop only if the nonunion subcontractor were removed from the job. The NLRB held this to be "coercion and restraint" within the meaning of clause (ii).

Subparagraph (A)—Prohibited Object: Compelling Membership in an Employer or Labor Organization or Compelling a Hot Cargo Agreement

Section 8(b)(4)(A) prohibits unions from engaging in clause (i) or (ii) action to compel an employer or self-employed person to join any labor or employer organization or to force an employer to enter a hot cargo agreement prohibited by Section 8(e). Examples of violations of this section are:

Examples of Violations of Section 8(b)(4)(A)

- In an attempt to compel a beer distributor to join a union, the union prevents the distributor from obtaining beer at a brewery by inducing the brewery's employees to refuse to fill the distributor's orders.
- In an attempt to secure for its members certain stevedoring work required at an employer's unloading operation, the union pickets to force the employer to join an employer association with which the union has a contract.
- A union pickets an employer (one not in the construction and garment industries), or threatens to picket it, to compel that employer to enter into an agreement whereby the employer will only do business with persons who have an agreement with a union.

Subparagraph (B)—Prohibited Object: Compelling Recognition of an Uncertified Union

Section 8(b)(4)(B) contains the Act's secondary boycott provision. A secondary boycott occurs if a union has a dispute with Company A and, in furtherance of that dispute, causes the employees of Company B to stop handling the products of Company A, or otherwise forces Company B to stop doing business with Company A. The dispute is with Company A, called the "primary" employer, the union's action is against Company B, called the "secondary" employer, hence the term "secondary boycott." In many cases the secondary employer is a customer or supplier of the primary employer with whom the union has the dispute. In general, the Act prohibits both the secondary boycott and the threat of it. Examples of prohibited secondary boycotts are:

Examples of Violations of Section 8(b)(4)(B)

- Picketing an employer to force it to stop doing business with another employer who has refused to recognize the union.
- Asking the employees of a plumbing contractor not to work on connecting up airconditioning equipment manufactured by a nonunion employer whom the union is attempting to organize.
- Urging employees of a building contractor not to install doors that were made by a manufacturer that is nonunion or that employs members of a rival union.
- Telling an employer that its plant will be picketed if that employer continues to do business with an employer the union has designated as "unfair."

The prohibitions of Section 8(b)(4)(B) do not protect a secondary employer from the incidental effects of union action that is taken directly against the primary employer. Thus, it is lawful for a union to urge employees of a secondary supplier at the primary employer's plant not to cross a picket line there. Section 8(b)(4)(B) also does not proscribe union action to prevent an employer from contracting out work customarily performed by its employees, even though an incidental effect of such conduct might be to compel that employer to cease doing business with the subcontractor.

When an Employer Is Not Protected from Secondary Strikes and Boycotts

In order to be protected against the union action that is prohibited under this subparagraph, the secondary employer has to be a neutral as concerns the dispute between the union and the primary employer. For secondary boycott purposes an employer is considered an "ally" of the primary employer and, therefore, not protected from union action in certain situations. One is based on the ownership and operational relationship between the primary and secondary employers. Here, a number of factors are considered, particularly the following: Are the primary and secondary employers owned and controlled by the same person or persons? Are they engaged in "closely integrated operations?" May they be treated as a single employer under the Act? Another test of the "ally" relationship is based on the conduct of the secondary employer. If an employer, despite its claim of neutrality in the dispute, acts in a way that indicates that it has abandoned its "neutral" position, the employer opens itself up to primary action by the union. An example of this would be an employer who, claiming to be a neutral, enters into an arrangement with a struck employer whereby it accepts and performs farmed. out work of that employer who would normally do the work itself, but who cannot perform the work because its plant is closed by a strike.

When a Union May Picket an Employer Who Shares a Site with Another Employer

When employees of a primary employer and those of a secondary employer work on the same premises, a special situation is involved and the usual rules do not apply. A typical example of the shared site or "common situs" situation is when a subcontractor with whom a union has a dispute is engaged at work on a construction site alongside other subcontractors with whom the union has no dispute. Picketing at a common situs is permissible if directed solely against the primary employer. But it is prohibited if directed against secondary employers regularly engaged at that site. To assist in determining whether picketing at a common situs is restricted to the primary employer and therefore permissible, or directed at a secondary employer and therefore violative of the statute, the NLRB and the courts have suggested various guidelines for evaluating the object of the picketing, including the following.

Subject to the qualification noted below, the picketing would appear to be primary picketing if the picketing is:

1. Limited to times when the employees of the primary employer are working on the premises.
2. Limited to times when the primary employer is carrying on its normal business there.
3. Confined to places reasonably close to where the employees of the primary employer are working.
4. Conducted so that the picket signs, the banners, and the conduct of the pickets indicate clearly that the dispute is with the primary employer and not with the secondary employer.

These guidelines are known as the *Moore Dry Dock* standards from the case in which they were first formulated by the NLRB. However, the NLRB has held that picketing at a common situs may be unlawful notwithstanding compliance with the *Moore Dry Dock* standards if a union's statements or actions otherwise indicate that the picketing has an unlawful objective.

Picketing Contractors' Gates

In some situations a company may set aside, or reserve, a certain plant gate, or entrance to its premises, for the exclusive use of a contractor. If a union has a labor dispute with the company and pickets the company's premises, including the gate so reserved, the union may be held to have violated Section 8(b)(4)(B). The U.S. Supreme Court has stated the circumstances under which such a violation may be found as follows:

> There must be a separate gate, marked and set apart from other gates; the work done by the employees who use the gate must be unrelated to the normal operations of the employer, and the work must be of a kind that would not, if done when the plant were engaged in its regular operations, necessitate curtailing those operations.

However, if the reserved gate is used by employees of both the company and the contractor, the picketing would be considered primary and not a violation of Section 8(b)(4)(B).

Subparagraph (B)—Prohibited Object: Compelling Recognition of an Uncertified Union

Section 8(b)(4)(B) also prohibits secondary action to compel an employer to recognize or bargain with a union that is not the certified representative of its employees. If a union takes action described in clause (i) or (ii) against a secondary employer, and the union's object is recognition by the primary employer, the union commits an unfair labor practice under this section. To establish that the union has an object of recognition, a specific demand by the union for recognition need not be shown; a demand for a contract, which implies recognition or at least bargaining, is enough to establish an 8(b)(4)(B) object.

Subparagraph (C)—Prohibited Object: Compelling Recognition of a Union if Another Union Has Been Certified

Section 8(b)(4)(C) forbids a labor organization from using clause (i) or (ii) conduct to force an employer to recognize or bargain with a labor organization other than the one that is currently certified as the representative of its employees. Section 8(b)(4)(C) has been held not to apply when the picketing union is merely protesting working conditions that are substandard for the area.

Subparagraph (D)—Prohibited Object: Compelling Assignment of Certain Work to Certain Employees

Section 8(b)(4)(D) forbids a labor organization from engaging in action described in clauses (i) and (ii) for the purpose of forcing any employer to assign certain work to "employees in a particular labor organization or in a particular trade, craft, or class rather than to employees in another labor organization or in another trade, craft, or class."

The Act sets up a special procedure for handling disputes over work assignments that will be discussed later in this material (see p. 38).

Publicity Such as Handbilling Allowed by Section 8(b)(4)

The final provision in Section 8(b)(4) provides that nothing in Section 8(b)(4) shall be construed "to prohibit publicity, other than picketing, for the purpose of truthfully advising the public, including consumers and members of a labor organization, that a product or products are produced by an employer with whom the labor organization has a primary dispute and are distributed by another employer."

Such publicity is not protected if it has "an effect of inducing any individual employed by any persons other than the primary employer" to refuse to handle any goods or not to perform services.

The Supreme Court has held that this provision permitted a union to distribute handbills at the stores of neutral food chains asking the public not to buy certain items distributed by a wholesaler with whom the union had a primary dispute.

Moreover, it has also held that peaceful picketing at the stores of a neutral food chain to persuade customers not to buy the products of a struck employer when they traded in these stores was not prohibited by Section 8(b)(4).

Section 8(b)(5)—Excessive or Discriminatory Membership Fees

Section 8(b)(5) makes it illegal for a union to charge employees who are covered by an authorized union-security agreement a membership fee "in an amount which the Board finds excessive or discriminatory under all the circumstances."

The section also provides that the Board in making its finding must consider among other factors "the practices and customs of labor organizations in the particular industry, and the wages currently paid to the employees affected."

Examples of Violations of Section 8(b)(5)

Examples of violations of this section include:

- Charging old employees who do not join the union until after a union-security agreement goes into effect an initiation fee of $15 while charging new employees only $5.
- Increasing the initiation fee from $75 to $250 and thus charging new members an amount equal to about 4 weeks' wages when other unions in the area charge a fee equal to about one-half the employee's first week's pay.

Section 8(b)(6)—"Featherbedding."

Section 8(b)(6) forbids a labor organization "to cause or attempt to cause an employer to pay or deliver or agree to pay or deliver any money or other thing of value, in the nature of an exaction, for services which are not performed or not to be performed."

Section 8(b)(7)—Organizational and Recognitional Picketing by Noncertified Unions

Section 8(b)(7) prohibits a labor organization that is not currently certified as the employees' representative from picketing or threatening to picket with an object of obtaining recognition by the employer (recognitional picketing) or acceptance by his employees as their representative (organizational picketing). The object of picketing is ascertained from all the surrounding facts including the message on the picket signs and any communications between the union and the employer. "Recognitional" picketing as used in Section 8(b)(7) refers to picketing to obtain an employer's initial recognition of the union as bargaining representative of its employees or to force the employer, without formal recognition of the union, to maintain a specific and detailed set of working conditions. It does not include picketing by an incumbent union for continued recognition or for a new contract. Neither does it include picketing that seeks to prevent the employer from undermining area standards of working conditions by operating at less than the labor costs which prevail under bargaining contracts in the area.

Recognitional and organizational picketing are prohibited in three specific instances.

A. When the employer has lawfully recognized another union and a representation election would be barred by either the provisions of the Act or the Board's Rules, as in the case of a valid contract between the employer and the other union (8(b)(7)(A). (A union is considered lawfully recognized when the employer's recognition of the union cannot be attacked under the unfair labor practice provisions of Section 8 of the Act.)
B. When a valid NLRB representation election has been held within the previous 12 months (8(b)(7)(8)).
C. When a representation petition is not filed "within a reasonable period of time not to exceed thirty days from the commencement of such picketing" (8(b)(7)(C)).

Publicity Picketing

Subparagraph (C) is subject to an exception, called a proviso, which permits picketing "for the purpose of truthfully advising the public (including consumers)" that an employer does not employ union members or have a contract with a labor organization. However, such picketing loses the protection of this proviso if it has a substantial effect on the employer's business because it induces "any individual employed by any other person" to refuse to pick up or deliver goods or to perform other services.

Expedited Elections under Section 8(b)(7)(C)

If an 8(b)(7)(C) charge is filed against the picketing union and a representation petition is filed within a reasonable time after the picketing starts, subparagraph (C) provides for an election to be held forthwith. This election requires neither a hearing nor a showing of interest among the employees. As a consequence the election can be held and the results obtained faster than in a regular election under Section 9(c), and for this reason it is called an "expedited" election. Petitions filed more than a reasonable time after picketing begins and petitions filed during picketing protected by the 8(b)(7)(C) proviso, discussed above, are processed under normal election procedures and the election will not be expedited. The reasonable period in which to file a petition cannot exceed 30 days and may be shorter, when, for instance, picketing is accompanied by violence.

Examples of violations of Section 8(b)(7) are as follows:

- Picketing by a union for organizational purposes shortly after the employer has entered a lawful contract with another union (8(b)(7)(A)).

- Picketing by a union for organizational purposes within 12 months after a valid NLRB election in which a majority of the employees in the unit voted to have no union (8(b)(7)(B)).
- Picketing by a union for recognition continuing for more than 30 days without the filing of a representation petition wherein the picketing stops all deliveries by employees of an other employer (8(b)(7)(C)).

Section 8(e)—Entering a Hot Cargo Agreement

Section 8(e) makes it an unfair labor practice for an employer or a labor organization to enter a hot cargo agreement. This section applies equally to unions and to employers. The discussion of this section as an unfair labor practice of employers has been treated as a discussion of an unfair labor practice of unions as well. (See pp. 21 and 22.)

Section 8(g)—Striking or Picketing a Health Care Institution without Notice

Section 8(g) prohibits a labor organization from engaging in a strike, picketing, or other concerted refusal to work at any health care institution without first giving at least 10 days' notice in writing to the institution and the Federal Mediation and Conciliation Service.

How the Act Is Enforced

The rights of employees declared by Congress in the National Labor Relations Act are not self-enforcing. To ensure that employees may exercise these rights, and to protect them and the public from unfair labor practices, Congress established the NLRB to administer and enforce the Act.

Organization of the NLRB

The Board, the General Counsel, the Regional Offices

The NLRB includes the Board, which is composed of five members with their respective staffs, the General Counsel and staff, and the Regional, Subregional, and Resident Offices. The General Counsel has final and independent authority on behalf of the Board, in respect to the investigation of charges and issuance of complaints. Members of the Board are appointed by the President, with consent of the Senate, for 5-year terms. The General Counsel is also appointed by the President, with consent of the Senate, for a 4-year term. Offices of the Board and the General Counsel are in Washington, D.C. To assist in administering and enforcing the law, the NLRB has established 33 regional and a number of other field offices. These offices, located in major cities in various States and Puerto Rico, are under the general supervision of the General Counsel.

Functions of the NLRB

The Agency has two main functions: to conduct representation elections and certify the results, and to prevent employers and unions from engaging in unfair labor practices. In both kinds of cases the processes of the NLRB are begun only when requested. Requests for such action must be made in writing on forms provided by the NLRB and filed with the proper Regional Office. The form used to request an election is called a "petition," and the form for unfair labor practices is called a "charge." The filing of a petition or a charge sets in motion the machinery of the NLRB under the Act. Before discussing the machinery established by the Act, it would be well to understand the nature and extent of the authority of the NLRB.

Authority of the NLRB

Enterprises Whose Operations Affect Commerce

The NLRB gets its authority from Congress by way of the National Labor Relations Act. The power of Congress to regulate labor-management relations is limited by the commerce clause of the United States Constitution. Although it can declare generally what the rights of employee are or should be, Congress can make its declaration of rights effective only in respect to enterprises whose operations "affect commerce" and labor disputes that "affect commerce." The NLRB, therefore, can direct elect ions and certify the results only in the case of an employer whose operations affect commerce. Similarly, it can act to prevent unfair labor practices only in cases involving labor disputes that affect, or would affect, commerce.

What Is Commerce

"Commerce" includes trade, traffic, transportation, or communication within the District of Columbia or any Territory of the United States; or between any State or Territory and any other State, Territory, or the District of Columbia; or between two points in the same State, but through any other State, Territory, the District of Columbia, or a foreign country. Examples of enterprises engaged in commerce are:

- A manufacturing company in California that sells and ships its product to buyers in Oregon.
- A company in Georgia that buys supplies in Louisiana.
- A trucking company that transports goods from one point in New York State through Pennsylvania to another point in New York State.
- A radio station in Minnesota that has listeners in Wisconsin.

When the Operations of an Employer Affect Commerce

Although a company may not have any direct dealings with enterprises in any other State, its operations may nevertheless affect commerce. The operations of a Massachusetts manufacturing company that sells all of its goods to Massachusetts wholesalers affect commerce if the wholesalers ship to buyers in other States. The effects of a labor dispute involving the Massachusetts manufacturing concern would be felt in other States and the labor dispute would, therefore, "affect" commerce. Using this test, it can be seen that the operations of almost any employer can be said to affect commerce. As a result, the authority of the NLRB could extend to all but purely local enterprises.

The scope of the commerce clause is limited, however, by the first amendment's prohibition against Congress' enacting laws restricting the free exercise of religion. Because of this potential conflict, and because Congress has not clearly expressed an intention that the Act cover lay faculty in church-operated schools, the Supreme Court has held that the Board may not assert jurisdiction over faculty members in such institutions.

The Board Does Not Act in All Cases Affecting Commerce

Although the National Labor Relations Board could exercise its powers to enforce the Act in all cases involving enterprises whose operations affect commerce, the Board does not act in all such cases. In its discretion it limits the exercise of its power to cases involving enterprises whose effect on commerce is substantial. The Board's requirements for exercising its power or jurisdiction are called "jurisdictional standards." These standards are based on the yearly amount of business done by the enterprise, or on the yearly amount of its sales or of its purchases. They are stated in terms of total dollar volume of business and are different for different kinds of enterprises. The Board's standards in effect on July 1, 1990, are as follows:

NLRB Jurisdictional Standards

1. *Nonretail business*: Direct sales of goods to consumers in other States, or indirect sales through others (called outflow), of at least $50,000 a year; or direct purchases of goods from suppliers in other States, or indirect purchases through others (called inflow), of at least $50,000 a year.
2. *Office buildings*: Total annual revenue of $100,000 of which $25,000 or more is derived from organizations that meet any of the standards except the indirect outflow and indirect inflow standards established for nonretail enterprises.
3. *Retail enterprises*: At least $500,000 total annual volume of business.
4. *Public utilities*: At least $250,000 total annual volume of business, or $50,000 direct or in direct outflow or inflow.
5. *Newspapers*: At least $200,000 total annual volume of business.
6. *Radio, telegraph, television, and telephone enterprises*: At least $100,000 total annual volume of business.
7. *Hotels, motels, and residential apartment houses*: At least $500,000 total annual volume of business.
8. *Privately operated health care institutions*: At least $250,000 total annual volume of business for hospitals; at least $100,000 for nursing homes, visiting nurses associations, and related facilities; at least $250,000 for all other types of private health care institutions defined in the 1974 amendments to the Act. The statutory definition includes: "any hospital, convalescent hospital, health maintenance organizations, health clinic, nursing home, extended care facility or other institution devoted to the care of the sick, infirm, or aged person." Public hospitals are excluded from NLRB jurisdiction by Section 2(2) of the Act.
9. *Transportation enterprise, links and channels of interstate commerce*: At least $50,000 total annual income from furnishing interstate passenger and freight transportation services; also performing services valued at $50,000 or more for

businesses which meet any of the jurisdictional standards except the indirect outflow and indirect inflow of standards established for nonretail enterprises.

10. *Transit systems*: At least $250,000 total annual volume of business.
11. *Taxicab companies*: At least $500,000 total annual volume of business.
12. *Associations*: These are regarded as a single employer in that the annual business of all association members is totaled to determine whether any of the standards apply.
13. *Enterprises in the Territories and the District of Columbia*: The jurisdictional standards apply in the Territories; all businesses In the District of Columbia come under NLRB jurisdiction.
14. *National defense*: Jurisdiction is asserted over all enterprises affecting commerce when their operations have a substantial impact on national defense, whether the enterprises satisfy any other standard.
15. *Private universities and colleges*: At least $1 million gross annual revenue from all sources (excluding contributions not available for operating expenses because of limitations imposed by the grantor).
16. *Symphony orchestras*: At least $1 million gross annual revenue from all sources (excluding contributions not available for operating expenses because of limitations imposed by the grantor).
17. *Law firms and legal assistance programs*: At least $250,000 gross annual revenues.
18. *Employers that provide social services*: At least $250,000 gross annual revenues.

Through enactment of the 1970 Postal Reorganization Act, jurisdiction of the NLRB was extended to the United States Postal Service, effective July 1, 1971.

In addition to the above-listed standards, the Board asserts jurisdiction over gambling casinos when these enterprises are legally operated, when their total annual revenue from gambling is at least $500,000.

Ordinarily, if an enterprise does the total annual volume of business listed in the standard, it will necessarily be engaged in activities that "affect" commerce. The Board must find, however, based on evidence, that the enterprise does in fact "affect" commerce.

The Board has established the policy that when an employer whose operations "affect" commerce refuses to supply the Board with information concerning total annual business, the Board may dispense with this requirement and exercise jurisdiction.

Finally, Section 14(c)(1) authorizes the Board, in its discretion, to decline to exercise jurisdiction over any class or category of employers when a labor dispute involving such employees is not sufficiently substantial to warrant the exercise of jurisdiction, provided that it cannot refuse to exercise jurisdiction over any labor dispute over which it would have asserted jurisdiction under the standards it had in effect on August 1, 1959. In accordance with this provision the Board has determined that it will not exercise jurisdiction over racetracks, owners, breeders, and trainers of racehorses, and real estate brokers.

The Act Does Not Cover Certain Individuals

In addition to the foregoing limitations, the Act states that the term "employee" shall include any employee except the following:

- Agricultural laborers.
- Domestic servants.

- Any individual employed by his parent or spouse.
- Independent contractors.
- Supervisors.
- Individuals employed by an employer subject to the Railway Labor Act.
- Government employees, including those employed by the U .S. Government, any Government corporation or Federal Reserve Bank, or any State or political subdivision such as a city, town, or school district.

Supervisor Defined

Supervisors are excluded from the definition of "employee" and, therefore, not covered by the Act. Whether an individual is a supervisor for purposes of the Act depends on that individual's authority over employees and not merely a title. A supervisor is defined by the Act as any individual who has the authority, acting in the interest of an employer, to cause another employee to be hired, transferred, suspended, laid off, recalled, promoted, discharged, assigned, rewarded, or disciplined, either by taking such action or by recommending it to a superior; or who has the authority responsibly to direct other employees or adjust their grievances; provided, in all cases, that the exercise of authority is not of a merely routine or clerical nature, but requires the exercise of independent judgment. For example, a foreman who determined which employees would be laid off after being directed by the job superintendent to layoff four employees would be considered a supervisor and would, therefore, not be covered by the Act; a "strawboss" who, after someone else determined which employees would be laid off, merely informed the employees of the layoff and who neither directed other employees nor adjusted their grievances would not be considered a supervisor and would be covered by the Act.

"Managerial" employees are also excluded from the protection of the Act. A managerial employee is one who represents management interests by taking or recommending actions that effectively control or implement employer policy.

The Act Does Not Cover Certain Employers

The term "employer" includes any person who acts as an agent of an employer, but it does not include the following:

- The United States or any State Government, or any political subdivision of either, or any Government corporation or Federal Reserve Bank.
- Any employer subject to the Railway Labor Act.

NLRB Procedures

The authority of the NLRB can be brought to bear in a representation proceeding only by the filing of a petition. Forms for petitions must be signed, sworn to or affirmed under oath, and filed with the Regional Office in the area where the unit of employees is located. If employees in the unit regularly work in more than one regional area, the petition may be filed with the Regional Office of any of such regions.

Procedure in Representation Cases

Section 9(c)(1) provides that when a petition is filed, "the Board shall investigate such petition and if it has reasonable cause to believe that a question of representation affecting commerce exists shall provide for an appropriate hearing upon due notice," if the Board finds from the evidence presented at the hearing that "such a question of representation exists, it shall direct an election by secret ballot and shall certify the results thereof." When there are three or more choices on the ballot and none receives a majority, Section 9(c)(3) provides for a runoff between the choice that received the largest and the choice that received the second largest number of valid votes in the election. After the election, if a union receives a majority of the votes cast, it is certified; if no union gets a majority, that result is certified. A union that has been certified is entitled to be recognized by the employer as the exclusive bargaining agent for the employees in the unit. If the employer fails to bargain with the union, it commits an unfair labor practice.

Procedure in Unfair Labor Practice Cases

The procedure in an unfair labor practice case is begun by the filing of a charge. A charge may be filed by an employee, an employer, a labor organization, or any other person. Like petitions, charge forms, which are also available at Regional Offices, must be signed, sworn to or affirmed under oath, and filed with the appropriate Regional Office that is, the Regional Office in the area where the alleged unfair labor practice was committed. Section 10 provides for the issuance of a complaint stating the charges and notifying the charged party of a hearing to be held concerning the charges. Such a complaint will issue only after investigation of the charges through the Regional Office indicates that an unfair labor practice has in fact occurred.

In certain limited circumstances when an employer and union have an agreed-upon grievance arbitration procedure that will resolve the dispute, the Board will defer processing an unfair labor practice case and await resolution of the issues through that grievance arbitration procedure. If the grievance arbitration process meets the Board's standards, the Board may accept the final resolution and defer that decision. If the procedure fails to meet all the Board standards for deferral, the Board may then resume processing of the unfair labor practice issues.

An unfair labor practice hearing is conducted before an NLRB administrative law judge in accordance with the rules of evidence and procedure that apply in the U.S. district courts. Based on the hearing record, the administrative law judge makes findings and recommendations to the Board. All parties to the hearing may appeal the administrative law judge's decision to the Board. If the board considers that the party named in the complaint has engaged in or is engaging in the unfair labor practices charged, the Board is authorized to issue an order requiring such person to cease and desist from such practices and to take appropriate affirmative action.

The 6-Month Rule Limiting Issuance of Complaint

Section 10(b) provides that "no complaint shall issue based upon any unfair labor practice occurring more than 6 months prior to the filing of the charge with the Board and the service of a copy thereof upon the person against whom such charge is made." An exception is made if the charging party "was prevented from filing such charge by reason of service in the armed forces, in which event the 6-month period shall be computed from the day of his discharge." It should be noted that the charging party must, within 6 months after the unfair labor practice occurs, file the charge with the Regional Office and serve copies of the charge on each person against whom the charge is made. Normally service is made by sending the charge by registered mail, return receipt requested.

Appeal to the General Counsel if Complaint Is Not Issued

If the Regional Director refuses to issue a complaint in any case, the person who filed the charge may appeal the decision to the General Counsel in Washington. Section 3(d) places in the General Counsel "final authority, on behalf of the Board, in respect of the investigation of charges and issuance of complaints." If the General Counsel reverses the Regional Director's decision, a complaint will be issued. If the General Counsel approves the decision not to issue a complaint, there is no further appeal.

Powers of the NLRB

To enable the NLRB to perform its duties under the Act, Congress delegated to the Agency certain powers that can be used in all cases. These are principally powers having to do with investigations and hearings.

Powers Concerning Investigations

As previously indicated, all charges that are filed with the Regional Office are investigated, as are petitions for representation elections. Section 11 establishes the powers of the Board and the Regional Offices in respect to hearings and investigations. The provisions of Section 11(1) authorize the Board or its agents to:

- Examine and copy "any evidence of any person being investigated or proceeded against that relates to any matter under investigation or in question."
- Issues subpoenas, on the application of any party to the proceeding, requiring the attendance and testimony of witnesses or the production of any evidence.
- Administer oaths and affirmations, examine witnesses, and receive evidence.
- Obtain a court order to compel the production of evidence or the giving of testimony.

The Act Is Remedial, Not Criminal

The National Labor Relations Act is not a criminal statute. It is entirely remedial. It is intended to prevent and remedy unfair labor practices, not to punish the person responsible for them. The Board is authorized by Section 10(c) not only to issue a cease-and-desist order, but "to take such affirmative action including reinstatement of employees with or without back pay, as will effectuate the policies of this Act."

Affirmative Action May Be Ordered by the Board

The object of the Board's order in any case is twofold: to eliminate the unfair labor practice and to undo the effects of the violation as much as possible. In determining what the remedy will be in any given case, the Board has considerable discretion. Ordinarily, its order in regard to any particular unfair labor practice will follow a standard form that is designed to remedy that unfair labor practice, but the Board can, and often does, change the standard order to meet the needs of the case. Typical affirmative action of the Board may include orders to an employer who has engaged in unfair labor practices to:

Examples of Affirmative Action Directed to Employers

- Disestablish an employer-dominated union.
- Offer certain named individuals immediate and full reinstatement to their former positions or, if those positions no longer exist, to substantially equivalent positions without prejudice to their seniority and other rights and privileges, and with backpay, including interest.
- On request, bargain collectively with a certain union as the exclusive representative of the employees in a certain described unit and sign a written agreement if an understanding is reached.

Examples of Affirmative Action Directed to Unions

Examples of affirmative action that may be required of a union that has engaged in unfair labor practices include orders to:

- Notify the employer and the employees that it has no objection to reinstatement of certain employees, or employment of certain applicants, whose discriminatory discharge, or denial of employment, was caused by the union.
- Refund dues or fees illegally collected, plus interest.
- On request, bargain collectively with a certain employer and sign a written agreement if one is reached.

The Board's order usually includes a direction to the employer or the union or both requiring them to post notices in the employer's plant or the union's office notifying the employees that they will cease the unfair labor practices and informing them of any affirmative action being undertaken to remedy the violation. Special care is taken to be sure that these notices are readily understandable by the employees to whom they are addressed.

Special Proceedings in Certain Cases

Special proceedings are required by the Act in certain kinds of cases. These include the determination of jurisdictional disputes under Section 10(k) and injunction proceedings under Section 10(1) and (j).

Proceedings in Jurisdictional Disputes

Whenever it is charged that any person has engaged in an unfair labor practice in violation of Section 8(b)(4)(D), the Board must hear and determine the dispute out of which the unfair labor practice arises. Section 8(b)(4)(D) prohibits unions from striking or inducing a strike to compel an employer to assign particular work to employees in one union, or in one trade or craft, rather than another. For a jurisdictional dispute to exist, there must be real competition between unions or between groups of employees for certain work. In effect,

Section 10(k) provides an opportunity for the parties to adjust the dispute during a 10-day period after notice of the 8(b)(4)(D) charge has been served. At the end of this period if the parties have not submitted to the Board satisfactory evidence that they have adjusted, or agreed on a method of adjusting, the dispute, the Board is "empowered and directed" to determine which of the competing groups is entitled to have the work.

The Investigation of Certain Charges Must Be Given Priority

Section 10(1) provides that whenever a charge is filed alleging a violation of certain sections of the Act relating to boycotts, picketing and work stoppages, the preliminary investigation of the charge must be given priority over all other types of cases in the Regional Office where it is filed. The unfair labor practices subject to this priority concerning the investigation are those defined in Section 8(b)(4)(A), (B), or (C), all three subparagraphs of Section 8(b)(7), Section 8(e) and, where appropriate, 8(b)(4)(D), Section 10(m) requires that second priority be given to charges alleging violations of Section 8(a)(3), the prohibition against employer discrimination to encourage or discourage membership in a union, and Section 8(b)(2), which forbids unions to cause or attempt to cause such discrimination.

Injunction Proceedings under Section 10(l)

If the preliminary investigation of any of the first priority cases shows that there is reasonable cause to believe that the charge is true and that a complaint should issue, Section 10(l) further requires the Board to petition a U.S. district court to grant an injunction pending the final determination of the Board. The section authorizes the court to grant "such injunctive relief or temporary restraining order as it deems just and proper." Another provision of the section prohibits the application for an injunction based on a charge of violation of Section 8(b)(7) (the prohibition on organizational or recognitional picketing in certain situations) if a charge against an employer alleging violation of Section 8(a)(2) has been filed and the preliminary investigation establishes reasonable cause to believe that such charge is true.

Injunctive Relief May Be Sought in Other Cases

Section 10(j) allows the Board to petition a Federal district court for an injunction to temporarily prevent any unfair labor practice after a complaint has been issued and to restore the status quo. pending the full review of the case by the Board. This section does not require that injunctive relief be sought, but only makes it possible for the Board to do so in cases when it is considered appropriate.

Court Enforcement of Board Orders

In the U.S. Court of Appeals

If an employer or a union fails to comply with a Board order, Section 10(e) empowers the Board to petition the U.S. court of appeals for a court decree enforcing the order of the Board enjoining conduct that the Board has found to be unlawful. Section 10(l) provides that any person aggrieved by a final order of the Board granting or denying in whole or in part the relief sought may obtain a review of such order in any appropriate circuit court of appeals. When the court of appeals hears a petition concerning a Board order, it may enforce the order, remand it to the Board for reconsideration, change it, or set it aside entirely. If the court of appeals issues a judgment enforcing the Board order, failure to comply may be punishable by fine or imprisonment for contempt of court.

Review by the U.S. Supreme Court

In some cases the U.S. Supreme Court may be asked to review the decision of a circuit court of appeals, particularly when there is a conflict in the views of different courts on the same important problem.

CONCLUSION

In this material the entire Act has been covered, but, of necessity, the coverage has been brief. No attempt has been made to state the law in detail or to supply you with a textbook on labor law. We have tried to explain the Act in a manner intended to make it easier to understand what the basic provisions of the Act are and how they may concern you. If it helps you to recognize and know your rights and obligations under the Act, and aids in determining whether you need expert assistance when a problem arises, its purpose will have been satisfied. More than that, the objective of the Act will have been furthered.

The objective of the National Labor Relations Act, to avoid or reduce industrial strife and protect the public health, safety, and interest, can best be achieved by the parties or those who may become parties to an individual dispute. Voluntary adjustment of differences at the community and local level is almost invariably the speediest, most satisfactory, and longest lasting way of carrying out the objective of the Act.

Efforts are being made in all our Regional Offices to increase the understanding of all parties about what the law requires of them. Long experience has taught us that when the parties fully understand their rights and obligations, they are more ready and able to adjust their differences voluntarily. Seldom do individuals go into a courtroom, a hearing, or any other avoidable contest, knowing that they are in the wrong and that they can expect to lose the decision. No one really likes to be publicly recorded as a law violator (and a loser too). Similarly, it is seldom that individuals refuse to accept an informal adjustment of differences that is reasonable, knowing that they can obtain no better result from the formal proceeding, even if they prevail.

The consequences of ignorance in these matters—formal proceedings that can be time consuming and costly, and that are often followed by bitterness and antagonism—are economically wasteful, and usually it is accurate to say that neither party really wins. It is in an attempt to bring about more widespread awareness of the basic law and thus help the parties avoid these consequences that this material has been prepared and presented as a part of a continuing program to increase understanding of the National Labor Relations Act.

INDEX

A

B

C

D

E

F

G

H

O

P

Q

R

S

T

U